# PRAISE FOR *HOMESCHOOLED TEENS*

*Sue Patterson's book is a gem; it is superb in many ways. Her extensive experience, careful observations, and wise perspective provide a framework for the poignant and perceptive comments of 75 people who are or were homeschooled. These comments have to do with a wide range of topics, from academics and college admission to dating and sibling relation-ships. I know of no better book providing a convincing case that young people who are homeschooled through middle and high school engage in learning in deep and meaningful ways and go on to live productive and fulfilling adult lives. Read this book if you're con-templating or anticipating homeschooling your kids through high school, are already doing it, or simply want to appreciate hearing from (and seeing in engaging photos) young people who are living full and rich lives.*

> — **Wes Beach** directs Beach High School, is the Teen Adviser for both the Gifted Homeschoolers Forum and the HomeSchool Association of California, is a colunminst for *The Homeschooler Post*, and author of *Forging Paths: Beyond Traditional Schooling* and his newest work, *Self-Directed Learning: Documentation and Life Stories*.
>
> www.beachhigh.education

*If you want to know what it's like to be a homeschooled teenager, the best way to find out is to ask them. Sue Patterson asked 75 teens and young adults who were homeschooling or had graduated from homeschooling to describe their experiences, with the help of a 30-item-questionnaire. This book is the result. It's a well-organized compilation of the respondents' answers to questions about their ways of learning, social lives, family relationships, hobbies, college experiences, careers, and more. I recommend it highly to anyone who is homeschool-ing, considering homeschooling, or curious about it.*

> — **Peter Gray**, Research Professor of Psychology at Boston College and author of *Free to Learn: Why Unleashing the Instinct to Play Will Make Our Children Happier, More Self-Reliant, and Better Students for Life.*

*Let's hear it from the kids! There is finally a big enough generation of grown-up home-schooled kids that it is possible to see patterns and grasp the diversity in their experiences. And who better to tell us about all that than the kids themselves! So, Sue asked and they responded! And responded. And responded. Sue has done a fabulous job of sifting through and organizing a LOT of material so that we, the readers, can really learn and enjoy what these fascinating young people have to say about what it was like growing up without school. Read straight through or skip around to topics that especially interest you. Either way, you'll find these young voices are fascinating and absorbing as they open a window for you to get a look into their unconventional lives. A great read. You'll find it hard to put down.*

> — **Pam Sorooshian**, is an economics professor at Cypress College in California, a homeschooling conference speaker, columnist for *The Homeschooler Post*, a Homeschool Association of California board member, and has been active in the homeschooling community for two decades.

*Reading Sue Patterson's **Homeschooled Teens** was like reading the sequel I never wrote to my own books. I've always said that anyone who wants to know whether homeschooling—especially unschooling—works should look at the kids, but Sue's approach is even better: she asks the kids. And as we homeschooling parents know well, our kids have plenty to tell us.*

> — **Mary Griffith**, author of *The Homeschooling Handbook* and *The Unschooling Handbook*

*Young people who have learned without school are wonderfully unique individuals, usually with a strong sense of self. They are also pretty "normal," as well as being really interesting, engaged, and passionate people who have had a variety of awesome experiences because they weren't held back by the constraints of school. This thoughtful book, full of their opinions, experiences, and honest comments about home-based learning, is proof. You will be reassured, then inspired. And they will provide you with some really great advice...so pay attention!*

> — **Wendy Priesnitz**, a homeschooling/unschooling pioneer, helped her two now-adult daughters learn without school in the 1970s and '80s. She has been a writer and journalist for forty years, and is the author of twelve books. She is also the editor of *Life Learning Magazine*, which she founded in 2002 after the demise of John Holt's *Growing Without Schooling* magazine. You can learn more about her and read more of her writing on her website at www.WendyPriesnitz.com and at www.LifeLearningMagazine.com.

*Homeschooled Teens is an extraordinary resource. Parents make decisions about their children's education and then the children live those decisions. In this book, Sue Patterson gives voice to 75 homeschoolers between the ages of 15–39+ about the effects of homeschooling in their lives, compiling the information from conversations and surveys.*

*What struck me again and again as I read this book was the author's ability to relate to young people and accept their point of view; her skill in presenting all of this information in such a readable, organized, and helpful format; her warmth; and her respect for each of the teens and young adults she interviewed. A reassuring, helpful, and fantastic resource for anyone involved in homeschooling or interested in this way of educating children.*

> — **Marty Layne**, mother of four and grandmother of two, has been leading workshops and running programs for parents, babies, toddlers, and children for about 30 years in Victoria and elsewhere in North America. Her book: *Learning At Home: A Mother's Guide to Homeschooling.*
>
> www.martylayne.com

*A vivid and honest survey about the joys, opportunities, and challenges of homeschooling teenagers. It describes how homeschooling impacts dating, socialization, sports, the high school prom, parent–child relationships, and other milestones of teenage development. The book contains many real-life examples that cover a variety of experiences with homeschooling, often told in the teens' own words. Read this book to learn how you can customize homeschooling to any teenager's advantage.*

> — **Patrick Farenga**, co-author of *Teach Your Own: The John Holt Book of Homeschooling*
>
> www.johnholtgws.com

*Sue Patterson has brought together a priceless collection of observations and insights from 75 homeschooled teens and young adults. With a wide range of experiences, interests, and goals, they candidly share details about their lives without school. I really loved how beautifully she framed the sections with her insights into their answers as well. From learning, to their social and family lives, to the question of college, it's a fascinating look at homeschooling during the teen years.*

> — **Pam Laricchia**, author of the book, *Free to Learn* and her website is livingjoyfully.ca.

# HOMESCHOOLED TEENS

75 young people speak about their lives without school

**Sue Patterson**

2nd Tier Publishing

Published by:
2nd Tier Publishing
13501 Ranch Road 12, Ste 103
Wimberley, TX 78676

ISBN 978-0-9862290-4-6

Cover design by Joyce Fetterol
Book design by Dan Gauthier

# CONTENTS

PREFACE   vii

INTRODUCTION   xiii

**GETTING TO KNOW THEM**   CHAPTER 1 – Who Are They?   1

CHAPTER 2 – Middle School and High School Experience   11

CHAPTER 3 – Homeschooling Reluctantly or Happily?   21

CHAPTER 4 – The Advantages of Homeschooling   35

**LEARNING**   CHAPTER 5 – Variety of Ways to Learn   55

CHAPTER 6 – Community College Classes   69

**SOCIAL LIFE**   CHAPTER 7 – Did You Find Enough Friends?   83

CHAPTER 8 – Peer Pressure   97

CHAPTER 9 – Dating   109

CHAPTER 10 – Going to Prom   123

**EXTRACURRICULARS**   CHAPTER 11 – Sports   135

CHAPTER 12 – Teen Employment   149

CHAPTER 13 – Enjoying Hobbies   161

CHAPTER 14 – Travel   177

**FAMILY LIFE**   CHAPTER 15 – Sibling Relationships   191

CHAPTER 16 – Relationships with Parents   205

CHAPTER 17 – Interacting with Other Adults   219

**POST HIGH SCHOOL**   CHAPTER 18 – College Experience   233

CHAPTER 19 – Pursuing Passions   247

CHAPTER 20 – A Non-College Career Path   261

**FUTURE PLANS**   CHAPTER 21 – Will You Homeschool Your Own Children?   269

CHAPTER 22 – Words of Advice for Worried Parents   285

CHAPTER 23 – What Are They Doing Now?   303

EPILOGUE   321

ABOUT THE AUTHOR   323

# In Gratitude...

I want to thank my family and friends for their patience with this book project. I know they thought this was the book that would never be finished! It did almost seem as if the world was putting all kinds of opportunities in my path to derail me, "You SAY you want to do this book, but do you want it more that THIS?" Some of the speedbumps have been: weddings, a grandbaby, grown children moving across the country, a mom with worsening Alzheimers, a husband who had a heart attack and an early retirement, an editor who went back to work because I took too long, a publisher whose office flooded and the book file was ruined. And yet, here it is. So my answer to that question is, "Yes. I do want this book to be released into the world."

As for the specifics, thank you to Diane Kallas for editing and proofing the manuscript. Thank you to Jamie Heston for helping with final proofing. Special thanks to Dan Gauthier and Shiila Safer at 2nd Tier Publishing who endured great hardships to get this book completed. Thank you for your stamina and persistence! Thank you to Pam Sorooshian for late night calls helping me find some clarity in how I wanted this book to present itself to you. Thank you to Tozi Gutierrez for showing me how to create my own graphics. Thank you to the friends and family—especially the homeschooling moms—who cheered me on, helping me continue with this project.

Thank you to everyone who shared the survey with their support networks and for many, their own children. Your enthusiams kept me from throwing in the towel!

A huge amount of gratitude goes to Joyce Fetterol who designed this exciting book cover. My ideas were oh-so-1980s and she brought me up to date! I love what she did with it and am forever grateful.

Thank you to the teens and young adults who answered so honestly and generously. They probably have no idea how much their responses will help families exploring this idea of home education for their teenagers or how many teens they may have rescued from miserable situations.

My heart is filled with appreciation and gratitude for all of these young people who simply shared their stories.

Thank you to my family for believing I COULD get this thing done! Thank to my husband, Ron, who provided for us while we were exploring our own home education path. His love, and unwavering support throughout the years cannot be matched. Someone asked recently how he was able to embrace this educational philosophy that's so unusual. He shrugged and replied, "I trusted my wife and I trusted my kids. It's as simple as that."

Most of all, I want to thank my own children. Thank you for your patience as you waited for me to finish paragraphs or editing, or sift through notes piled high on the computer desk. Thank you for being the wonderful, curious strong young adults that you are! You jumped onboard with this alternative way of learning, and continued to trust that I knew what I was doing! I didn't really know—but I saw how you learned best and continued to make adjustments along the way. I have such deep respect and love for the three of you. I'm in awe of how incredible each of you are in your own ways!

I love you all.

Thank you.

# PREFACE

As a homeschooling parent, I spent a lot of afternoons at parkdays chatting with other moms. I wanted my kids to have fun with their friends, but I was also on a mission. I wanted to pick the brains of parents with children older than mine *and* I wanted to see how their kids acted, specifically, their teenagers. While my younger kids played, I was a veritable secret agent—eavesdropping, scrutinizing, interrogating—looking for evidence that homeschoolers were maturing into the kind of people I wanted my kids to be. I justified my behavior, then and now, by recalling all the anxieties that populated my homeschooling world. Yes, we all worried if our kids would learn to read or draw or stop counting on their fingers and toes, but more than that we worried about our children getting into college, making friends, having a full, rich life, among other things.

Sometimes my fears for my kids were specific:

- *Will they miss the various activities associated with adolescence? What about prom? Dating? Graduation ceremonies?*
- *Will this choice close doors for them? Will they get into college or get a job?*

Other times my fears were vague, shadowy and overwhelming:

- *Will I be warping them somehow?*
- *Will they hate me later down the road?*

I wasn't the only parent asking these questions twenty years ago and I believe there are parents still asking them today.

Something else has happened over time though. Years have passed, and those teens that we knew when my own children were little, are grown now—many are homeschooling children of their own! The homeschooling "movement," no longer a new phenomenon, has also grown. We no longer have to speculate about how these kids will turn out—they're out in the world, happily living their lives. And now we have an opportunity to hear directly from the teens and young adults who lived and thrived on this alternative educational path.

Today, the U.S. census indicates maybe 4% of American children are homeschooled. I'd caution against relying on any numbers too much, as we are a particularly difficult group to count. States vary on their legal interpretation of the term "homeschooler." Many categorize homeschooling families as small private schools and therefore have no jurisdiction or interest in them. Schools have their own problems managing the attendance systems they've already put in place—letting families make their own decisions for their teens is a much better idea!

Most of us went to a brick and mortar school, and the concept of homeschooling is fairly new. Our parents sent us off to school because that's just what everyone did. And while many of us had experiences in middle schools and high schools that were less than stellar, we accepted it as a given… like death and taxes. And while true homeschooling pioneer parents were quietly removing their children from the school systems in the 60s and 70s, it wasn't until the 1980s that this movement home became more noticeable.

John Holt, an educational activist, founded the bimonthly publication *Growing Without Schooling* in 1977 that networked homeschoolers worldwide. He began his work life as a teacher, but ultimately became disillusioned with the school system. He wrote ten books, the first published in 1964 and his last two—*Learning All the Time* (1989) and *A Life Worth Living* (1990)—published posthumously, that would guide families as they navigated the uncharted waters of home education. Holt's appearance on the Phil Donahue show in 1981 raised the visibility of homeschoolers and escalated the controversy. It also rallied families unhappy with their own school situation.

Parents homeschool for a variety of reasons, but during the 1980s and 1990s in the United States, religious homeschoolers took the forefront. While there might not have been more of them, they were certainly outspoken and in the news. They left many with the impression that only conservative religious families opted out of the public school system.

As time progressed, and the educational system continued to deteriorate, more families explored homeschooling. They saw schools as bent more on molding instead of encouraging youth to flourish. These families wanted their children to have an experience with learning, different from what schools or the more rigid homeschooling-at-the-kitchen-table variety provided.

Then, in the last two decades, virtual schools, hybrid programs within the school system, and charter schools, came into existence and families had new options for educating their children.

Our family began homeschooling in what I consider the middle wave of homeschoolers. We were an active-duty military suburban family. I had never considered homeschooling as something we would choose to do. Yet, after I sent my oldest child off on the bus to Kindergarten and first grade, it became clear that this wasn't the best place for him. His school experience was squashing his cheerful exuberance about learning. I began to look around at my options.

We lived on Lackland AFB and I knew one family who homeschooled. Their teenagers were cheerful and articulate—they had no problem chatting with their mom's friend. I wanted to know more about their experience. They were happy. And normal. That was important to me then.

Our family was transferred to Alaska and chose to take that as our first break with the school system. We immersed ourselves in the homeschooling community but discovered that finding teenagers proved to be a little tricky. Occasionally, families we knew had one "older" child… often only about 12. My kids were 2, 5, and 7. I really wanted to look down the childhood road a little further and see how to prepare for a homeschooled teen. But we tended to gravitate or cultivate support groups with children of the younger age. We were still using flyers and hard copy newsletters to communicate back then. Email lists were just beginning and AOL provided message boards that linked us to the outside world. Homeschooling books and magazines by Linda Dobson, Cafi Cohen, Mary Griffith, Helen and Mark Hegener helped us figure out this unique path we had chosen.

We continued to move with the military, from Alaska to California and then to Texas. We had fabulous opportunities for meeting other homeschooling families at statewide and regional conferences, campouts and get-togethers as well as local parkdays and field trips. California, with its large number of homeschoolers, had plenty of teens for me to observe and watching the homeschooled teens interact with their families warmed my heart. These families seemed to be moving through adolescence with communication and respect. All the preconceived ideas about rifts between teens and adults disappeared before my eyes. While the relationships between these adolescents and their parents varied, it seemed more dependent upon the parenting style and nothing to do with the fact that they were homeschooling.

Still, even though the popularity of homeschooling was increasing, parents happily home educating their younger children appeared to have doubts about their ability to provide the right educational environment for their older child.

In the late 1990s and early 2000s, we attended several homeschooling and unschooling conferences. Panels of teens fielded questions and shared their experiences. Parents wanted to talk to these teens to find answers that might allay their fears. The teens responded with grace and candor. They were funny and interesting and pursuing a variety of fascinating paths. But conferences only happen annually, and some parts of the country never get to witness these teen panels. My vision of this book was to remedy that.

Now that my own homeschooled teens are grown, I found myself in an interesting position. We had created friendships over the years with other families locally as well as across the United States. Because I participated in a variety of online email lists and message boards throughout the years, I knew a lot of people who would be interested in a book about homeschooling through adolescence.

In September 2011, I created a survey of thirty questions asking about various aspects about the life of a homeschooled teen. I shared the survey on the internet, through blogs, social media, and email lists. I was incredibly fortunate with how many people were interested in participating. After three years of gathering data and collating responses, seventy-five people from ages 15–39 had shared candidly about their lives. I'm so happy to be able to share it all with you here in *Homeschooled Teens*. I loved talking with so many of the survey respondents. They were thrilled with having an opportunity to let people know how much they enjoyed their homeschooling experience. Reading and listening to these teens and young adults reaffirms my own belief that homeschooling is the best option for teenagers.

It is my hope that this book will reassure other families who are frustrated with the school system but worry that a dark cloud will hover over their teen if they choose to home educate. I want parents to see that homeschooling is not just an option for younger children. In fact, when a parent takes a good look at what's happening in high schools across the country, watching their teens withdraw and feel powerless in their own lives, I want to fling open the school doors and help them release their teen. The whole world is waiting to engage with them—there's no reason to continue with an antiquated system that is doing more damage than good.

Choosing to homeschool allows these teen years to be a true transition into adulthood with parents walking alongside, offering resources and guidance. It's my hope that *Homeschooled Teens* gives you the information you need to bolster your courage and step out into this fabulous adventure with your teenager!

# INTRODUCTION

While *Homeschooled Teens* will be a fascinating read for anyone interested in home education, it was specifically written for two different sets of parents. First, those parents who have been homeschooling their younger children but find themselves hesitating about continuing this path for the teen years. Secondly, for those families who haven't considered homeschooling before now, yet find themselves looking at options for their children who are unhappy and withering in high schools across the country.

The 75 teen and young adult respondents address the concerns that parents, grandparents, aunts and uncles often have about homeschooling. Everyone wants to figure out the right choice for their child. *Homeschooled Teens* will shed a little light on the subject by answering the specific questions that parents worry about.

When you read *Homeschooled Teens*, you'll notice that the bulk of the book contains direct comments from the 75 survey respondents. Try to hear their voices as they describe candidly what their lives were like.

The first section of the book basically introduces everyone to our participants. Readers will notice where they lived as teens as well as the style of homeschooling their family practiced. Information is also given to identify those teens who spent any time at all in school as well as those who never set foot there. The respondents who attended school prior to homeschooling are often blunt about what their experiences had been. Their families opted to break with the status quo and seek an alternative.

The survey respondents share how they felt about being a homeschooler during their adolescence. Some are younger, and still homeschooling and their responses often reflect the exuberance of youth. Others have the benefit of looking back on their teen years and assessing what went well and what could've been a little different. It might be helpful to occasionally glance back to this first chapter, identifying where the teen or young adult lived and what style of homeschooling was used. This might help parents identify states where more homeschooling opportunities exist and might even help them in their thoughts about deciding how they plan to approach learning with their teenager.

The majority of the teens and young adults in the survey did not go to middle or high school. Most had interactions with public school peers during this time period though—through sports, clubs, church, and a myriad of other activities and venues. Some attended middle school and then came home to learn, usually because of bad experiences in the schools. If parents are not sure about what's happening in middle schools and high schools around the country, these respondents will shed some light. Whether they attended school for any amount of time during their teen years or simply talked with their public and private schooled peers, this chapter will demonstrate a startling difference in the lives of homeschooled teens.

When parents hesitate about home education through middle school and high school years, they often focus on what they feel their child will miss. Understandably, no parent wants to place their child at a disadvantage. The surveyed teens and young adults share what they see as their advantages because of homeschooling: their approach to learning, their real world opportunities, their freedom to make choices, avoiding unnecessary stress, better socialization as well as better influences in general.

Parents sometimes worry about how their teen will learn more difficult subjects like algebra, chemistry or history. Several chapters focus on examples of the various ways teens learn in a home setting. The truth is, it's not always at home. And parents may be relieved to discover that the teacher isn't always them! Homeschooled teens learn in informal small groups centered around a topic of interest. Homeschool support groups often create opportunities out in the community. Sometimes people form co-ops with classes one or two days each week, led by parents with a particular expertise. Community-based activities and classes are also available to teens during the day, evening, or weekend.

Many of the survey respondents took community college classes as a teen, sometimes for dual credit. It's very common now for homeschooled teens to expect that they will be tapping into the community college system for all kinds of classes. Sometimes they take the class for credit and sometimes because it's fun or something they're interested in. Nevertheless, homeschooled students—regardless of their family's chosen educational method—adapt well to the college setting. Any fear that they won't be successful is quickly eliminated. Colleges have noticed that homeschoolers are particularly good students overall, partly because they choose to go to college because they want to, and not just because it's what's expected after twelfth grade. Community colleges are accepting homeschooled teens at younger ages and they are doing remarkably well there too.

The next section of the book sheds light on the teens' social life. Parents are often concerned about this aspect. Realistically, awkward teens exist in public schools, private schools and homeschooled communities. No one has a corner on that market. I'm not really sure why parents forget how many teens seemed odd when they went to school, yet, parents continue to worry about creating oddness with their educational choices. The respondents address many of the specific socialization questions parents might have, talking openly about finding friends, peer pressure, dating and even going to prom.

Because homeschooled teens are out in the world, that's where they find their friends. They're not limited to only those born in their birth year—their friends' ages are irrelevant. They make friends based upon shared interests, much the same way adults make friends. These teens and young adults didn't experience peer pressure to the degree that their public and private school peers may have. Many wrote about avoiding it altogether. For those who did experience some peer pressure, they were able to find solutions and deal with it. Not having to cope day-in, day-out with a bully was an enormous advantage to our homeschooled teens. Readers will see how openly the respondents share about the various paths they've taken. For me, it was striking to see how they haven't been influenced to conform, at least not to the same degree as those in school.

Sometimes the socialization question has to do with dating... will their teen find boyfriend/girlfriend experiences if the family chooses to homeschool? While some families are not embracing this concept, others will read that homeschooled teens have fairly similar experiences as their schooled counterparts. Some homeschooling communities are smaller, so those interested in finding dating prospects do much the same as they do in finding friends in general: they widen the circle, meeting people because of shared interests in the community. Those who were disappointed in their teen dating life quickly found that after the high school years, they had no problems once they got to college or out into the work world.

Interestingly, missing out on going to prom is another question parents frequently have when they're thinking about teen socialization. Most likely, this has to do with a rite of passage that adults cling to—whether it's realistic or not. As one teen wrote, "to stay in a high school just so I can maybe be asked to prom? No thank you." Those teens who wanted to attend a prom, found one because their homeschooling community created one, they went with a public schooled friend to theirs, they went to one of the larger homeschool groups who hosted a prom in a bigger city, or they went to plenty of local dances. The need to check that box, so to speak, is more in the heads of parents than in the teens themselves.

Another section of the book is devoted to "extracurriculars" namely, sports, jobs, hobbies and travel. For those with a rigorous academic focus, this term seems most applicable. These teens were focused on their studies and their other interests had to be fit in around their scheduled learning activities just like school kids do. For many of the teens, though, these extracurriculars were a large focus of their adolescence—and from the comments, one of their favorite parts!

Americans love their sports—and families considering homeschooling their teens wonder if they're closing the door on this particular aspect of the adolescent's life. But home educated teens who want to find sport activities, either team or individual, have no problems accessing a variety of sporting options. Many of the young adults found sports that they've been able to carry into adulthood with them. Others tapped into local leagues (homeschooling and otherwise) and some even found ways to play part-time for the local high school. What's really awesome to me is that they're able to find a sport based upon their interest, and not just because that's "the big deal" in their local high school. And those who are not inclined to play sports felt no pressure to play.

Many of the respondents found employment as teenagers. Their flexible schedule gave them significant advantage in finding a job. Several were even able to find jobs in an area they had some career interest, giving them a lot of insight into whether they'd really like to work at that job later, as an adult.

Traveling was an enormous perk for the teens and young adults surveyed. More than 80 percent wrote about their travels with their families or solo during the teen years. And one third of those surveyed have traveled internationally. It's hard to find statistics about the opportunities for travel that teens in schools have, but this seems like most would have limited time to indulge. My speculation is that their freedom to incorporate learning opportunities into a trip, along with not being bound by the school calendar, all combined to make travel a fabulous benefit for homeschooled teens.

With seventy-five teens and young adults sharing, so many different hobbies are represented! Readers will be delighted to see how homeschooled teens are pursuing passions, identifying and learning new skills, and stepping out into the world to see what's out there to enjoy. Without being cramped by the school experience, homeschooled teens found hobbies that fell into categories like athletics, animals, arts, cooking, reading, community service, political action, computer games, science, travel and club activities. The young adults were able to look back at their adolescent hobbies and identify how one led to another, with some carrying over into adulthood and even careers. They were exposed to a wealth of different interests and activities throughout their teen years.

Parents often worry about the impact home education will have on their family life. When I first considered homeschooling, I remember a woman telling me that she didn't want to be "The Teacher" in her child's life. She said it as if teacher was synonymous with policeman or prison warden! She felt it would negatively impact her relationship with her child. But when asked about their parent/teen relationship, these teens and young adults reported having really good healthy relationships with their parents. They appreciated the time and effort their parents had spent with them and wrote very little about the power struggles so many teens in school experience. When children know that their welfare is a priority for their mothers and fathers, it's amazing how that relationship can shift.

The respondents report better than usual sibling relationships as well. The pecking order of school grade levels is removed with homeschooling, as is the peer pressure that causes teens to worry about their younger or older sibling affecting their social status. Instead, being around their brothers and sisters so much, fostered a closer relationship for many of our survey respondents—one of compassion, empathy, and general enjoyment.

Society often has the misconception that homeschooled children are isolated from other adult influences, fearing that if the parents mistreat or neglect them, no one will notice. The survey respondents dispel this notion right away. Homeschooled teens interact with coaches, mentors, instructors, club leaders, bosses, volunteer coordinators as well as parents of their friends, relatives and adults in their places of worship. From the descriptions given, teenage homeschoolers are far from isolated!

The next section of the book focuses on questions that emerge about the period of time after the middle and high school years. What comes next for these homeschooled teens? Sometimes it's college, sometimes it's a career without college, but more often than not, they're pursuing the passions they discovered as teenagers.

When parents have fears about college, they usually fall into two different areas: they worry that the teen won't be able to get into college and they worry about how the teen will cope with college life once they're there. While the surveyed teens and young adults share the steps they took to get into college and what that path looked like, the big take-away is that they had very little problem with college admissions. More than 80% of those over eighteen attended a university. Universities across the country are finding homeschooled youth to be excellent college candidates and these homeschooled teens and young adults are sharing first-hand how that's been their experience as well. They describe their college life, what came easily to them as well as where they struggled a little. But their struggles were small, and overall they found that they were well-prepared for the college experience.

Again, looking at those 18 years of age or older, just over one quarter of those surveyed found careers that didn't include a 4-year college. Several acquired the necessary training through trade schools or community college certification programs. Others took a passion and turned it into a career.

Because so many of the homeschooled teens enjoyed a variety of hobbies throughout adolescence, I wondered if these were passing phases or something they'd carry with them into adulthood. Many of those surveyed wanted to learn more about their particular interest, and studied it at a higher learning institution. Often, this was one more step on their path toward a paid career. These young adults recognized that having their parents' support for what started as a hobby, ended up being exactly what they needed to translate that hobby into a way to earn a living. Other grown homeschoolers simply continue to enjoy the hobbies that they started as adolescents.

The final section of the book asks questions about the future. Whether or not they would homeschool their own children seemed like it would be an important indicator as to whether they enjoyed their homeschooling experience. Several of the grown homeschoolers are already doing just that! They list a variety of reasons why they've chosen to home educate.

Over half of all the survey respondents anticipate homeschooling their own children. They were quickly able to identify reasons they believe homeschooling offers the most advantages. Interestingly, just under half offered a "maybe," in response to the question of home educating their own child. While many thought there was a strong chance that they would, they saw factors that might prevent them from making such a choice. They didn't want to simply jump on the bandwagon, but instead wanted to weigh everything and make a decision when the time comes. Sounds like good decision-making skills to me! It will be interesting to follow up with these survey respondents in a few years to see what they ended up doing.

One of my favorite chapters is here toward the end. When asked what they'd say to a worried parent, these homeschooled teens and young adults shared heartfelt and encouraging responses. I was reminded of those parkdays and conference panels over the past two decades, where home educated teenagers were sharing their stories with parents who had questions. And now, many more parents can find answers that will clear up so many questions about whether or not they should make the choice to homeschool through the teen years.

The final chapter shares what each of these homeschooled teenagers or young adults are doing with their lives now. I love reading about so many diverse paths. Because they were homeschooled, they are discovering more about themselves as well as exploring new adventures. The younger respondents, still immersed in their teen years, are full of excitement and promise. They're happy to let people peer into what their lives look today. Those "graduated" homeschoolers who were so candid as they reflected on their adolescence, seem to have a confidence that serves them well as they find their way in the adult world.

I hope that we will get to talk with these homeschooled teens and young adults again. Perhaps we can touch base with them periodically, following the course of their lives, seeing where their paths twist and turn.

It's been an honor to talk with them and share their thoughts with you. I'm sure their responses will help shine some light on issues that parents may have as they make the decision to homeschool their teenager.

CHAPTER 1

## Who Are They?

The teens and young adults who answered the survey had a wide range of experiences during their adolescent years. Their remarkable childhoods have led them on unique paths to adulthood. This book charts some of the choices they made and paths that they took. Some are still pursuing their education outside of institutions, while others are enjoying college and careers, and some are even busy homeschooling their own children!

While most are from the United States, one lived in Canada and another in Israel during what would have been their high school years. And while most of the young adult respondents still reside in the United States, a few now live in Europe and Canada. The chart at the end of this chapter represents the states and countries where these teens and young adults lived.

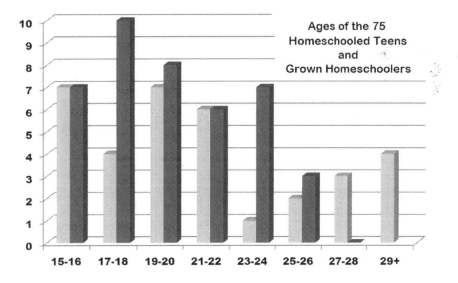

Ages of the 75 Homeschooled Teens and Grown Homeschoolers

Many of the respondents have resided in more than one state, so that's indicated in the chart as well.

The majority of those represented here began homeschooling in their younger years, and simply continued through their adolescence. Some attended the primary grades before making an educational change, while others attended school through middle school and only left institutional learning during high school.

In our family, my oldest went to kindergarten and first grade, and then we brought him home. During that first year of, what I called, our educational experiment my middle child went off to kindergarten, because I was unsure about how our days would flow and I mistakenly thought kindergarten would be good for her. Truthfully, I also wanted the time and space to figure out "this homeschooling thing." School wasn't a happy or enriching time for her, and when she finished the year, she never went back. My youngest child, benefiting from her siblings' experiences, never went to school until, at fifteen, she wanted what seemed to her to be an exotic adventure: attend the local public high school. She shares her experiences in the chapters ahead. (Spoiler: she ended up only going for a year and half. Once one tastes freedom, it's a little hard to give it up.)

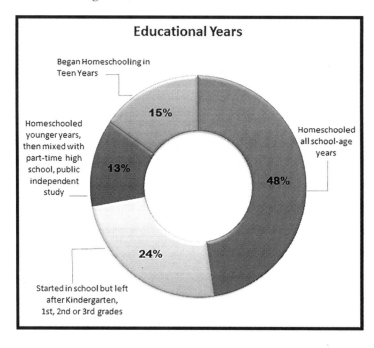

When the general public hears the term "homeschooling," they often have no idea what the kids do all day or how the families function. The truth is, no simple answer exists to that question. Every family is unique and each chooses methods based upon their own philosophy about life and learning. Sometimes they duplicate the classroom in large and small ways, simply because it's familiar. Sometimes they reject anything that looks like institutional learning. Sometimes they embrace different choices depending on each of their children, or the year, or the opportunities they have in front of them, or the goals their kids discover. And it's not unusual for families to change their style of homeschooling along the way. Parents and kids both discover new ideas and invent original ways to learn and incorporate this into their growth process.

However, homeschooling does tend to fall into certain broad categories or styles. The 75 survey respondents identified five different methods (and one "catch-all" method for all the "uncategorizable" approaches) that they employed. This chapter is organized around those styles. Each respondent is introduced based on the homeschooling style their family used most and then each shares a little about their educational path. Here are the five-plus-one home-schooling methods: unit studies, school-at-home, co-ops, topic- or textbook-based, unschooling, and "do their own thing."

## Homeschooling Methods

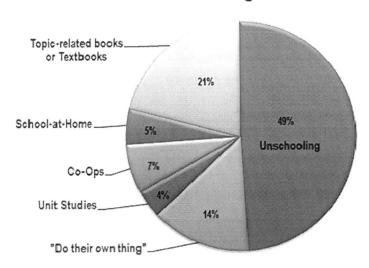

Topic-related books or Textbooks — 21%
School-at-Home — 5%
Co-Ops — 7%
Unit Studies — 4%
"Do their own thing" — 14%
Unschooling — 49%

## *Unit Studies*

In homeschools that are primarily organized around unit studies, the families, or often groups of families, focus on a topic to study in depth, until another subject is chosen. The theme is used as a springboard to a wide variety of school subjects relating to that topic, so that math and writing and reading and history and science may all revolve around dinosaurs or medieval weaponry or rap music. Children of all age levels participate in the topic as suits their developmental readiness, but everyone studies the topic.

These respondents used unit studies as their primary style:

**Elizabeth, 19,** homeschooled until she was 17, using some independent study offered through the public school system, in California.

**Risa, 21,** homeschooled kindergarten through high school, in California.

**Sarah H., 21,** homeschooled through high school, in North Texas.

## Co-Ops

A slightly more formalized educational option, co-op families attend classes outside of the home, usually for a fee. These classes are led by participating parents or hired teachers and usually meet only a couple of days per week.

These respondents used co-ops as their primary style:

**Carver, 18**, from age 5 through 17, in California

**Chant, 15**, since age 11, in Maryland and Colorado

**Grace, 19**, for all of her school-aged years, but included independent study from 5th grade on, in California

**Kelli, 21**, from 13 to 18, in Texas

**Micah, 16**, since birth, in Tennessee

## A few textbooks, more topic-related books

Families in this category look for interesting books to provide the core of their learning experiences. They may use textbooks, but often they supplement these with more in-depth books on specific subjects.

These respondents used topic-related books or textbooks, (although trying not to replicate school) as their primary style:

**Alaina, 25**, homeschooled from 2nd grade until she was around 15 when she combined homeschool with community college, in Oregon

**Beth, 20**, homeschooled always, in New Jersey

**Caitlin, 27**, homeschooled from age 11 on, in California and Oregon

**Emily, 16**, homeschooled her whole life, in Oklahoma

**Hannah J., 22**, homeschooled from age 3 to 17, in Illinois

**Kaci, 18**, homeschooled from age 9 on, in Texas

**Kate, 15**, homeschooled since birth, in Texas

**Katie F., 24**, homeschooled from "0 to graduation," in Wisconsin

**Kevin, 20**, homeschooled from 2nd through 4th grades, and then again for 11th and 12th grades, in Texas

**Nancy, 15**, homeschooled since age 7, in Georgia, New York, Connecticut, and New Jersey

**Nathan, 22**, homeschooled after Kindergarten in school, in Massachusetts and New Mexico

**Sarah B., 29**, homeschooled her whole life, in New Jersey and Pennsylvania

**Skye, 22**, homeschooled from age 13 and up, in Texas

**Sophie, 19**, homeschooled from preschool until age 16, in California

**Trina, 16**, homeschooled "all her life," in Oklahoma and Georgia

**Zach, 24**, homeschooled from age 0 to 19, in Pennsylvania

**Tess, 27**, homeschooled from age 10 through high school, in Pennsylvania

## Similar to School

These families chose to follow the type of curriculum that most schools use. They use textbooks, tests, grades, and, most likely, set times of day to learn. Often, you might hear homeschoolers refer to this style as "school at home."

These respondents used school at home as their primary style:

**Alsatia, 18**, homeschooled kindergarten through 12th grade, in Florida

**Caroline, 24**, homeschooled age 6 to 18, in Maryland

**Hailey, 18**, homeschooled ages 13 to 14 and 16 to 18, in Florida

**Nicholas, 26**, homeschooled age 14 to 18, in Ohio

## Unschooling

Those who chose this method do not follow the scope and sequence of school. Instead, unschooling families approach learning in a more natural way. Unschoolers follow the interests of the child. Parents seek out resources and opportunities to fuel the child's learning at home or out in the community.. Typically, there are no tests, subjects, grades, or pre-determined curriculum. The unschooled teens and young adults were our largest group of participants

These respondents used unschooling as their primary style:

**Aiden R., 16**, always unschooled, in NYC, Texas, and Georgia

**Aiden W., 23**, after 3rd grade, in Oregon, Ohio, and Tennessee

**Brenna, 22**, from age 7 through 18, in Florida

**Alyssa H., 17**, 4th through 12th grade, in North Carolina

**Alyssa P., 18**, all except tenth grade and half of eleventh grade, in Texas, California and Alaska

**Ari, 21**, went to public school in 1st grade and then unschooled, in New York, Wisconsin, Texas and Georgia

**Cameron L., 24**, from age 12 to 18, in South Carolina

**Cameron PT., 20**, from age 1 to 17, in California

**Dakota, 20**, from age 7 to 19, in Texas

**Hannah T., 18**, a "lifelong unschooler," in Texas and Ohio

**Jackson, 20**, from age 0 to 20, in Texas, California, and briefly in Chicago, Illinois

**Jared, 22**, always, in California

**Joseph, 19**, for the entirety of his pre-college life, in New York

**Julia, 15**, from age 6 onward, in New Hampshire

**Katie P., 20**, after kindergarten, in Alaska, California, and Texas

**Kirby, 26**, always, in New Mexico

**Laura, 24**, from age 5 to 17, in Puerto Rico, Oklahoma, Alaska, Texas, and Virginia

**Laurel, 21**, from age 8 on up, in Oregon

**Michael, 22**, after kindergarten and 1st grade in public school, in Texas, Alaska, and California

**Mike S., 16**, all his life, in Texas

**Molly N., 19**, age 3 to 18, in Oregon

**Molly S., 20**, age 7 to 18, in California

**Rose S., 20**, always, in California

**Rosie, 24**, her whole life (until she went to the university), in Israel and in the U.S.

**Rosie D.**, 30, from eighth grade on, in New York

**Roxana, 25**, since age 6, in California

**Rowan, 18**, from age 0 to 18, in Texas

**Roya, 27**, from age 10 and up, in California

**Rebecca, 39**, age 14 to 17, in Indiana

**Sarah D., 19**, from age 0 to18, in Illinois, Iowa, Kansas, and North Carolina

**Sarah P., 17**, from "birth until now," in Texas and California

**Simcha, 17**, always, in Massachusetts and Vermont

**Skylar, 26**, from age 4 to 17, in California

**Tony, 15**, from age 6 onward, in New Hampshire

**Wendelyn, 34**, from age 8 to 18, in Indiana

***Zoe 24***, from age 6 up, in Chicago, Illinois

## *"I did my own thing."*

This category is open to interpretation! If a survey respondent didn't feel he or she fit into any particular category, this category was their only logical choice. Additionally, if the teens weren't aware of their homeschooling style or if it changed throughout the years, they often selected "I did my own thing."

Those teens and young adults who categorized themselves as "doing their own thing" include:

**Alatheia, 16**, homeschooled from 7 through the present, in Florida

**Alyssa A., 16**, since she was 4 years old until now, in Florida

**Anastasia, 18**, "for all ages," in BC, Manitoba, and Alberta, Canada

**Crystal, 15**, since birth, in Texas

**Emma, 18**, from age 7 through now, in California

**Tori, 18**, until 10, then part-time from 11 to 12 years old, at 15, and again at 17 years, in Alaska

**Kristin 19**, from age 0 to 18, in North Carolina

**Steen, 15**, since age 4, in Florida and Georgia

**Sunny, 17**, from age 4–16, in 47 states (RV travel with family for seven years)

**Teagan, 20**, from 0 to 16, in Ohio and Colorado

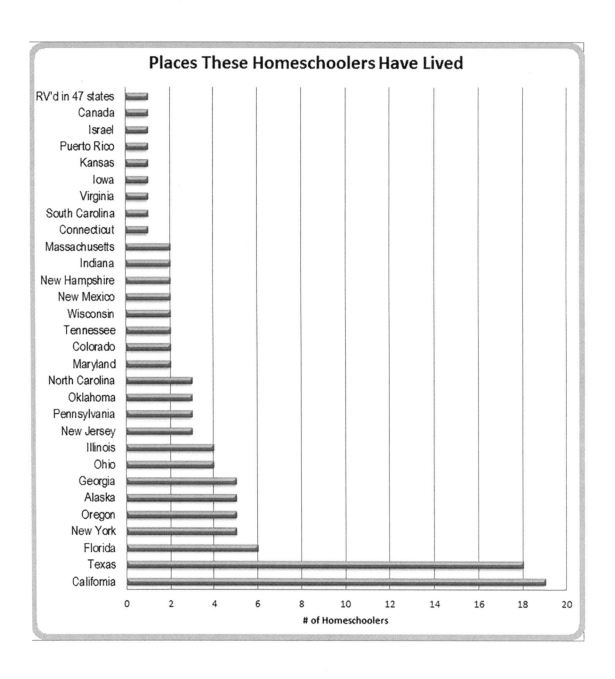

*Kelli and Kaci out in the backyard*

*Katie P. and Alyssa P. - sisters*

CHAPTER 2

# Middle & High School Experiences

Early adolescence is a particularly vulnerable time for many. While most American parents send their kids off to middle school and high school, others are rethinking their children's social and education environment, wondering if institutional learning and peer pressure are the best experiences during these years.

Many people consider middle and especially high school to be important American rites of passage. Families that were happily homeschooling younger aged children sometimes fear that they might miss out on essential social experiences by not attending during these older years. Some parents feel that school offers a better academic environment in the later grades, believing homeschooling to be fine for younger students, but not rigorous enough for teens. Despite educational reports demonstrating the superiority of homeschooling during adolescence, these fears persist. Occasionally parental fear of "harder subjects" means that they doubt their ability to continue to teach or mentor their child. And sometimes they worry that their decision to opt out of formal education may prevent their child from getting a college degree and entering a career they might enjoy.

> ### *How Old? What Grade?*
>
> Middle schools typically include seventh and eighth grade children, typically 12–14 years old.
>
> Some areas include 11–12 year olds (sixth graders) as well.
>
> High school ages are traditionally 14–18 year olds.

None of these fears are rooted in reality.

Take a few minutes to consider specifically what your teen wants from a middle or high school experience. Ask them directly and also think back (as objectively as possible) to your own time in high school, weighing the happy and sad experiences, the challenging against the dull. Remember that the reality of schools today is different than the glossy, fuzzy memories we have of high school more than a decade or so ago. More problems have bubbled to the surface in schools. Considered objectively, institutionalized settings do not look like the best place for teens to grow, learn and thrive.

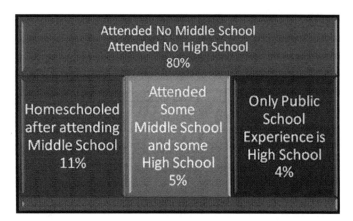

Bullying and antisocial behaviors seem to peak in the middle schools. Unfortunately—but perhaps because—so many kids this age struggle with their self-confidence. A lot of research has been done on this demographic. Data shows when this middle school age group is gathered by the hundreds and educated separately (from the high school and the elementary schools), both the learning and the behavior suffers.

Teens in grades 6–10 are most often involved in bullying. School bullying statistics identify that nearly **77% of all students have been bullied**, either mental bullying or verbal abuse. This bullying often results in teens with poorer self-esteem, depression, anxiety, and even suicidal thoughts. Statistics reveal that students are seeing an increase in violence in their schools and the incidents of cyber-bullying is on the rise.

We hear a lot about high stakes testing, with middle and high schoolers spend their days preparing for these tests. Many parents simply accept this as part of how school is today. And, I suppose they're right. Unfortunately, a high price is paid for a few extra test score points. Teens are conditioned to believe that their test scores matter more than learning. The cognitive skills they would have gained by exploring and discovering take too long and cut into test preparation time.

The *Middle School Journal* described high stakes testing as simply recalling facts—the lowest form of thought—and questioned if: "they may be lobotomizing an entire generation of young people."

Some respondents had first-hand experience in middle and high schools, while others offer opinions based on what they observed about their schooled peers.

## *Those with Middle School Experience*

Middle school can be a difficult time for many kids. Sometimes, families that didn't see any problems during elementary school years—or noticed some issues but thought they would work themselves out— discover that once their children reach middle school age things get a lot worse. Younger teens, and even pre-teens, come home with stories about the problems they're facing in the classroom and the lunchroom. When parents weigh the pros and cons, they often decide that it's not worth it for their child to stay in school. This group of homeschooled teens and grown homeschoolers had been in school up until their middle school years.

Middle schools are typically referred to as the "weak link" in the chain of public education. It was created to form a bridge to high school. While that sounds like a good plan, it often turns into more of a holding tank. Children who "did well" in elementary schools must wait for those who didn't to catch up. Supposedly this allows all kids to start high school with roughly the same skill set. But when you add in high stakes testing, and an increasing amount of homework, this age group loses their chance for more exploratory experiences. Any interests in the arts or sciences like journaling, dramatics, music or even scouting or reading for pleasure—all have to be set aside for what the schools have determined are the academic pursuit du jour. Then when you add in negative experiences like bullying or being bored, parents found themselves eager to explore their options. Here are their candid comments about what it was like for them in middle school.

**Hailey, 18:**   I attended a traditional public school until the seventh grade. I was big into horses and natural training methods and convinced my mom to let me do full-time online homeschooling so that I would have more time with the horses. I ended up going back to school for the eighth

> ### *Caitlin, 27*
>
> I attended school until seventh grade in Ottawa, Canada. My last year in school was among the most difficult and painful times in my life. I would come home almost daily from the bullying of the other kids. It took several years of homeschooling to regain my self-confidence.

grade and suffered through to finish my sophomore year. I hated high school. It wasn't that I wasn't popular or didn't have any friends; I did have a few select friends, and even was voted onto the homecoming court every year. I just always felt like there was so much more to life than the petty, trivial problems and topics that my peers were concerned with. I was ranked number one in my class on completion of the 10th grade, so it wasn't that school was too hard. On the contrary, I floated through my classes and the teachers loved me. Yet I yearned for more.

**Nicholas, 26:**   I attended grade school through 7th grade. The experience was okay, but I had trouble with my grades. I think the two things that contributed to the trouble were being picked on by other kids, and not getting individualized attention due to the large class size.

**Kelli, 21:**   I attended middle school for two years. I left about three months into eighth grade. Public school had always been a shaky experience for me. After 9/11 and many incidents at my upper middle class middle school, I began to feel very unsafe there. It was not a place of peace or even academic challenges for that matter. I awoke one day and told my mother that I did not want to go back. I felt that I was not learning anything of value. Instead, I was memorizing for Friday's fill-in-the-blank tests and moving on without real application of the content I was being taught..

**Cameron L., 24:**   I attended just one year in middle school through sixth grade. I had gone to school up until that point, this was the year my mother decided to take me out of school. Throughout that year she told me it was okay to question my teachers, that grades didn't matter, to not take the tests I wasn't ready for, particularly a French test. She and I both disliked my French teacher and thought that taking this test was not worth it because I hadn't learned anything from her to begin with. I believed everything my mother was telling me, even though I was somewhat reluctant and unsure of the dramatic change we were making. I went along with it because I knew my mother was brilliant and was clearly not going to "ruin" me.

> ### Rebecca, 39
>
> I attended sixth and seventh grades in middle school. I had my small group of close friends and one absolutely wonderful teacher in particular that made the experience bearable. But overall the experience was a negative one. I was bored, uninterested, not in the right "clique." I spent a lot of time reading through a medical dictionary of my mom's... mysteriously "contracting" many diseases over the course of those 2 years in an attempt to not have to go to school.

**Skye, 22:**  I attended middle school. In terms of education, I often found myself bored because of the pace of and restrictions of information teachers were allowed to discuss, science in particular. In terms of the social aspects, I was often ignored by "friends" unless they needed me for support or what-have-you.

## *Those with High School Experience*

A few of the teens and young adults spent some time at the local public high school. Their experiences were all quite different—some trying it briefly, others using the school part time, and some going full time for the final years. School districts across the country vary in how, or if, they embrace homeschoolers, so a few were able to go for part-time classes or sports participation.

It's not surprising that some wondered what it would be like to go to school. Who doesn't speculate about the color of the grass on the other side of the fence? Between the media and marketing hype, much of society is centered on the institution of school. Teens would have to live in a bubble to avoid all of that. And, minds encouraged to inquire might end up pondering the "what if's" of institutional learning.

Nine of the surveyed respondents share their experiences.

**Sophie, 19:**  I attended two different charter schools. I was part of Horizon charter school for half of sophomore year and all of junior year, and then I was a student at Smith Flat Charter/ Charter University Prep for all of senior year. Prior to that though, I had been homeschooled.

**Alsatia, 18:**  I took one class at the local high school for the last three years of my education and also attended classes at FLVS in both middle and high school if that counts as going. I would describe the experience as more of a social outing than anything else.

**Elizabeth, 19:**  I attended junior high and high school part-time and then went to the high school full-time as a senior.

> **Grace, 19**
>
> I did "split site," which means I was allowed to take 1-3 classes at the a junior high or the high school through Davis School for Independent Study. I didn't mind having a class or two because I did it mostly to participate in choir and science. I sometimes found students' priorities, behavior towards teachers, and behavior towards each other a little off-putting. However, it was always easy to find people with similar attitudes. High school was easier than junior high because it was a much bigger campus.

**Steen, 15:**   I attended ninth grade summer school. It was quite enlightening not horrible but not terribly enjoyable either. Being around youth my same age was a very different experience. I had a tendency to hang around the teachers mostly and discuss my interests such as politics and coaching football instead of talking to the youth who were often acting immaturely.

**Zach, 24:**   I took a few classes in high school and played soccer on the high school team during my senior year. I found the little experience I had with high school to be a rather poor learning experience. The lack of skills of the people in the class often ended up stifling my learning. The group project aspect was something that was hard to get as a homeschooler though.

**Tori, 18:**   I attended middle school and high school. I went part-time for sixth and seventh grade, but I went full-time during eighth grade. I thought my classes were very fun, but it was hard socially. Everybody seemed to know each other, and I didn't have enough classes to get to know people really well. Once I started eighth grade I found a group of friends with whom I have remained friends through high school and even college. I liked high school when I first started, but I went part-time for the second half of my semester. I think that's why I struggled throughout the rest of my those years. People didn't see me so it was hard to keep close to people. I went part-time for my senior year. I was ready to be out of high school.

**Kevin, 20:**   I liked it, but it seemed to go at too slow of a pace for me. I got my work done quickly, and then just sat around. I don't like school in general though. Haha. It wasn't too bad.

## Those who did not attend Middle School or High School

The majority of survey respondents never attended middle or high school. While some had early experiences attending the elementary grades, others did not attend any

---

### Alyssa P., 18

After having been un-schooled, I attended public school full-time my sophomore year and I left in February of my junior year. My mom kept calling it "An Experiment." I made the drill team, and that was one of the main reasons I wanted to go. I discovered I was smart at things I didn't realize. Plus, I saw that I interact with people in a much better way than they did—probably because I had never been to school.

formal classes until college. Nevertheless, they interacted with friends and neighbors, hearing about school experiences and forming opinions. In spite of the push from society to attend school, they chose to continue homeschooling throughout their teen years.

Something striking about all their comments is the variety; even though none of these respondents attended middle school or high school, each of their perspectives was different.

**Emma, 18:** I did not attend any school at all. Many of my friends did though and I heard about all of the drama. Most of the time, I'm glad that I missed all that drama and peer pressure and daily stress of school.

**Molly N., 19:** No. Legally, I was registered at a charter school for high school but never actually attended classes. I received credit through community college.

**Nathan, 22:** I went to kindergarten only. I was with friends I had known all my life so the experience was definitely good.

**Micah, 16:** I attended a co-op for middle and high school.

**Sarah P., 18:** I did not attend middle or high school. However I am currently attending Austin Community College, and have been for several semesters. It is sort of like high school for me.

**Kaci, 18:** I was homeschooled throughout all of those years. I'm nowhere near upset about missing out on the high school experience. I'm proud to say I'm homeschooled and that it worked really well for me.

**Cameron PT., 20:** I've been to both middle and high schools while doing volunteer work. Kind of crappy and cramped places. I hate those dinky little desks.

**Aiden R., 17:** I have never gone to school but I have been in schools during school hours meeting friends for lunch, and it seemed stressful.

---

**Simcha, 17**

I spent three weeks in school when I was nine years old. For that entire time, I sat at a desk for hours. I'd write what was on the blackboard and then watch the other kids looking out the windows and stare at the walls. I felt that it was silly to sit at a desk doing nothing when I could be home learning. After those weeks, we got the papers giving us authorization to homeschool and I never went back.

---

**Zoe, 22**

I never attended middle or high school. Until I attended college, my longest stint in the Chicago public school system was a couple weeks of kindergarten before my parents pulled me out.

**Rosie, 24:**   I was homeschooled all my life, until attending the university. (I did complete an organized high school curriculum though to get a diploma)

**Jackson, 20:**   I attended no formal educational institutions until starting college classes at Austin Community College.

**Rowan, 18:**   I have not attended any school of any kind. I did "shadow" at the Griffin School in Austin, Texas, for one day. I was initially very excited about joining the school at age 13, but I didn't pass the math test needed to get in and it was out of my family's budget. In the end, I was happy not to have gone.

**Katie P., 20:**   I started homeschooling after half-day kindergarten. I never attended middle school or high school. I'm glad that I didn't. I feel that if I had, I would be a completely different person than I am now. I most likely wouldn't have had the courage to do what I am doing now, studying at the New York Film Academy.

**Jared, 22:**   When I was 18 years old, community college became the first official "classroom experience" I ever had. Before then, I had never spent any amount of time in a classroom.

## School Shootings

While none of us want to think about the idea of school shootings, they exist—not just in our country but also around the world. When respondents began talking about stress that was associated with attending school, the horrific images from the news were sometimes at the heart of their concerns. We don't have good statistics on bullying in the school years, but we do have objective information about the most violent incidents that we've seen in schools.

Without trying to frighten anyone, let's look at the data about shootings on school campuses. The chart shows the number of middle and high school shootings recorded. It does not include colleges, universities or other locations, nor does it include death by stabbing, which also occurred occasionally. The school shooting statistics for countries outside of the United States are also included, as this is clearly not just a US problem.

## School Shootings

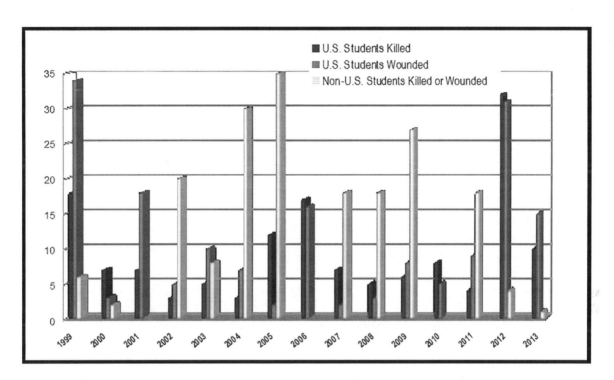

Hundreds of thousands of children attend school and never experience any of these terrifying events. But when a school goes on "lock-down" or a student makes a threat, the deaths of the students represented in this table comes flooding back to many children and teenagers' minds.

*Jackson, enjoying life*

CHAPTER 3

## Homeschooling Reluctantly or Happily?

Some of the first questions posed to the respondents were "Were they happy to be homeschooling through their teen years? Did they have a choice?"

After nearly 20 years of talking to fellow alternatively-minded parents, I've concluded that if everyone is not on board with the desire to home educate, you are likely to create a rough time ahead—for all involved. Opening an on-going dialogue between you and your teenager is the best route toward ensuring success. Some of the questions you might ponder together are:

- *What makes them want to homeschool?*
- *What do they see as drawbacks?*
- *How do they visualize their day?*
- *How do they think it will affect your relationship with them?*
- *What role would they like to see their parents fill?*

Most of the respondents expressed no reluctance about their atypical education at all. Many of these were homeschooled throughout their younger years, so continuing as a teenager was not an unusual option for them. However, others, who spent some earlier years in school, were well aware of what they were leaving behind. While several of the respondents harbored some doubts or questions about the educational process when they hit their teen years, only a handful of these transitioned to public high school. And, of these, many attended traditional school only part-time or briefly, often just to see what it was like.

As parents, we want the best for our children. We want them to be happy. Out of the 75 teens and young adults surveyed, all of them were happy with the unique educational path their families chose for their adolescent period.

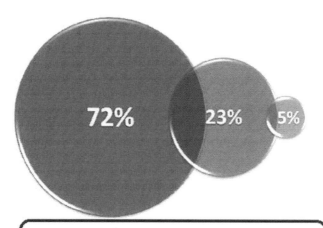

72% **Glad to be Homeschooled**

23% **Some Reservations but Continued Homeschooling**

5% **Left Homeschooling to Try High School**
(part-time, full-time, or temporarily)

## *Happily Homeschooling*

### More Opportunities, Options, and Advantages

Several of the respondents found that they had more opportunities by not going to a brick-and-mortar school. They felt they were able to learn far more than their peers who had all of their studies predetermined by a school board. When they had more say in their own educational path, they were much more engaged with the learning. Others found their involvement with extracurricular activities was increasing and the flexibility that came with designing their own schedule allowed them to pursue their interests. Having an adjustable schedule offered them the opportunity to be more involved in the community and life in general—instead of just reading about it or waiting for their lives to start after graduation.

**Risa, 21:** When I was 14 years old, I was accepted into a prestigious International Baccalaureate high school program at a public school. My parents let me decide whether

---

### *Michael, 22*

I was glad to learn at home even though we weren't home that much! We learned everywhere! I always felt a little sorry for those who were trapped at schools on beautiful days or when we were out in the real world doing cool stuff. I knew they were bored out of their minds there. Yeah, I was definitely glad to be homeschooled.

I wanted to attend or continue homeschooling. I chose to homeschool because I loved it so much. I have no regrets.

**Molly N., 19:**  I am very glad about homeschooling. I was given the option of going to high school as a teen but refused. I didn't feel I would have benefited from it.

**Kate, 15:**  I was, and still am, glad to be homeschooled. It has provided so many opportunities to advance my education.

**Teagan, 20:**  I was very glad with the decision—I always loved being homeschooled, and as a teen I was getting more and more heavily involved in my extracurricular pursuits, so I looked forward to having the time and opportunity to devote to them.

**Anastasia, 19:**  I was absolutely glad about homeschooling as a teen. By then I was over my occasional childhood desire to "be like other kids" and was grateful for the opportunities homeschooling provided.

**Mike S., 16:**  I am currently loving my way of life and I'm very confident that I can achieve my goals in the future, so I would say I'm quite glad about homeschooling.

### Avoiding Drama

A few of our respondents couldn't help but mention feeling relieved to have avoided much of the drama that seems to correlate with going to high school. They were able to skip the gossip, peer pressure, stress and "pointless drama" they watched their public school peers endure.

**Aiden W., 23:**  I was pretty happy. All of my friends who attended school seemed so caught up in superficial stuff. School was all they ever talked about. I was enjoying reading and exploring too much to want my life wrapped up so tightly.

**Sunny, 15:**  I was very glad to avoid (most) pointless teenage drama that comes with school. I am very grateful, in general, to be homeschooled during my teen years.

> *Katie P., 20*
>
> I was very glad to homeschool. It gave me the chance to accomplish so many more things. I could audition for many plays being produced in my community, go on trips with my family, write books, and many other things that I wouldn't have been able to do because of the time that public school requires.

> ### *Joseph, 19*
>
> Since it was all I knew, I had a very limited frame of reference. Growing up with friends who were in school, however, I definitely think it was the right choice for me. I wouldn't have wanted it any other way.

> ### *Skylar, 26*
>
> Homeschooling was all I knew. I was a big advocate for it, and it was too much of my identity to give up. So, no, I was never reluctant about it.

**Aiden R., 17:**   I was glad for homeschooling because I didn't have to be stressed about getting up at 7:00 A.M. and getting ready or anything like that.

### Continuing As Usual

Because many of the teens and young adults surveyed had homeschooled through their elementary school years, continuing was natural; it was simply a way of life for them. They'd grown quite comfortable with the independence and freedom associated with home education.

**Rose S., 20:**   I was glad, but I had homeschooled the whole way through though, so it was in no way a change for me.

**Laura, 24:**   I had never considered going to high school—it was firmly rooted in my mind that I would continue homeschooling until college.

**Rosie, 24:**   I was always homeschooled, as were all of my brothers, so for me it seemed normal.

**Jackson, 20:**   I was glad to homeschool, as it was how I had been raised up until that point.

**Katie F., 24:**   I was so happy that my mother decided to continue to educate us at home even though some of my homeschooled friends were starting to ship off to schools for high school.

**Sarah D., 19:**   I'd always been homeschooled, and I was happy to continue homeschooling.

**Cameron PT., 20:**   I always loved homeschooling. I was quite smug about not being in school for most of my childhood. I still am really.

**Alyssa H., 17:**   I had a lot of friends who had been homeschooled and who were going to go to public school for their high school years. Many of them asked me to go, but I always told them that I couldn't make it in a public school, I couldn't be happy there. So I was glad to continue homeschooling.

**Nathan, 22:**   As a teen, I had already been homeschooled for eight years so it was not that bad. I was active in many programs for homeschoolers.

**Tony, 15:**   As a teen converting to unschooling instead of homeschooling, I was very excited.

**Rowan, 18:**   I have always been very, very thankful to have been homeschooled. I do not make that assessment only from what others have said about their experiences, but also from how I see that I have developed. I do not force myself to do things that do not fulfill me, and because of this I feel fulfilled. I also remember much more of what I have learned than many of my schooled friends.

**Sarah H., 24:**   I had always been home schooled, and never really had a desire to go to a public or private school, so I would have to say I was glad about it.

**Zach, 24:**   I was always happy to be homeschooled.

## Happy to Leave School

Others who had attended public or private schools knew all too well what they were leaving behind when they made this educational leap. Their responses show that their parents involved them in the decision and that made a big difference in their happiness with the educational choice.

**Skye, 22:**   Homeschooling was my idea, so I wasn't reluctant at all.

**Caitlin, 27:**   I was extremely excited about homeschooling, mostly because it meant I would no longer have to go to school.

**Alsatia, 18:**   At age 14, I was given a choice to go to public high school with my cousins but I chose not to. In truth I just saw it as another four years of school. By homeschooling, I had the ability to be more flexible with my schoolwork which is something I definitely miss now that I am graduated from it.

> ### Kelli, 21
> I was relieved above all things. After many years of feeling out of control among the chaos of school, I was free to take an active role in my education and make my own decisions (that is, if they were mature and relevant to my education).

**Hailey, 18:** Homeschooling was my idea. My mom wouldn't have ever agreed to it if she would have had to do any teaching. She's not the type of mom that would do well homeschooling her children, but I found out about online homeschooling and she came around.

**Zoe, 22:** Honestly I can't remember ever regretting being homeschooled. I know my parents talked to me for a long time when they first decided to take me out of school and I think that was the hardest part for me because I didn't understand why I was doing something different than all of my friends. But as I became integrated into the homeschooling community I lost that apprehension.

**Hannah J., 22:** I'm very glad for homeschooling, so much so that my parents used the "threat" of high school as a disciplinary measure on occasion. :)

**Kaci, 18:** I had no reluctance at all. I was very happy to get out of public school.

**Chant, 15:** I was glad for homeschooling as no one really liked me through elementary school and when I joined my home school co-op, every time I saw my friends I felt needed.

**Rebecca, 39:** I was glad! Relieved. We loosely used a curriculum for the first year which I hated but it took up very little time. After that first year, my parents switched to an entirely interest-led, unschooling approach. This I LOVED. I have to say that I did admit to my mom years later when I was researching homeschooling my own child, that I seriously thought they had stopped homeschooling us after that first year. My head was so filled with how school and homeschooling was "supposed" to look that while I wouldn't change anything from those years, I did think we weren't homeschooling any longer. The active and intentional facilitation that my parents did was so important and crucial, but without that prepared curriculum I had difficulty seeing what we were doing as homeschooling. Once I was researching homeschooling—and more specifically unschooling—over a decade later, my perspective got a pretty big shift. When I read about interest-led learning and

---

**Kevin, 20**

I was glad to homeschool. I got to do the work at my own pace, which was usually pretty fast. And then I had the rest of the day to chill or hang out with friends.

---

**Zoe, 22**

As a teen, I don't think I ever regretted not being stuck in school. All my friends who went to school ever did was complain about how horrible school was!

unschooling when my oldest was 6 or 7, I shared with my parents what my thoughts were way back then. My mom was appalled that I had thought that—simply appalled. She asked why I hadn't said anything, asked what was going on, why things shifted? Honestly, I hadn't known why they'd changed their approach but there was no way I was going to say anything to bring their attention to the lack of formal prepared curriculum. Why on earth would I jinx the good thing I had going on? :)

**Attitude About Parents**

Even though this question was primarily about their happiness or reluctance to skip high school, a good number of the teens and young adults expressed their feelings about their parents choosing home education for them. Being in such close proximity with their parents every day, these teens and young adults often develop a closer relationship with their parents. It was easy for them to see the impact this educational choice had on their entire family. Families that emphasize good communication reap the benefits of appreciative teens and an overall close parent/teen relationship.

**Sarah B., 20:**   My parents always gave me the option to go to public school, so being homeschooled was something that I wanted.

**Emily, 16:**   I consider being homeschooled one of the greatest gifts my parents gave me. God has blessed me in many ways through this lifestyle. I have never wanted to go to school and I definitely don't feel like I am missing out!

**Nicholas, 26:**   I was glad and excited to try it out. I remember hearing my parents discuss the option and I was very hopeful that they would homeschool me.

> ### *Rose, 30*
>
> I was glad! It was very much something I pushed my parents to do. It was my parents who were concerned about letting me off easy. They thought I needed to learn to put up with social pressures. They worried I would never learn to get up to an alarm clock. It only took a few months for them to realize that I would be just fine.

## *Experiencing Some Reluctance*

Some who participated in the survey expressed they'd felt some reluctance at various points during their teenage years. While their parents may have researched the homeschooling option, many of the teens have not. In the face of so many options, it's not surprising that they might question their choices and educational path. But, as you'll read in the comments below, they continued to homeschool.

**Crystal, 15:** I was happy, although I thought several times about asking if I could go to school for a year or two, but I'm glad I didn't.

**Sophie, 19:** When I was younger, being homeschooled was great. I got to do school when I wanted as long as I got it done that day, and I didn't have to wake up early. As I got older, I wanted to be around more people my age so I had to find other ways and I got involved in youth group and such.

**Brenna, 22:** I initially considered attending the International Baccalaureate program as a high school student, but quickly decided that I wanted to unschool during the teen years; I wanted the freedom to explore my own passions, and I knew that I wouldn't have the time to do that in school.

**Cameron L., 24:** My mother sat me down in our den one afternoon and asked, "So... would you rather be homeschooled-- have school at home with tests and grades and field trips, or be unschooled, learn at your own pace, and, frankly, do whatever you want?" As a 12 year old, I naturally chose the latter. I think she wanted me to choose unschooling because with her months of research she was beginning to understand the logic behind it.

Honestly, unschooling was a random choice for me. I had asked to be taken out of school and homeschooled a year earlier, but it was my mother who researched and came across unschooling. I had no idea what it was. So when she said, "Do whatever you want," I was sold, but then I got a lot of negative responses from my friends and everyone at school. I was constantly told I would never get an education, that I'd be living "on the streets" as a "drug addict," and that I would never qualify for college. So, yes, I was very reluctant at first because of all the negativity that was being tossed at me from people I cared for a lot. It even came from some of my extended family. They thought my

---

### Molly S., 20

Around the age of 13, a few of my homeschooling friends were going off to high school. That, along with angst rebellion instincts, tempted me to go to high school slightly. I knew, though, that it would mostly get in the way of doing the things I really wanted to do. It's hard to say how I felt about homeschooling as a teen, because that was the normal state. Going to school would have been a change.

---

### Hannah T., 18

There were a few moments when I was around 11 or 12 years old that I remember wanting to try out institutionalized schooling. But after spending time with a large group of traditionally schooled kids, I also remember that desire going away pretty quickly!

parents were going crazy. But the interesting thing is that it turned out quite the opposite: It was my friends who became drug addicts while I went on to see the world, travel, and create some very meaningful things. I still see some of those friends, but it's fascinating how wrong they all were.

**Roya, 27:**   When my mother told me we were going to homeschool I was furious—I was excited about school. I gave her the silent treatment for a week—until she bribed me with new office supplies! She then asked if I would try it for three months, and then I could decide whether or not to go back to school. After day one, when she took us to Sea World, I never looked back!

**Carver, 18:**   I was reluctant to continue homeschooling during some of my teen years.

**Julia, 15:**   There was a little worry about being "different" from other kids, but beyond that simple worry at age 6, I had no other opinions.

**Emma, 18:**   There were times that I thought going to high school would be an easier more streamlined approach to education but when I really thought about it I liked my homeschooling situation much better.

**Alaina, 25:**   I was very happy to homeschool as a teenager. I did look into high school briefly but decided against it. My parents did not want us attending middle school but they were okay about high school. They fully supported what I wanted to do.

**Alyssa A., 18:**   In a way, I was both reluctant and happy. In my freshmen year of high school (9th grade) I considered going to public school just because I had heard of this artsy school nearby. The sole reason why I didn't go was because the idea of public school terrified me. It still kind of does. While this decision has been with me throughout my entire high school career (is that right to say that?), I'm glad that I have been homeschooled. All of my life, it has provided me opportunities like volunteering, programs, and internships

---

### Simcha, 17

I thought about going to school on and off for about two years. All of my friends went to school and I figured if I went too, I would see more of them. My parents made it clear that if I ever wanted to go to school, all I had to do was ask and they would see that I had the chance. I thought about it, and concluded that it was not worth it to start going to school when I was happy where I was.

---

### Laurel, 21

As a teen, I was 100% in love with homeschooling. Okay, maybe 99.9%, because even the happiest of unschoolers have occasional doubts. I quit school after 2nd grade, though, so I had a bit of time to adjust to the idea.

that I probably wouldn't have found if I had been in a public or private school.

**Sarah P., 18:**   I have always enjoyed homeschooling, however I have experienced a few phases of fear that I was not educated properly, and fear that I would not succeed at Austin Community College. I always wanted to homeschool, though, and enjoyed the social aspect of it.

**Steen, 15:**   Whether I was happy or reluctant depended on my mood, but overall I was glad, as it is what I have done my entire life.

**Wendolyn, 34:**   I was very lonely as an adolescent when I was unschooled. There were little to no social resources for homeschoolers at that time [1992–1997]. As a teenager, I got involved in musical theatre, worked at a library, a vet clinic, a drive-in, a child care ministry and as a nanny. These activities helped me meet more people, which was the one thing I had originally felt was lacking.

**Kristin, 19:**   Having been homeschooled all of my life, I had no thoughts of going to school when I became a teen. I appreciated the free time that I had to read and do my own things, and I didn't want to go to school and deal with homework, cliques, and organized sports. I did start thinking about going to school the summer before my sophomore year, because I enjoyed socializing in my dance classes, and I wanted more of it outside of dance. However, it became clear during my summer camps that although I really enjoyed hanging out with some teens, others irritated me to no end. By the fall, I realized that there was no way I could put up with lots of other teens for hours on end, while doing something that I wasn't passionate about.

The other time that I was reluctant about homeschooling, and considered going to high school was during my junior year. I had been through a string of foot injuries, making dance difficult. I could no longer take as many dance classes, and this cut down on my time out of the house and with friends. It was hard for me to register for non-dance classes, because I didn't have a driver's license yet and everyone else

---

**Dakota, 20**

I felt a little of both, reluctant and happy at different times. I feel like I missed out on some of the social stuff of high school, but at the same time, I gained a close group of friends through homeschooling.

---

**Jared, 22**

At times, the idea of going to school appealed to me. But I never got the urge to actually take any classes. If I had really wanted to take a class though, I most likely would have.

in my family was busy and unable to drive me to regular weekly meetings. I got very lonely and depressed sometimes, and that was the hardest year of high school for me.

## The Homeschooling, Public School Mix

A small number of the teens in the survey did have some experience in public high schools, after being homeschooled for most of their lives. Their reasons for going were all unique. And whether they went part-time, temporarily, or later in the teen years, they felt their homeschooling years were instrumental in preparing them for success.

**Alyssa P., 18:**   I was very glad about homeschooling for the most part. We had a lot of fun, plus it was all I knew. When I reached about 14 or 15 years of age, I started to think about other options. My mom let me go to high school when I said I really wanted to be on the drill team. I was afraid I wasn't academically up to it, and in some ways, I was behind. My age group was tenth grade, but nothing I had done prior to going to high school would "transfer in." So I took two summer semesters and studied for a couple of CBE's (Credit by Exam). I passed them. And then by my Junior year (eleventh grade) I was caught up with my age group. I had no trouble at all with the academics. So much of the work was pointless though. I didn't do well with the "group punishment" idea. This is what they do when two or three people do something wrong and the whole group is punished. That was incredibly frustrating, since I was always following their rules. Teachers had been lied to so often, I guess, they always assumed all the students were lying—me included! There was so much distrust all around. The drama was irritating, some of the things that happened there were really dumb, and I felt like I was wasting my time staying in school. In the end, I stayed only a year and half. That was enough for me.

**Tori, 18:**   I remember literally sobbing at my mother's feet, begging not to go to school full-time during my eighth grade year. I liked homeschooling because I could learn the way I wanted. I learn best by doing, not taking notes about

---

**Kristin 19**

I seriously considered going to school my senior year, but I thought it would be silly to have to get used to everything about public school when I would only be there for one year. I had other things to consider, my job, dance, and theatre – which were all easier to pursue as a homeschooler. I was also fiercely independent and didn't want my whole day dictated by adults who didn't know me at all.

Not to mention that I still found most other high school students annoying.

---

**Grace, 19**

I had homeschooled my whole life and I knew I didn't want to go full-time to the junior high or high school.

But I was able to take a class or two each year so there was never really a question for me.

it. I think homeschooling was very beneficial to me because I was a slow learner, and my mom just worked with me at my own pace. I couldn't read until I was eight years old, but I advanced four grades in a year. I graduated from a public high school in the top ten percent of my class, which is proof that kids don't have to learn to read at age four to be smart and succeed. I also feel that going to public school better prepared me for college work, because the systems are more alike. I also think it improved my social skills to be put in public school for a period of time.

**Elizabeth, 19:**   Because I had been homeschooled since I was in kindergarten I wasn't reluctant to be homeschooled. However as I got older I did want to see what the public school was like and I knew I eventually wanted to go full time to the local high school. Attending junior high part-time (a California option) was a perfect way to start my transition into the public system.

---

### Alyssa P., 18

I was hoping for more friends, since we had moved to our neighborhood when I was 13 years old. But that didn't really happen.

Going to high school was fun for a little while, but the gossiping and lying got to be too much for me to tolerate. The dance team was fun for a while too, and I'm happy for the experience, but I was very glad to get back to unschooling, where I had much more say over my day!

*Alyssa P., Katie P., Kirby, and Cameron L. meeting for BBQ in Austin, Texas*

*Jared had a lot of time to practice with his camera*

*When you look at friends who went to school, do you see advantages to homeschooling?*

## CHAPTER 4

## The Advantages of Homeschooling

Our unconventionally educated respondents were asked about the advantages they experienced as compared to their schooled friends. I asked them to think about some of the troubles they were able to avoid, simply because they learned at home—some of their answers might surprise you. Invariably, they reported tremendous advantages because of being homeschooled and they fall into six categories:

- *They have a happier approach to learning.*
- *They've been exposed to real world opportunities.*
- *They have the freedom to make choices.*
- *They've been able to avoid unnecessary stress.*
- *Their socialization opportunities are better.*
- *They have better influences.*

### *Approach to Learning*

One of the main advantages is simply the opportunity to protect your teen's natural love of learning. As parents, we notice that very young children are like sponges when it comes to new experiences; their curiosity propels them into learning new skills and ideas. One reason we don't see this attitude toward learning as they get older, might be because society gets in the way. Schools decide what and when they're going to learn. The natural internal motivation of a child to explore and discover has been stifled and replaced with the schooled child's resistance. Forcing the school's plan for learning on children, year after year, teaches them that their choices must be shelved so that the system's choices for them remain the priority.

| Advantages of Homeschooling | Avoided by Not Going to School |
|---|---|
| ⅄ more free time<br>⅄ working at their own pace<br>⅄ meeting people of all ages<br>⅄ taking early college classes<br>⅄ traveling during "the school year"<br>⅄ maintaining a better attitude toward learning<br>⅄ exploring subjects their own way<br>⅄ more opportunities simply due to the flexible schedule<br>⅄ more self-discovery<br>⅄ healthier food<br>⅄ stronger work ethic<br>⅄ meeting more people with shared interests<br>⅄ more independent decision making<br>⅄ more comfortable with adults<br>⅄ individual attention<br>⅄ increased self-confidence<br>⅄ better family relationships<br>⅄ decent sleep<br>⅄ more flexibility<br>⅄ a better life! | ⅄ peer pressure<br>⅄ stress<br>⅄ academic restraints<br>⅄ aversion to learning<br>⅄ unnecessary competition<br>⅄ bullying<br>⅄ apathy about life<br>⅄ early morning tiredness<br>⅄ stifling of creativity<br>⅄ schedules that are someone else's plan |

When families opt out of this institutional approach, they have the opportunity to change all of that. They can remove the obstacles that interfere with the drive to learn. They can tailor their teen's education to his or her interests, strengths and weaknesses – a truly personalized learning situation that sustains the enthusiasm for learning that was so obvious in their children's younger years.

**Mike S., 16:**   I think one of the many advantages is learning how to choose what's best for yourself. Some people I know that have a more heavily structured education don't seem to have much passion for one subject over another. I also think that having more time to reflect and think about everything gives me a deeper connection. I feel like all of my current relationships with my family and friends are healthier than those of other teens.

**Sunny, 17:**   I feel like it's a lot easier to be taught when my parents taught me and my two siblings. They only had to focus on three kids rather than a whole classroom. We got to move along a lot faster and we didn't have to wake up at 7:00 a.m. ;)

**Molly N., 19:**   I think that the education system in the U.S. is a huge failure and those going into university are ill-prepared and unmotivated, largely due to their experience. My peers in university often have to take remedial classes in college, are burnt out, and don't really know how to tap into their creativity. Unschooling allowed me to direct my education.

**Nicholas, 26:**   The biggest advantage I had by homeschooling was the individualized attention. Schools often fit 30 kids or so into one classroom with one teacher. If you have trouble or don't understand something, it is difficult for the teacher to stop and address one student's needs. There were other children in my class (when I went to school) who would have benefited from the one-on-one teaching that I got when I switched to homeschooling. I doubt that they did as well as I did in the rest of their academic career.

---

*Michael, 22*

From an education standpoint, teens in school didn't receive anything more than me. In fact, my opportunities to learn what I wanted, where I wanted, how I wanted, gave me MORE of an advantage over those cooped up in school. I never had an aversion to learning—which I believe school itself creates.

I had

UNRESTRAINED EDUCATION.

I had no restraint with regard to learning. Not from a teacher or a curriculum or a school.

> ### *Jackson, 20*
>
> Up until starting college classes, I had the advantage of not having had subjects shoved down my throat. I grew up with a love of learning because I never "had" to do any of it. Every time I hear someone talk about how they "hate math" or "don't like to read," I cringe, wishing they had had a chance to explore those subjects on their own terms.

> ### *Zach, 24*
>
> The advantages I see are the ability to learn on my own and be proactive. And I'm more involved in problem-solving, as opposed to needing to be told what to do.

**Wendelyn, 34:**   I have noticed when I talk to people that had traditional schooling, they have a difficult time thinking outside the box—almost as if there is no other way to do things than the way it was done with them. People expect you had specific training, degrees or schooling when you do something well. I also see that there are few people who continue to learn and grow as an adult. They seem to have the mentality that they learned everything they need to know through school and don't need to continue once they were done. They also feel like school is the only place you can learn efficiently. I try to be open minded, and continue to seek experiences, people and literature that will help me become a better person.

**Roya, 27:**   I think the biggest advantage I have is this drive to keep on learning. Even in my graduate program, where most of the folks who have no interest in school have been weeded out, there is resistance to learning.

**Katie F., 24:**   I found that I still have a love of learning that many people I have met who went to a public school don't have. I never learned to hate learning and, being homeschooled, I have the tools at my disposal to learn anyhow and anywhere instead of just in a classroom with a teacher.

**Elizabeth, 19:**   Since Davis has a very good public school system and is very safe I don't think I avoided any big problems such as bullying or incidents such as that. But I did avoid having to do a lot of busy work in the classroom and I was able to get ahead in some subjects, such as math.

**Tori, 18:**   I think my biggest advantage was that I had been taught to be motivated about learning by my mom during homeschool. I still will never understand people who just don't do their homework. To me, it's not an option. I try my best because that is what I have been taught to do. Also, homeschooling allowed me to work on my strengths, so when I'm trying to learn something, I can usually pick the easiest way for me to learn something or complete a task.

**Anastasia, 19:** My freedom to study (and in some cases NOT study) has been invaluable. My interests in mathematics, biology and other sciences all blossomed through exposure to sources that simply wouldn't have been available in school.

**Hannah T., 18:** In college I found I had lots of advantages over most of my traditionally schooled peers due to my unschooling background. The most obvious advantage was my ability to self-teach and learn on my own, something most homeschoolers and unschoolers discover early on. My views on the world also seemed much broader than my peers, and I tended to ask more questions in the classroom which definitely aided in my learning experience.

## *Real World Opportunities*

Homeschoolers have an enormous advantage when it comes to living in the real world. They aren't confined to 180 days of classroom attendance, or limited to only reading about fascinating places or events. Instead, they are able to move freely in the world, exploring their communities and interacting with a wide variety of people. Ironically, many people think homeschoolers are sheltered and lacking exposure to "real life," while, in fact, the opposite is true. Teens who are not burdened by the constraints of all-day classroom sitting are out in the world making friends in their neighborhoods, in clubs, and at community activities; they are working, volunteering, attending community college classes, and traveling the globe. The teens and young adults who felt their opportunity to interact with the real world was their big advantage, share their thoughts in this section.

**Risa, 21:** I believe that I benefited from homeschooling because of the wealth of available opportunities that would have otherwise been impossible for me. Because I was homeschooled as a teen, I was taking college classes when I was 16 years old, working (including for CA State Department of Parks and Recreation), and traveling extensively. These are all experiences that have shaped me as a person

> ### *Katie P., 20*
> I believe that my advantage was that I got to do so many things: travel, tons of dance classes, and every community theatre opportunity. Public school takes up so many hours of the day that it would have been hard, if not impossible, to be able to have had all the awesome experiences I've been able to have.

and been influential in my college years—and would never had happened if I had attended public school.

**Skylar, 26:**   I was exposed to so much more as a homeschooler. I could pursue my interests to their end, and I found what I really love—grief support and death and dying. I'll be returning to grad school in the fall to continue my education and further my career path.

**Hailey, 18:**   Because I homeschooled, I got to live in Germany for my junior year of high school. While they were memorizing facts for a history test, I was learning how to navigate the Berlin subway system. While they were gossiping in class and ignoring the teacher, I was talking with activists and the yogi next door. They are pursuing monetary and superficial success and comfort, I am seeking passion and spiritual fulfillment every day of my life.

**Kristin, 19:**   Since I basically developed and followed my own curriculum during high school, I had to be very motivated and self-driven to get my work done every day. I also juggled a part-time job, dance, and theater, on top of my schoolwork, during high school. In college, time management wasn't difficult for me. I was easily able to complete my homework and study for tests, whereas a lot of my friends who had gone to school had a hard time focusing on schoolwork and meeting deadlines. I didn't expect to just automatically make good grades, like some people did, so I worked hard and generally got a lot out of my classes. Homeschooling gave me a strong work ethic.

**Steen, 15:**   I had the ability to be around the people I wanted to be around, all around the world—people of much more maturity and those that truly shared my interests. I have been able to do so many amazing things that if I was stuck in a classroom I would not have been able to do. My perspective on life and what is important is very different and my consciousness about the world around me is much greater.

**Alsatia, 18:**   Well for one thing, I got the college credit of an advanced placement course with a LOT less work.

---

### Zoe, 22

The first thing I always think of is, that I got an actual childhood. When you go to school you sit at a desk from 8A-3P (not counting gym class which seems like a torture on a whole different scale). After school, kids have to go home and do hours of homework. It's much harder to have good relationships with your family, simply because you don't get to spend a whole lot of time with them. You also get used to only socializing with kids your own age. Age has never made a difference in who I choose to be friends with. I also see in some (obviously not all) people, that the fun of learning has been removed.

As a homeschooler I got to dictate my own curriculum, so I got to learn what was actually interesting or useful to me, not what someone else had decided I should know.

**Sarah P., 17:**   I have the advantage, first, of meeting young people and adults of varying ages. I am involved with the grand span of ages that comes with the real world of college, competitive dance, etc. I am able to cope with and converse with everybody, without the fear of adults that sometimes accompanies schools (i.e., principals, teachers.) I have also never developed school avoidance habits, as many do or must to cope with school life. I have been involved with the homeschool community, which, though it doesn't work for some people, I find to be much more accepting and helpful, without fear of bullies.

**Molly S., 20:**   I have had more time to do theatre, music, dance, voice training, etc. I have had time to learn about several things because I didn't have to take history six times.

**Jared, 22:**   There seems to be an artificiality that is accompanied with school; homeschooling puts you in the real world, not a fake environment. I think that being out and about in the real world conversing with adults about anything and everything contributed a lot to my social skills.

**Caitlin, 27:**   I became a much more self-confident person, and learned to figure out how to get what I wanted without necessarily following the conventional path. I have friends ranging in age from teenagers to 65+, many of them I met while I was homeschooling. I was able to have many experiences that would not have been possible if I spent most of my days in school.

## Freedom to Make Choices

When families send their teens to school, I don't think they consider how much freedom they're asking their child to give up. Most parents went to school themselves, so they give little thought to sending their children down a similar path. Studies show that giving children and teens more freedom allows them time and opportunity to gain practice, improve confidence, and become more self-reliant. Homeschooled teens have the freedom to follow their passions, both dipping their toes in new activities and pursuing

> ### Kelli, 21
>
> By far the clearest advantage I experienced was the freedom I was given. I was free to discover who I was morally, spiritually and politically in the privacy of my own home without fear of judgment from my peers.
>
> I was free to fail and start again, as needed.

> ### Jared, 22
>
> Homeschooling gave me the freedom to be who I wanted to be. It allowed me to shape my future and make the choices I wanted to make.
>
> It didn't hinder me in any way.

interests on a deeper level than would have been available if they were at school. Sitting in a classroom, all day every day, with each hour pre-planned for them, robs them of opportunities to gain these skills.

Sometimes families fear giving teens freedom because they worry that chaos will result. But when parents are well-connected with their teen, they are in a much better position to know how much freedom that teen can handle. These teens and young adults felt that having freedom to be involved in the many choices of their day was one of the biggest advantages of homeschooling:

**Teagan, 20:**   The advantage I have always felt I had as a homeschooler is the freedom to choose my knowledge. Unlike a traditional public school education, I was able to pursue the knowledge that excited me, as opposed to just the knowledge that the school board decided I should have. If I wanted to spend six months studying almost nothing but the history of Tudor England (which I did, at age thirteen), for example, I could.

**Ari, 21:**   I had the ability to travel more, create my own schedule, and focus on my random passions.

**Alyssa H., 17:**   When I look at my friends who go to school I notice that they never really have time to do what they want… they don't get to read what they want or chase after their dreams. They get up, go to school, come home do homework, go to bed, and then do it all over again. I am able to study what I want and do all sorts of things that other kids will never get to do.

**Nancy, 15:**   I have a chance to study at my own pace, I also can add bible study in which is something I wouldn't be able to do in public school.

**Cameron PT., 20:**   Less bullying, tons of free time to doodle and play with army men, while they had to waste their days on irrelevant activities. I ended up going to college and doing just as well or better than them without studying at all, whereas they spent twelve years prepping for it.

---

### Skye L., 22

When I think of advantages I've had, I think of freedom. Some of my advantages included:

- Worked at my own pace
- Travel opportunities
- Greater autonomy over education/knowledge
- Increased time on subjects of interest
- No penalties for late work or sick days
- Extremely flexible schedule
- Minimal peer pressure and/or potential alienation
- Better food/more choices

---

### Hailey, 18

When I look at my peers stressing over SAT and ACT scores, sweating rivers over college applications, a nd pulling their hair out trying to find a career path at 18, I feel bad for them. There they are, taking years off their lives stressing like that over something as insignificant as standardized test scores, and I want to throw my arms around them and say "There is another way!"

I think it would have been awful to have wasted all that time on something that matters so little.

**Sarah H., 24:**  I avoided a lot of negative peer pressure. I was also able to study more things that interested me, like art history, and spend more time studying subjects I chose.

**Kaci, 18:**  Well, a lot of people I know who went to public school are really into drama, parties, and all those negative things. Parties don't always have to be about getting drunk or doing drugs. I think my advantage was that I didn't get into much of that. I kept away as best as I could, and taught myself to say no.

**Sarah H., 24:**  I think I avoided a lot of negative peer pressure. I was also able to study more things I was interested in, like Art History, and spend more time studying subjects I chose.

**Grace, 19:**  I didn't have to worry about the SAT exam, or the social hierarchy or what "group" I wanted to be a part of. You just don't have that in a homeschool community. The only bad experience I ever had was being on one of the high school girls' sports teams.

I had more choices: did I want to do full time or independent study? How many classes (if any) did I want to take at the high school? Did I want to graduate from the high school and go to a four year college or did I want to skip a year or two and go to community college? Because of these options, I didn't feel rushed and I didn't feel a lot of pressure to figure out my life/career path at seventeen. I didn't feel like a failure when I chose to give myself more time.

I've also noticed that on average, friends of mine that were mostly homeschooled have an easier time conversing with adults than my public school friends.

**Trina, 16:**  School kids are very hung up, have bad judgment and often have very bad character. Some people say that their bad character is due to the parents but since public schoolers are only around their parents a few hours a day

> ### *Rebecca, 39*
>
> I had freedom and flexibility. So many people assume that traditional high school is the *only* way to achieve this one particular desired end result.
>
> But it's not. There are many paths that can be taken. And once you come to that realization, the fact of the matter is painfully obvious… traditional school is a complete waste of time.
>
> You can achieve whatever you want without spending a minimum of 7 hours each day (add homework on top of that), 5 days a week, 9 months a year, for 13 years of it sitting in a classroom.
>
> Yep. Definitely freedom and flexibility.

at most, they are more likely to get character traits from friends and the people they are with most of the day.

## Avoiding Unnecessary Stress

The news is full of heartbreaking stories of teenagers struggling with stress. Whether they're worried about fitting in or competing with their peers, clearly a problem exists. When teenagers are homeschooled, certain stressful situations can be minimized if not completely avoided. It's not that they live a stress-free life—no one is so lucky to have that!—but so many stressful situations only exist when a person is trapped in an institutional setting with others similarly fenced in.

These teens and young adults think that avoiding the stress of going to high school was their biggest homeschooling advantage:

**Tess, 27:**   I feel like I skipped a whole lot of pressure and torture associated with public school. While some people have the hang up that "High School is Life," I was lucky enough to have the experience that school was vehicle to a destination, and not the ride of life itself. Also, I had health problems and not having the stress and pressure of a public school experience made my problems more manageable.

**Jared, 22:**   I had friends who were homeschooled and friends who went to school and I noticed a few differences between the two groups. Homeschoolers tended to be more laid back and chill. I felt a bit more comfortable around them. I wasn't worried that they might judge me or anything I did or say. For example, the topic of math: my school friends would almost always freak out when I told them I wasn't doing the same math as they were. That never happened with my homeschooled friends. I definitely felt no peer pressure with them. My friends who went to school were a bit more pushy and seemed to be on the fast track. They also seemed much more stressed than my homeschooled friends. After spending two years coaching the Davis High Junior Varsity tennis team, and seeing the way they have a group of close friends they hang out with and

---

### Wendelyn, 34

I lived a very sheltered life growing up but I feel like it made me an emotionally stronger person. My husband, who went to public school, has some emotional damage from his school experiences.

### Emma, 18

I never had to endure the constant stress of deadlines, peer pressure, little sleep, not having time to do fun stuff, bad teachers, and drama.

whatnot, sometimes I feel that I sort of missed out on that experience. On the other hand, I would have missed out on the homeschooling experience if I had gone to school, and I wouldn't trade that for anything.

**Laurel, 21:**   I rarely suffered from stress as a teenager. That was the most obvious difference between my schooled friends (and some homeschooled friends) and myself, I think.

And now that those friends are in college, or recently out of college, I'd say the stress thing still applies. I've got no student loans to pay off, no pressure from my family to follow the career path I supposedly chose in college, and no strong desire to escape from my life in some way. I'm not saying every kid in school has to deal with these things, but the majority of my degree-seeking friends experience some, if not all of these problems.

**Aiden R., 17:**   I was never stressed because I didn't have to get homework done on some time line. And I didn't have to wake up early like they do!

**Caroline, 24:**   I never had to deal with bullying which some of my friends experienced. I also never had to deal with lousy teachers (I remember some of my friends talked about teachers screaming at them and throwing chairs). Drug abuse was big at a lot of the local high schools. I didn't get into it as a teen, which, in my opinion was a good thing. While this may just be my nature, homeschooling taught me that going against the crowd is ok. Peer pressure is huge and I certainly felt it, but I also could look at it and recognize it as such and make a decision based on that knowledge. This was not the case for most of my public schooled high school friends. Most importantly, most of my friends in high school learned to dislike school at an early age. They didn't like learning and, while they did well, they found school to be a chore. I grew up with parents that focused on us being competent academically, but, because I did not have the rigid structure encountered in public high schools, I never had to deal with sitting bored in a class or doing busy work. In my opinion, those and similar things taught my friends that learning happens in school and not elsewhere and that learning is a chore.

---

**Alatheia, 16**

I think I am more socially adaptable than many of my school friends, and I'm more confident in different social situations. For example, I strike up conversations with people who interest me. One day, I was in the museum, and complimented a man on his bow-tie, which freaked out my school friend who was with me. The gentleman in question turned out to be the CEO of the museum, and offered us a tour of the archives!

---

**Crystal, 15**

I can carry on a conversation with people of a wider age range than many people who went to school. I think I have a better relationship with my family than a lot of teens that I know that did go to school. And, I avoided a lot of bullying.

## Sarah B., 20

I find that there are a few advantages that I have over my friends that went to public school. I am much more comfortable talking to professors and adults in general because of spending time talking to my parents and my friends' parents all through my life. I find that a lot of the people I know that went to public school have a much harder time interacting with people of different ages. I also found that it was difficult for a lot of my friends to study on their own. They did not know what to do or where to look for extra help if the way a teacher explained something did not make sense to them.

## *Better Socialization*

Unfortunately, "social reasons" are often touted as one of the reasons a parent avoids homeschooling their teen. I think it's funny because, when I was in school, we were always being told, "You are not here to socialize!" And yet worrying about finding friends is often a big obstacle for parents and teens making this decision. But remember, school doesn't guarantee a happy social life. Just being near hundreds of other teens on a daily basis doesn't mean healthy or satisfying friendships. Those of us who went to middle schools and high schools need only to pause for a moment to remember situations that didn't go well at all. When children are basically trapped eight hours per day, five days per week, the environment can easily become a breeding ground for negative social behaviors. Bullying, avoidance, creating artificial "pecking orders" become common schooled kid behaviors. It's not surprising since these children and teens have to find some way to adapt to this situation that most cannot escape.

Parents of homeschooled teens can find situations for their adolescents to socialize with others in much more positive ways. Sometimes it is as easy as participating in homeschool support groups or joining clubs that share your teen's interests.

Homeschooled teens are not limited to interacting within their age group. They can learn from and befriend people who are younger or older, forming relationships based on affinity and connection rather than proximity and age. These friendships are formed in the same way that adults interact with each other once they're out of school! Keeping everyone solely grouped with their own age mates is artificial and does nothing to help adolescents join "the real world."

Another socialization advantage is that parents of homeschooled teens are often more involved with what's happening in their teens' life. They're not so out of the loop that they can't offer support and guidance for how to gracefully learn to get along with others. By the time an exhausted teen gets home from a day of drama in high school, they seldom want to share it with the people who might actually be able to help them. Homeschooling can change this dynamic in many ways.

These teens and young adults believe that "socialization" is one of the big advantages of homeschooling through their teen years.

**Hannah, 22:**  I didn't have to use up energy being more social than I can tolerate. Also, since I essentially went at my own pace from 7th grade onward, I was able to get ahead in science-related subjects as well as develop self-study habits and a love of learning that serve me well.

**Alyssa P., 18:**  One of the troubles I see school kids encounter is the "approval" factor. I never could figure out why they ALWAYS wanted other people's "approval." They couldn't decide anything without checking with everyone else first. Then, as they got older, they couldn't decide what college they wanted or what they wanted to study, without seeking everyone else's input. I guess they were conditioned to think like that. When I went briefly to high school, I never heard any adult ask "Where do you want to go? What do you love to do and what do you want to study?" It was always, "Go to a VERY prestigious (the more expensive—the better) college." Being homeschooled, I was able to figure out what I wanted to do and then my family helped to support me so I could achieve it. Another social advantage I have is my ability to talk to adults as people. I don't see them as The Enemy.

**Kristin, 19:**  The most obvious advantage I noticed while I was in high school was that I didn't have to deal with all the social junk that goes on in school. Snobby girls, bullies, cheating boyfriends, I never had to deal with any of this. This meant that I avoided betrayal, teasing, and heartbreak. When I got to college, I wasn't as jaded as most other students. This allowed me to be very friendly and open, and I made friends fast and gained people's trust fast.

However, when I did actually have an experience with lying and betraying friends, it was a big shock. I knew that people couldn't always be trusted, but I hadn't expected my close friends to hurt me that much. If I had gone to school, I probably would have had that experience earlier on, and might have even been able to avoid it once in college. However, I would

---

**Nathan, 22**

I definitely was able to avoid bullying. There are probably some bullies out there, but I think they are more the exception than the rule. The thing that made homeschooling better was that once I was away from that situation, it was over. But people who go to school have to see that person who bullied them almost every day.

prefer to have dealt with that kind of thing once I was 19 years old and fairly strong and independent, instead of when I was 13 or 14 years old and still shy and impressionable.

**Chant, 15:**   I don't have to mess with any bullies at all, I don't have any distractions during my school work, and I can work at my own pace.

## Better Influences

When a family chooses to homeschool, their relationship with each other can be strengthened. And when relationships are good, parents are in a better position to offer guidance along the way. Because they're not seen as an enemy or out of touch, these parents have a chance to be much more involved in their teens' lives, and to notice quickly when their teen is having a rough time. Something as simple as having more time together means that the parent has time to offer problem solving or simply have some influence when their teen faces some of the tougher choices that await. These teens and young adults felt that homeschooling throughout their teen years offered them the advantage of having better influences in their lives.

**Alaina, 25:**   What I might think is a benefit, someone who went to school might have experienced as well. It just depends on how involved a parent was in the raising of their child. My education included a lot of travel and museums as well as creative problem solving. I feel this has allowed me to have a very creative outlook on life.

**Kevin, 20:**   I'm not really sure about any advantage or disadvantage. I think it all falls on how they are brought up. Whether it's homeschool, public school or otherwise, it's how they make their choices after school. I've seen both ends of the spectrum.

**Emily, 16:**   Most kids can only relate to and get along with people their own age. Homeschooled kids are used to being around a variety of ages at all times. They function well with any age group. When you home school you have many more opportunities to do and experience more than a classroom.

> ### Rowan, 18
>
> The schooled children, adolescents and adults I have met seem to experience anxiety over issues that seem like they could be resolved by letting go of the need to please others. They seem to focus so hard on getting good grades that they absorb no knowledge.

> ### Beth, 20
>
> I had a strong family connection. I wasn't sexually active. I had better values, wasn't easily pressured, was more of an individual thinker. I was more self-reliant and I graduated early.

You get to experience life, not just sports, prom, and school work… which sadly, is what children are being taught to believe is life. When you are homeschooled you are prepared for adulthood. You are not left, even expected, to act like an immature kid. You are held to higher expectations, not held down by low expectations and only shown how to be a kid. Kids do not grow up to be kids. Kids grow up to be adults. Homeschooling prepares you for the challenges of adulthood!

Most kids look to their peers for guidance. Their peers who have as little or less life experience and wisdom as themselves. My parents are my role models. They teach me to follow Jesus' example! God gave children parents for a reason. Being homeschooled has been a wonderful gift. My parents have sacrificed so much to give me this advantage. I can never repay them fully! They have given me so many blessings, the blessing of friendship with my siblings, the blessing of safety, the blessing of freedom, the blessing of knowing God's voice, the blessings of being homeschooled! I am thankful to them and to God who has called them to homeschool!

**Laura, 24:**   I don't think I had as much peer pressure as public schoolers and I definitely was a lot more sheltered in certain aspects. I am grateful that I didn't "know" about certain things until I was older because once something's in your mind, it's really hard to get it out.

**Tony, 15:**   I think the worst aspect of the school system is that it does not promote curiosity, or open-minded thinking. Not only does it not promote those, the environment had some unintended side effects, due to separating kids not only by age, but also the grades they get. This, combined with the social pressure applied by putting so many kids in an unnatural environment, can create some very unhealthy behaviors in children. Bullying and the misconception that one person is better than another, is possibly the worst idea that can be spread! It's quite horrid that we send our children to a place that promotes that kind of thinking. This idea can lead to things such as dictatorship, and arrogance. These are just a few things that are wrong with the school system we have in place, and that is the advantage

---

**Sarah D., 19**

The biggest benefit I got from being homeschooled was the chance to really know my siblings. Because we were all home all the time, we learned to take care of each other and get along with people of different ages, or people with different interests. We never had to deal with bullying or cliques.

---

**Joseph, 19**

Traditionally schooled friends of mine who have very specific interests (like me and computers) often found themselves feeling very restrained, academically, sometimes having that specific interest or passion weaned out of them by the conformity-based public (or even private, sometimes) education they were receiving.

that I have – the advantage of not being in an environment that promotes such ideas.

**Rowan, 18:**   I believe that being raised by stable adults has helped me not criticize others, not get caught in drama, and be able to make choices based on what feels right to me and not make decisions because others, adults or peers, are saying that is what they want of me.

**Joseph, 19:**   I was able to avoid a lot of social pressure that would have certainly shaped me and who I am for the worse. While I did have some minor social issues in college, they were not nearly major enough to prevent me from making a ridiculous number of friends, and I've overcome those issues since then nonetheless.

**Kate, 15:**   My advantange, unlike some public schooled kids I know, I didn't learn about drugs and sex in middle school.

**Micah, 16:**   There is more pressure to excel in homeschool because you work so closely with your parents, but less peer pressure for drugs and alcohol use than in public schools.

**Simcha, 17:**   I have never done drugs or drank anything stronger than a glass of red wine at a wedding or dinner party. I've never been sent to

---

### Rose S., 20
### *What I Avoided by Skipping School*

- Bullying
- Teasing
- The stifling of creativity
- Public humiliation brought about by teachers and other students
- The stifling of the love of learning that all children are born with, and few adults have managed to retain
- The sheer exhaustion of being in the same place hour after hour, day after day, year after year
- The pressure to do things that I might not want to do, such as smoke, drink, sneak out, cheat, etc.
- An untrusting relationship with my parents
- A false idea that I can only talk to people who are exactly my age, not younger, not older.

*And this is only a small, small sampling of the negative things I avoided by not going to school.*

talk with a "counselor" nor have I ever felt the need to kill myself because I cannot meet up to the "social standard."

**Aiden W., 23:** I never had people tell me I couldn't do or be what I wanted. Some friends of mine had their dreams crushed and gutted like juicing oranges by teachers. That's not entirely true. My third grade teacher was a juicer. So I did experience that. My mom had to work kind of hard to help me see that I wasn't stupid after that. I'm quite confident in myself intellectually now.

## Teens & Sleep

In some comments, the homeschooled teens and young adults have mentioned getting to "sleep in" or avoiding stress because of not having to get up so early. At first glance, this may appear flippant. But science actually backs them up. We all know that when children reach puberty, their hormones begin to kick in. What we sometimes don't know is that those hormones can have an effect on a person's sleep cycle. The melatonin that increases at night that makes us naturally feel sleepy decreases significantly during adolescence. Add to that, light—artificial or natural—also inhibits the production which means that their body clocks, their circadian rhythms, are shifting.

> **Translation:** *Teens' bodies are physically geared to staying up later at night. Because they still need a good 9+ hours of sleep, that means they'll need to sleep later in the mornings.*

This certainly does not correlate with a typical high school schedule. Research shows that teens in school settings are basically sleep deprived. This can lead to increased stress, impaired memory, and inhibited creativity. It certainly interferes with learning. Any of what people consider the typical difficulties teens might experience are worsened if they're sleep deprived. It's not about power struggles and undermining authority, as some parents fear, it's something biological.

When parents of teens opt to homeschool, they're not forced to duplicate those high school schedule times. Teens can stay up late and then sleep in. This ensures that they get their full 9.25 hours of sleep needed, to be well rested and ready to explore and learn without being grumpy.

When parents ask their children to go to bed earlier and get up earlier, they're really working against nature. It's not the end of the world to do it, but why set up a problem situation? Why turn it into a power struggle?

When my kids were teens at home, I let them sleep late in the mornings and go to bed at whatever hour they wanted. It looked upside down compared to the rest of the world's schedules. Homeschoolers (and "schoolers" – as the kids used to call them) would ask me, "How will they be able to hold down a job—follow a schedule—adhere to expectations—if you never impose any on them as children?" Well, it turned into a non-issue. It would have been like practicing the act of waiting in line. Or working on eating. Sounds ridiculous, right?

One more advantage exists when parents work WITH their teen's natural inner body rhythms. Some of the best teen-parent conversations happen during those late hours. My teens were often feeling more relaxed, winding down from their day at 11 pm. Those late night conversations were real treasures, giving insight into what was happening in their lives—what they were nervous about or looking forward to—and they were open to listening to me about suggestions or stories of what I had seen in the past.

**Rebecca, 39**   We didn't have a sleep schedule. We stayed up and slept in, generally. Although, once I was 16 and working at the vet clinic I had to be into work by 8:00 a.m. at the latest to care for the dogs and cats in the kennel. The library was later... 10:00 a.m. or so. But I also remember napping! I'd take care of the dogs and kennel and then, if I wasn't staying to tag along with the vets on farm calls that day, I'd head home and take a snooze. I am a night owl by nature so going to bed early never really worked out very well. Naps—yes. But I loved that job, it was worth it.

My almost 15 year old stays up till 1:00 or 2:00 a.m. and sleeps till nearly noon more days than not. Her homeschooled (not unschooled) friends that she's up late messaging and chatting with stay up that late and then are awakened consistently early—7:00 a.m., schoolwork or not. It baffles my daughter. Her thoughts are, "no wonder they're so moody and grouchy all the time."

> ### Carver, 18
> By homeschooling, I avoided early morning tiredness.

> ### Michael, 22
> A big advantage for me was that I was able to go to bed when I was sleepy and get up when I felt rested. People were always afraid that I wouldn't be able to hold a job or get to college classes on time because I hadn't been "training" myself for that. Nothing was farther from the truth. I had several jobs where I had to get up early, and I just set my alarm and was out the door. No practice needed!

I think the freedom to get as much sleep as she needs, when she needs it has been a huge benefit for my teen. Her health and body, her emotional state, and our relationship are all better.

**Katie P., 20:**   When I was 15, I went to stay with my grandma in Dallas so I could attend a month-long intensive drama program. I got up at 5 a.m., checked email, fixed breakfast, showered, dressed, and caught the city bus to go downtown. And when I worked at Barnes & Noble, I often had to open the store at 7:00 a.m. I just went to bed a little earlier the night before so I could get enough sleep. After a while, I was just poking my head into my parents' room waking them up to tell them I was heading off to work. They didn't have to even get up!

✑ ✑ ✑

*The bottom line is that teens do have wacky sleep schedules. And parents really don't need to worry about it. Take advantage of the benefits that come with those late nights. Chat with them about Life in the kitchen over nachos – even if it's midnight! Talk to them about what you've read or learned about sleep and body rhythms. No one needs to rehearse getting up early. They will do it when they need to.*

*Rose S., Roxana, and Roya hanging out together*

*Kate taking notes*

*What were some of your various learning environments?*

## CHAPTER 5

# A Variety Of Ways To Learn

Homeschoolers know that classroom settings and more formal learning environments are not the only ways to learn. Taking advantage of the flexibility to use the whole community and tailoring those resources to fit the individual learner is a major characteristic of homeschooling. Most people are unaware of the opportunities that are available to independent learners today. And with the convenience of email lists, social media, and support group newsletters, families are able to connect, share and plan together.

### *83% report participating in a variety of group learning settings*

Some teens do well on their own, while some prefer learning with others. Many parents and teens are interested in finding group learning situations and there are a variety of ways to achieve this. Some families create small study groups with other families interested in the same topic. These classes can be offered in participants' homes or in community establishments, depending on the topic. Sometimes parents will coordinate having an expert on a particular subject talk or offer experiential or apprenticeship opportunities. Other families join co-ops (cooperatives) or school-type settings called "One Day Academies," or some other slight variation of this term, where groups of families hire teachers to teach a particular course. Sometimes the parents take turns teaching subjects themselves in a larger group setting. Homeschool support groups often sponsor field trips or set up group classes in the community – based on the participating families' interests.

Families aren't restricted to one particular learning environment so they can mix and match what works for their teen, what's best for that particular topic, or for any reason they choose. As homeschoolers network and communicate more, made easier by the Internet, parents and teens are finding interesting pursuits out in the community, all over the country. The concept of a lone student huddled over a book at a kitchen table with mom leaning over his shoulder can be put to rest. Teens are out in the world taking classes and teaching classes, volunteering and working, dabbling and delving deep, learning and exploring.

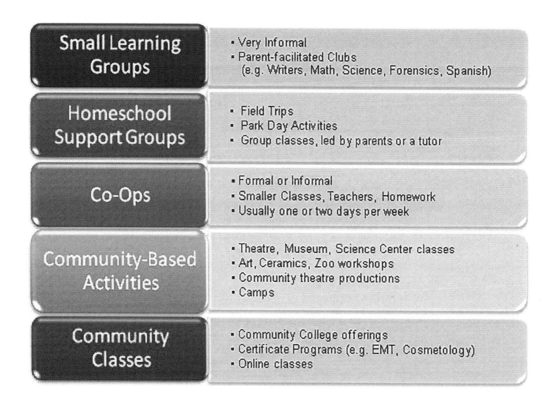

| | |
|---|---|
| **Small Learning Groups** | • Very Informal<br>• Parent-facilitated Clubs<br>  (e.g. Writers, Math, Science, Forensics, Spanish) |
| **Homeschool Support Groups** | • Field Trips<br>• Park Day Activities<br>• Group classes, led by parents or a tutor |
| **Co-Ops** | • Formal or Informal<br>• Smaller Classes, Teachers, Homework<br>• Usually one or two days per week |
| **Community-Based Activities** | • Theatre, Museum, Science Center classes<br>• Art, Ceramics, Zoo workshops<br>• Community theatre productions<br>• Camps |
| **Community Classes** | • Community College offerings<br>• Certificate Programs (e.g. EMT, Cosmetology)<br>• Online classes |

## Small Group Learning

Visualize six to eight friends, sprawled on couches and the living room floor, watching early American history on DVD. Or maybe a group huddled around a microscope at the kitchen counter sharing observations and drawing conclusions. Or a writing group run by the teens themselves, meeting in the local library's small study rooms (free for public use and often with no waiting list during the day!) So many possibilities exist when families choose this approach for learning particular topics.

One advantage of small learning groups is the social life it inspires outside of the class. Because schedules can be flexible they can completely accommodate all the group members. And if the participants aren't friends beforehand, that will likely change once the course is underway. And who doesn't enjoy learning with friends? All this approach requires is that parent or teen simply see a need and find the resources to fill it. No need to rely on institutions or "experts" to set up programs for them. Using small group learning, parents are actively and competently setting up a variety of learning opportunities for their homeschooled children.

Another benefit that comes with learning in small informal groups is that the kids grow up seeing their parents actively modeling problem-solving and resource-marshalling. With relatively no experience in a topic, anyone can seek resources within their circle of acquaintances, the internet and the larger community. Teens learn through this that any curiosity or interest can be pursued and how to creatively meet their own intellectual needs. Instead of relying on others to bring information to them, self sufficiency is reinforced with this small learning group style. They learn how to be lifelong learners.

Here are some teens with experience in studying in small groups.

**Sarah P., 17:**   When I was younger, I was involved with some casual writers clubs and math clubs that met once a week/biweekly. I have taken a number of recreational classes in that format. I never attended co-ops.

**Dakota, 20:**   I took a World War II class with some friends; it was fun despite all the death. I still find myself spouting random bits of knowledge about WWII every now and again.

**Beth, 20:**   We were able to meet with other homeschooled kids to learn. It was great.

**Sarah B., 20:**   I took some classes with a few other homeschoolers that I knew. I also took other classes my parents taught, or one of my friends' parents would teach us.

> **Tess**
> My group learning settings gave a lot of fun social experiences.

> **Kate, 15**
> I've taken personal finance and academic writing classes with other homeschoolers.

> **Risa, 24**
> I greatly enjoyed all the different methods of class work and thrived on the versatility of my education. It taught me to work well in different environments and fostered deep self-motivation.

**Risa, 21:** My homeschool experience used a lot of different class environments. My family participated in group, unit-studies where 3–4 families would focus on similar topics and themes. Once, for example, our unit study group focused on the Lewis and Clark expedition for a semester. We studied the history and international context of the Louisiana Purchase (History/World Civics), wrote in historical journals as if we were members of the expedition (English), memorized botany and plant classifications (Biology), and finally traveled to Oregon/Washington to follow the last 400 miles of their journey ourselves. It was an incredible experience for all of us and we never forgot the things we learned.

**Katie P., 20:** I attended a few learning groups while I was homeschooling as a teen. One was to study Hinduism, another was about World War II, and a third was Spanish. They weren't subjects that piqued my interest, but it made it easier to learn when I was with my friends. We did a lot of field trips through Girl Scouts and we learned a lot in 4-H meetings too.

**Emma, 18:** I took some group classes that homeschool parents taught and I do think they were good for me because it forced me to socialize. Now I take classes at the local community college; I don't necessarily "make friends" but I do talk to peers in class which helps with the whole social skills thing.

**Anastasia, 19:** I've only taken a few individual classes, and mostly with other homeschoolers. I can't say that they were very good experiences and I've found self-guided learning much more efficient.

**Alaina, 25:** We did some study groups or learning with friends. It was sporadic.

**Crystal, 15:** I did certain classes with smaller groups. It was really was great to be able to take a class with several people and not just by myself.

**Alyssa P., 18:** We did a group study with about ten other teens at different families' homes for different subjects. Of-

---

### Kristin, 19

My biology lab was all homeschoolers, and we learned a lot of lab techniques that I have since used at college. Since it was a homeschool class, all of the other students were bright, motivated, and had their own interests, which made them interesting to talk too. No one was judgmental and we all helped each other out. It was a great class. The other homeschool classes I was in were similar, with great teachers, practical knowledge, and fun students.

ten it tied in with something big happening in the community. Sometimes we met with a tutor (for Español) and sometimes a mom organized it using the Teaching Company DVDs and movies that matched up.

**Alyssa H., 17:**   Yes, I took a few classes with other homeschool teens: a research paper class, speech class, Latin group, an Enviro-thon team and a few other classes. Not often though, because I spent a lot of my time working or reading (because if you hadn't guessed by now I'm a bit of a book worm!).

**Skylar, 26:**   My homeschool group sponsored classes while I was middle school age—science, math, writing, etc.

---

### Elizabeth, 19

Many parents of the other homeschooled kids held classes once or twice a week, with 5 to 15 kids attending. I took marine biology, math, writing/English, cell biology classes, and U.S. history classes, among others. The classes were held at the home of the parent that was teaching the class. I think this was a perfect way to take classes because it allowed us to get out and interact with other students and teachers instead of only meeting with one teacher once a week.

I was able to work with other students and learn how to be in a group setting. This also taught me time management, since we only had classes once or twice a week, I really had to lay out a schedule and plan out when to get everything done. I think that helped a lot when it came to managing my time in college.

---

## Co-Ops

Co-ops come in many different shapes and configurations. They can be just a step more formal than small learning groups. Or, they can be quite formal with bylaws, fees, and a variety of expectations. The groups tend to be larger than other group learning options, so you often find them in church classrooms, simply because the space is available during the week.

Our family participated briefly in a few different Co-ops, since we moved around often. When my kids were in their early teens, our homeschool support group connected us with a co-op run by a committee of moms. They chose a particular time period or event, and then the participating families provided resources and activities to support the theme. This particular co-op was a lot of fun for my kids because the activities were hands-on, interactive, and entertaining. I think they'll always remember what they learned there. Some co-ops are like this—relaxed enough that the teen could choose their own level of involvement, based upon their interest.

Later, we participated in a much more formal co-op, primarily to connect them with other teens. They took a gym class and an art class, both very structured. It served our purpose of meeting people, but for a variety of reasons, we opted out of the co-op after a year.

**Skye, 22:**    Yes, I took some classes at a co-op with some friends. It was just one of the many ways I/we maintained a social life.

**Micah, 16:**    I took classes at a co-op which was fun to be with others my age, but it was really not a lot different than what I did at home because at home you still have the same assignments to complete.

**Nicholas, 26:**    Another homeschool friend and I tried classes with an already established group. The problem was that most of the kids were much younger and were teaching things we had both learned a long time ago. Approximately a year after that, my mother started a group of homeschoolers with the same religious belief. This group was wonderful. The group had members from Ohio, Indiana, and Pennsylvania. We were able to take many great field trips that would sometimes last several days. One time we all traveled around Ohio visiting the 8 locations of Presidents that came from Ohio. Overnight we would all stay at the home of a fellow homeschooler that lived in the area. This is a trip that would have been nearly impossible for a school to do. I also took Latin lessons with a fellow homeschooler.

**Michael, 22:**    I had a ton of group learning experiences. At first, it was primarily within whatever homeschooling community we were in. We had a blast learning about Egypt and China and the Civil War through a co-op.

---

**Sophie, 19**

I was involved in a co-op for a while. It was helpful because a bunch of local homeschoolers got together to learn and we were all taught by parents. It made us more motivated because there was some competition and at the same time the parents were totally involved.

---

**Ari, 21**

When I was younger I went to Friday Co-Op in Austin. Later, I did group studies at friends' houses in History, World Religion, English and Spanish.

The parents all set up a variety of hands-on experiences for us and each week, we'd get together with a bunch of other kids and basically play with our learning. Sometimes they brought in other people to show us stuff. We had big "Mad Science" days in the library activity center or some other community building. The guy did cool science experiments with us and we loved it. One dad we knew was a doctor. He got a really good microscope and showed us a lot about microbiology. Another time we had a small group of people interested in acting. So one of the parents found actors to come show us how to write screen plays and do improv. Another time, someone came to show us about what it's like to live with disabilities, where we personally experienced various disabilities. Since I'm in Nicaragua now, the only word that comes to mind is the Spanish word meaning workshop: "*charla*." We had a lot of *charlas!*

**Rowan, 18:**   From age 4–11, I was involved in a group called Friday Co-Op. I learned an awful lot and really enjoyed it. The kids voted on what classes they wanted and the parents volunteered to teach classes. I believe that it was a good thing for me.

**Carver, 18:**   I took several homeschool group classes, they furthered my learning.

**Katie P., 20:**   In my early teens, we lived in California where we had a large support group with lots of kids my age. We did group activities while we lived there, studying Egypt, ancient China, art, backyard theatre, and Choral singing. If we had stayed there, I probably would have continued with those co-op type activities, if they interested me and could fit in my schedule.

**Zoe, 22:**   I took several classes in a group setting. Overall they were positive experiences.

**Kristin, 19:**   I took a few classes, such as a lab class, but most of my studying was done on my own, with books that I found. The classes I took were great, though.

---

*Molly S., 20*

My parents put me in tons of classes: fine arts, sports, science, math, performing arts, dance, choir, language, English, history, economics… These were mostly before I started at my community college, but some afterwards as well.

---

*Alyssa A., 18*

I did take some co-op classes, some of which my mom taught. These provided a way of talking to people my age and it was fun being able to be around people doing the exact same thing you are.

**Hannah J., 22:**   I participated in a co-op through middle school, but not during high school. The quality of classes was variable; I tend to learn more on my own than in classes, but participating in a group was still beneficial.

**Chant, 15:**   We set up small group activities, which gave me social experiences and I made a lot of friends.

## One Day Academy/Umbrella School

The One-Day Academy is one the most formal of all the homeschool options. The classes imitate school classes, with the exception being that the teen often only goes one or two days each week. They employ teachers, who are sometimes parents with an expertise in a particular area, but just as often, teachers available for part-time work. Families simply pay for classes. Several towns have "One-Day Academies" that have been meeting for so long that they have their own facilities. Umbrella groups/schools vary from state to state, often provided by private schools that offer a homeschool option. Umbrella schools spring up in states where homeschoolers are trying to accommodate various regulations. Families who aren't comfortable with handling all aspects of their teen's education or are looking for the familiar school-type setting for their teen often choose these daytime academies. These are the teens and young adults who took classes in some of these more formal homeschool settings.

**Kelli, 21:**   Yes, I did take classes! I loved every minute of it too because it allowed my sister and me to socialize and make even more friends without being negatively over-saturated. We had time to be with friends, learn from others and gain new experiences. However, we were also allowed alone time where we could decompress and have time to rest and think.

**Kaci, 18:**   I took classes for three years at a one day academy. I enjoyed it at first, but later started to feel unwelcome. It was a very up-tight Christian co-op, and my beliefs were different.

> ### Caitlin P., 27
>
> Yes, I took many classes through Saturday Academy, a program available in Portland. I also took some classes arranged through the homeschooling community, such as a Latin club.

> ### Nathan, 22
>
> I took an art class with a group. I was in a theater group and did some daytime groups. They were great experiences for me because they helped me find friends outside those I already had.

**Trina, 16:**  I did take some more formal classes. It was stressful and, in the end, I learned more at home than I did in the classes. The other kids there were more into hanging out with their friends than actually learning. Most of the schoolwork was busywork that didn't really help me learn anything and I ended up going home and learning it all over again on my own.

**Caroline, 24:**  I took classes once a week for high schoolers in our umbrella group. Through that program I took chemistry, biology, and composition. The exposure to a lab environment was very good for me as it led to pursuing a job field and eventually to my current job, which can be laboratory intensive. The composition class was incredibly important for me. My mother always struggled with teaching her children to write (so she thought, I disagree), but having another set of strict eyes to pick apart papers was useful. Actually, I'd credit that class with making all the papers I ever wrote in college a breeze. The teacher was tough and exacting and I'll forever love her for it.

**Sarah H., 24:**  My dad started a school with some other homeschool families, and he and my mom taught classes. It was a really good thing, I think. It was a great chance to socialize with other kids and we had a really good time. We even had a choir for a time. I really look back at our little school as some of the most fun I had. I met my best friend there, and we have been friends now for over twelve years.

## Community Classes

You'd be surprised how many community resources a homeschooled teen has! And, certainly, more exist now than ever before. Communities are realizing that homeschooling families are an untapped market, which translates into more opportunities. When my kids were younger, we approached businesses to set up some sort of activity. They'd often find instructors and create a reduced price structure for us, since we were often arriving with multiple kids in tow, during the day when their business was slow. Now, communities that have active homeschool networks have learning experienc-

> **Cameron L., 24**
>
> I crashed a few college courses in sociology at USC in Columbia, SC. I took a 6-week course with the National Outdoor Leadership School learning outdoor leadership, group dynamics outdoor navigation and first aid.

> **Michael, 22**
>
> As an older teen, I did less with the homeschool group and more just out in the community—Teens Make a Difference Day, Quiz Bowl competitions, 4-H, community theatre, scouts.
>
> Yeah, I did lots of group stuff!

es already in place. Parents who aren't homeschooling yet might not be aware of some of the options available to homeschooled teens. And in communities that don't have opportunities set up, all it takes is a parent willing to help get one started! These teens and young adults share some examples of the classes they took in their communities:

**Mike S., 16:**   I took acting classes, and a few piano lessons. I've never taken any formal math classes, writing classes, psychology classes, etc. I still enjoy the aforementioned subjects, but I prefer to learn things when I feel it's necessary to learn them in order to achieve my goals.

**Molly S., 20:**   We went on a lot of field trips to museums, manufacturing, we definitely toured the little pretzel place by the mall once. I was also in book club. I was part of a group of kids (I think ages 6–17) who were guided through, but we did it ourselves, all the steps of creating a student film, by a mom in our group who had been in the film industry for a while. We even bought lights and equipment. I think the fact that I was exposed to so many kinds of things was very helpful in deciding where I fit and what I want to do. Although, I really enjoyed my physics class, learning about the way the world works, and I always loved math class... Well, you can see how much I am dwelling on the performing arts aspect of everything because that's where my heart lies.

**Jackson, 20:**   I only took theatre classes, no other formal classes that I can think of.

**Alyssa P., 18:**   I took some art classes at the local museum and theatre classes at a local community theatre. I also took dance classes and was on a competitive cheerleading team.

**Julia, 15:**   I take dance and I find that it is an incredibly valuable experience for teaching co-operation, respect, team work, fun and creativity. For the most, part students want to be at dance and the teachers want to

---

### Roya, 27

I took classes and basically lived at the ceramics studio between the ages of 13 and 20. I grew up there, learned about responsibility, clay, and ideal communities. I joined Girl Scouts, swim team, and a Shakespeare theatre group. I participated in poetry workshops at parties, conferences, and even campouts. We participated in Living History events through the homeschool groups as well as the local museums.

So much learning through all of these activities!

teach dance, this makes for better attitudes and experiences than school would ever afford.

**Emily, 16:** I enjoyed taking art classes, zoo classes, and science classes.

**Katie P., 20:** I also took a number of dance classes, musical theatre classes and intensives, voiceover as well as general acting classes as a teen. These also led to more classes with individual instructors in voice and dance.

## And Still More Teen Opportunities to Learn

Sometimes parents may feel like detectives, out combing the community looking for ways to foster their children's learning. But teens and kids can also do the research and discover a variety of resources to further their education. Many find ways to create or combine some of the opportunities that are available in the community too.

**Risa, 21:** I also took many online classes: Great Books (where I read Homer, Plato, Dante, Nietzsche, Darwin, St. Augustine, and Rousseau, among others), biology, and Greek. These online classes are available to homeschool students across the country and not only did I receive an amazing education (that I still reference now that I'm in college), but I made numerous friends from other states who I still travel to see.

**Elizabeth, 19:** I went to the high school part-time.

**Hailey, 18:** I took only online classes.

**Rebecca, 39:** I took two classes at the community college during my teen years.

**Kevin, 20:** I did my own classes on the computer and in books. It was a good thing. I could go at my own pace, decently fast.

---

**Alyssa P., 18**

When I was 17, my mom did the paperwork to declare me "graduated," and I enrolled in a 10-month cosmetology program. I completed it in what some people called my "senior year."

---

**Nicholas, 26**

I took EMT-Basic classes during my "senior" year in homeschooling. I think using the community college is a much more popular option now, I didn't use it back then. What a great option using the community college is though! Much of the material is similar and you can be finishing high school with a degree or close to it!

**Joseph, 19:**   I took several types of classes throughout high school—a number of group classes with other homeschoolers, which were primarily discussion-based. I had a one-on-one environment with tutors for subjects like math, piano, and Latin. When I took sciences in high school, it was in a community college setting, so it was definitely good for me (and impressive to college admissions) to have that experience early on. I also attended the Johns Hopkins Center for Talented Youth Summer Program for three years, which was a fantastic opportunity to meet like-minded students who attended standard school programs. All-in-all, a good variety.

**Hannah T., 18:**   I did an at-home college level forensic anthropology course, and read many college level text books to expand my knowledge base. Other than a forensic camp I attended for a couple of weeks I never really had any routine classes or groups I went to.

**Grace, 19:**   I homeschooled until fifth grade. Then, I did independent study/homeschool groups/co-ops, threw in some split site, CHSPEE'd (California High School Proficiency Examination) out of high school and went to community college in my "senior year."

**Kristin, 19:**   I tried one year to take classes at a community college, but due to budget cuts, they were considering whether they would still allow high schoolers to take college level classes, so I opted not to take the classes.

**Beth, 20:**   I started the "Jump Start" program at my community college at the age of sixteen, the same year I graduated from homeschool/high school.

**Sophie, 19:**   I attended 2 different charter schools. I was part of Horizon Charter School for half of sophomore year and all of junior year, and then I was a student at Smith Flat Charter School. I did University Prep for all of senior year.

**Rose, 30:**   I audited a couple of classes, one with my grandmother who had just discovered that our community college let her take classes for free, and one at a university in the class of a friend who was a professor.

---

### Jared, 22

My approach to academics was to not have an approach to academics.

I didn't follow any sort of curriculum. I didn't really study any textbooks.

I remember having one math book that I would work in whenever I wanted to (which was hardly ever).

Although I did participate in group activities, I didn't do them often.

I went on the field trips that our group would organize and other things like that. Basically, I led the way.

Whatever subject sparked my interest is the one I pursued, which brings us back to filmmaking; it sparked my interest, and I pursued it.

I think it's safe to say that I was a pretty loose unschooler.

*Ari, Aiden R., Kaci, Alyssa P. goofing off with friends
between theatre classes*

*Kate taking online community college classes*

*Did you use the local community college?*

## CHAPTER 6

## Community College Classes

Many non-traditional learners take full advantage of their local community college system while they are in what would be called their "high school years." As homeschooling has become more well-known, community colleges have changed regulations and restrictions to allow younger students without a high school diploma to attend. While each community college system has its own rules and expectations, and some states offer more colleges and programs than others, homeschooled teens are using them to test the waters of college, to begin degrees or complete certification programs.

**Homeschooled Teens & Community College**

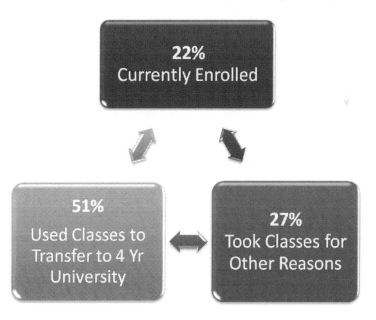

Some students use the community college system as a cafeteria-style educational option so they can take what they're interested in and leave the rest. Some took community college classes as dual-enrollment classes, meaning that the class "counted" for both high school and college credit. Community colleges often offer technical or vocational classes that might lead to a career or a hobby. Classes that may be difficult to provide at home-like science labs, foreign language, art or theater classes – may be offered at the community college. Many homeschooled teens started with classes that simply looked fun to them. Families that chose this route found that it gave their teen a better chance for success, helping them overcome any anxiety about stepping up to the college level.

Some students choose community college classes because they are less expensive than taking the same class at a university. Students can complete one or two years of courses—usually all of their lower division general education requirements—and then transfer to the university as sophomores or juniors. Often, these transfer students can avoid the SAT or ACT exams, since they will have already proven their ability to pass collegiate level courses.

My son graduated from college (Magna Cum Laude even!) without ever taking the SAT or ACT tests. After taking 30 college credits at the local community college, he was able to transfer to the nearby state university as a sophomore. He bypassed the SAT/ACT tests that cause so much teen stress.

It's not unusual for homeschooled teens to be a little nervous about taking community college classes at a younger than usual age. But typically, once they start the class, they discover there's nothing to be worried about. None of the homeschooled teens or young adults surveyed had any trouble with the classes or the environment. In fact, most of them loved it!

### *73% Use (or Plan to Use)*
### *the Community College system*

While there is certainly no rush to get started with college classes, teenage homeschoolers are often making plans and community college often plays a large part. One hundred percent of the teens surveyed planned on making use of their local college at some point.

**15-18 Year Olds'
Community College Experience**

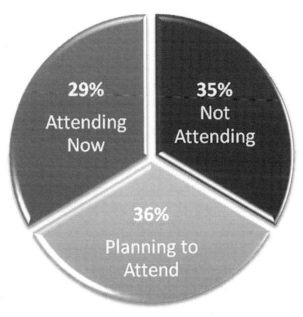

29%
Attending
Now

35%
Not
Attending

36%
Planning to
Attend

## *Dual Enrollment for 15-18 year olds*

Dual enrollment, sometimes called concurrent enrollment, is often offered by community colleges to allow eleventh or twelfth graders to take college credit courses that will count as high school credits and college credits simultaneously. Community colleges are recognizing that homeschoolers, with their sometimes murky approach to grade level, are often ready to take community college classes at a younger than usual age. Some colleges have specific programs to ease homeschoolers into the college class environment, often with fees waived when requirements are met. These classes are typically more academic, as opposed to classes for fun.

For those who want to transfer to universities, community college classes are a wonderful way to take some necessary courses and master some new material.

Some homeschooled teens are very aware of being "dually enrolled." That's usually because their state has made allowances for it or their particular community college sets it up that way. But many others simply take classes and are "dually enrolled" by default because they're still under the compulsory schooling laws of their state. They are taking college classes without having to jump through the application and testing hoops to attend a four-year college.

That may all sound a bit confusing! So let's read how these teens and young adults used their own local community college system.

**Risa, 21:**    Yes! I began taking classes at the local community college (as well as California State University—Sacramento) when I was sixteen. I was able to complete my high school requirements while simultaneously receiving college general education credit. I was able to interact with my professors in ways that helped shape my career choices and even had the opportunity to intern with various organizations making me a competitive college applicant once I graduated. Overall, it was a fantastic experience.

**Alyssa A., 18:**    I have taken dual enrollment classes at my local college since my junior year (11th grade) of high school..

**Beth, 20:**    I started the "Jump Start" program at my community college at the age of 16, the same year I graduated homeschool-high school.

**Brenna, 22:**    I dual-enrolled at a local community college for two years during the "high school years." I took several classes each semester and began building a transcript. I didn't find community college particularly challenging after being unschooled for several years—I was used to focusing on projects intensely, and I was able to do the same thing with my college assignments.

**Jackson P., 20:**    Yup! I took community college classes! Austin Community College (ACC) has what they call an "Early College Start" program, in which students can take two classes per semester for free.

**Hailey H., 18:**    I am still dual-enrolled at the moment actually. I take a few online courses through Florida Virtual School and the rest of my classes are either at the community college campus or through their online classes to save a bit on gas

---

### Katie F., 24

I did a couple classes for dual credit. Since I was able to work at my own pace, I was able to work ahead in my high school work and take college classes as well to get core credits off my plate for when I attended college full-time.

---

### Alsatia, 18

I enjoyed taking classes at community college. I graduated high school with 28 credits. This coming spring (only one year after high school graduation) I will be graduating from St. Johns River State (formerly Community) College with my Associate's of Arts degree. I call that a win!

money. Community college is a hit or miss thing though. I have a few classes that are quite simply glorified high school classes, but I have taken a few that really engaged me and left me wanting to know even more about the subject matter.

**Teagan, 20:**   I took approximately one class per quarter (mostly personal interest courses, i.e. art appreciation, French, fiction writing) for two years, from the ages of thirteen to fifteen. From then until I was seventeen, I was full-time (five classes per quarter) at the same community college, garnering a 4.0 GPA the entire time. This allowed me to rack up plenty of experience and good, inexpensive college credits that transferred with me when I moved on to a four-year school. As per my mom's communications with the Ohio school board, I technically graduated from high school at age sixteen. I had always intended to attend college, and taking community college courses only reinforced that intention.

**Sarah P., 18:**   I took classes during what would have been my senior year in high school.

**Skye, 22:**   Yes, I took community college classes. I graduated high school two years earlier than my publicly schooled peers, and by the time they were getting ready to graduate high school, I had an associate's degree.

## Classes for Fun

Enrolling in non-academic classes like pottery, dance or poetry can be a wonderful step into new experiences. Homeschooled teens taking this approach often choose topics they are eager to explore, so their interest is piqued. As they successfully complete these courses, and their familiarity with the demands of college classes increases, so does their confidence. While many of those surveyed took classes for fun at the community college level, these grown homeschoolers have more to share with you.

**Rebecca, 39:**   I took a writing class and a typing class when I was 16 years old. I began taking regular classes the next year.

> ### Rose S., 20
> For the first several years, I took mostly theater and dance classes. I treated the community college more like the parks and recreation department of the city. I used it as a resource for getting the instruction I wanted, plus the resources I couldn't get as easily elsewhere (such as access to a piano and accompanist, a barre, a giant room with a mirror, etc.).

> ### Laurel, 21
> I took some classes at community college. Most of them weren't credit courses, however. I just took an occasional class if it looked interesting to me.

**Rose S., 20:**  I started taking classes at the community college at 13 for fun, and I am still to this day taking classes. At about seventeen, I started taking "real" academic classes. Basically, at that point, those classes started to look fun. I felt like I was using the college as a resource.

**Dakota, 20:**  I took math, welding, and gymnastics.

**Roya, 27:**  I started taking community college classes when I was 13 years old. My first class was a voice class through the music department—but that same semester I believe I also took Psychology and English. I became really quickly involved with the ceramics department, and it was my home away from home for about eight years. I loved taking college classes, loved being the "little sister" to all my older classmates, loved having teachers whose jobs were to read and review my writing, loved all of it. I took a full course load at community colleges (except for a few semesters I took breaks for travel) until I transferred as a junior to a university at the age of 20.

## Transcripts and Entrance Exams

Some community college districts make it very easy for teens to attend. As homeschoolers continue to succeed at community colleges, it's easier for others to sign up. The application process may require transcripts and unless your child is signed up with a program that is basically duplicating school at home—possibly by mailing materials or checking in online—you're going to have to create them yourself.

*Don't panic!*

It's not as hard as it sounds. I've created transcripts for each of my children and each one looks a little different. When you opt for a truly individualized approach, would you expect anything else? Families who chose more traditional curriculum courses might have an easier time translating their homeschool work into a transcript, because they can simply plug in the course their child completed, assign the grade, and give the credit. But for those who have chosen a looser approach, you will need some mental flexibility in

---

### Katie P., 20

My test scores for community college were not the best. I waited a year and took them again. In the end, I opted to just take the developmental classes, which actually helped me a lot. I feel like I was able to trade 12 years of math classes, for instance, and condense it down to 3 semesters!

I'm glad I went to community college because it made me realize I didn't want to attend a 4-year college. I only want to act, so the conservatory route was a much better choice for me.

translating learning to a transcript. Remember that in high schools around the country, gifted programs are often set up in a way that mirrors how students unschool or use unit study approaches in their homes. These programs grant credits and create transcripts based on various factors, and you can, too. Sometimes it is just the length of time a student was present, and other times the student has studied a subject in depth but that translates to a variety of classes. And, if the teen had been dually-enrolled, the transcript is simple to create.

I had the experience of translating an internship into a "recognizable" transcript. At fourteen, my daughter participated in an internship at a natural make-up company. She learned about mixing organic substances, the necessity of clean environments, the laws that were required, as well as customer skills, taking inventory, making sales, and using the cash register. She also worked on models' make-up at photo shoots and fashion shows. She did this for ten months, which I translated into two semesters. For her transcript, we counted this internship as satisfying course requirements for Business Management, Business Math, Science, Ethics in the Workplace, as well as Make-up Artistry for Fashion Shows and Make-up Artistry for Photography.

**Rebecca, 39:**   My mother hodge-podged together a transcript for a local community college. The administrative staff really had no clue what to make of us. So my mom kept bringing in my homemade transcript for their review and every time they told her that something else was usually on the transcripts they had seen. She'd take mine home and add that aspect in. Translating activities, interests, work and other experiences was easily done and not an issue at all. My non-traditional courses were not questioned. I transferred from the small local community college where I took a couple classes during my high school years to a larger community college when I was 17 or 18. It was there that I declared a major and obtained an associate degree in my field of interest.

> ### Rebecca, 39
> I took the SAT on two different occasions and did pretty well. At least I didn't completely bomb the math section despite not having any formal math beyond pre-Algebra in 8th grade at the local public school—which I very nearly did bomb.

> ### Molly N., 19
> I took community college classes full time. I graduated with an associate degree (dually with my high school diploma) when I was 16.

**Michael, 22:**   I did the practice tests for the community college entrance exams. I had no problem with the reading and I squeaked by the math. But I had a little trouble with the writing component. They wanted me to write about the topic: "No Pass/No Play." Luckily, because we have a lot of lively political dinner conversations, I was familiar with it. But what I didn't realize is that they wanted me to take a position and write a persuasive paper on it. I simply wrote my thoughts, trying to see both sides of the argument. Well, that wasn't what they wanted, so they failed me. When I got home, we figured out how to write a simple 3-part formula for a paper: Introduction, 3 supporting arguments, Conclusion. They didn't really want to read my ideas, just do the formula. So when I went back in, that's what I did. And I passed without any problem. Interestingly, the second topic was "School Uniforms—For or Against." Evidently, they're all school-related topics. I found that to be really odd.

## Taking Classes...

Community college classes can be such a wonderful entrance into formal classroom settings. All of the teens and young adults surveyed were overwhelmingly satisfied with their experiences, receiving good feedback from teachers and adapting well to this new learning modality. Even when they started in their early teens, they shared that they enjoyed the experience and were successful.

**Roxana, 25:**   I was 14 years old when I started taking classes at the community college where my mother had been teaching for years. I was pretty comfortable on the campus and in the classrooms, because for years I'd already been spending time around the campus, sitting in the corner of my mom's classroom while she taught, following her around while she dropped by to pick up paperwork. I was very nervous about the actual class work, though—I thought I would be missing some vital information that everyone learned in high school—not about the actual class content (my first semester, I took classes in HTML, beginning voice, and opera history), but about how to take a test, when I was allowed to ask a question, how to write a formal

> ### Alaina, 25
>
> I started community college the quarter before I turned sixteen. It was a very rewarding experience. I learned how to survive in a college atmosphere and developed more traditional study skills.

essay, etc. My midterm exam for opera history included an in-class essay portion, which had me pretty terrified. My mom gave me about five minutes' worth of tips – how to have an introduction and a conclusion, a reminder to put in everything I knew, and the suggestion that I print (since my handwriting was, and is, pretty illegible). I wrote an essay on the musical themes of La Traviata and got 100%. Turned out, I didn't need four years of high school English to figure out how to write about a topic I loved – five minutes and a back-up pencil was enough.

**Tess, 27:**  I really think that taking community college classes was an incredible opportunity.

**Cameron PT., 20:**  I started attending community college lightly at seventeen. It's been quite easy, although the first semester was a bit of a culture shock. It's been a lot of fun cutting my teeth on things people wouldn't expect me to be good at, because I've never really learned/practiced them before.

**Sarah B., 20:**  I took a few classes over at a community college. They were good experiences. I took them with a few of my other homeschooled friends. We fit in perfectly even though we were a few years younger than the other students. I especially enjoyed Chemistry, because of the labs.

**Michael, 22:**  When I first started my community college experience, I noticed that my level of excitement was massively different from the other kids from school. I was going into something completely new and it was the same old song and dance for them. But I definitely felt a little jittery about going to a formal educational environment and start taking things like standardized tests and writing research papers. Still, I felt excited about the new challenge. I always wanted to participate in class both on the community college and university levels. I was always outspoken. I even went so far as to argue with professors over content, something the other students never did. I remember one time when I argued with my Psychology professor about the results of what she wanted to label "permissive parenting." She was going on and on about how kids from "those

> ### *Jared, 22*
> I loved the experiences I had in the community college system. Smaller class sizes and more one-on-one time with the professors was awesome. I think it was a great stepping stone for me.
>
> It also is a great alternative for kids who don't wish to attend a university right after high school, like me. It gives you time to breathe and find out what your passion truly is while still allowing you to pursue a college degree.

> ### *Skylar, 20*
> I started attending community college at age 13, and by age 15 I went full-time. I played sports, joined clubs, hung out with people both my own age and typically college-aged students. I thrived in the environment.

kinds of homes" are so wishy-washy and lazy, they can't do anything for themselves. I told her that made absolutely no sense. If kids are doing whatever they want, doesn't that imply that they are doing things for themselves? She didn't take kindly to being questioned in front of the class. I told her I came from what she would call a "permissive household" and I'm arguing my point right now. That's the opposite of wishy-washy. She really meant "absent" parents—and mine certainly were not that! But she wanted a comparison of parenting styles. And she clearly had a preference. I didn't bother to list out for her that I had earned my Eagle Scout award, held several offices in 4-H, organized community service events, had a job at Target, performed in community theatre, and traveled to Japan as an exchange student. Not really the slug she was implying I would be!

When I went from unschooling to community college, the high school graduates seemed to treat it as a means to an end. They wanted to "get this over with so I can get on with my life." I can't tell you how many times I heard that phrase. For me, each new experience was a new challenge, a new adventure. So the main difference between me and kids from school was attitude: I loved learning. It was a positive experience for me. I also had an appreciation for learning things outside my major, like philosophy. Almost all other students complained about how it was stuff they were never going to use, so why learn it. I always wanted to say, because it's interesting! Just because I'm not a volcanologist nor ever will be doesn't mean I wouldn't find learning about a volcano totally awesome. I just look at learning differently. I think this was directly related to being unschooled. The "school-at-home" homeschoolers who were taking the classes with me, were still anxious and stressed about the cosmetic elements of education like grades, professor recommendations, and the competition aspect (class ranking). They weren't stressing about learning the material, they weren't really focused on that part at all. It was odd to me. They were more similar to the school kids than me. They didn't have unrestrained ed-

---

**Sarah D., 19**

Yes, and it was a wonderful experience. I got to figure out how to deal with many of the social aspects of a school environment and the academic schedules and deadlines, years before having to deal with the stress of leaving home.

---

**Caitlin, 27**

I started community college classes at age 14.

I took math from college algebra through calculus, writing, biology, and chemistry.

ucation like I did. But I did fine with it. My teachers all commented that they enjoyed teaching students who want to be there!

**Emma, 18:**   Yes, at age 14 I started taking one class each semester, when I was sixteen I started taking two classes per semester. So far I have really liked all my community college classes and professors.

**Hannah J., 22:**   Yes, I took community college classes when I was 15-17 years old. I started with one class the summer after sophomore year, progressing to full time at the end of my senior year.

**Joseph, 19:**   I took all of my sciences at Mercy College, while continuing my previous homeschooling regimen (working with tutors and taking classes with other homeschooled teens).

**Katie P., 20:**   I took some community college courses when I was 18. At first it was okay. I was taking classes so I could get my hours to transfer to a four-year college. But soon it started to conflict with some of my acting projects and I found it harder to go to some of the auditions my agent set up. I felt that I had to choose between the two. So I decided to skip the hours and go to a conservatory (which is doing only classes in your major).

**Zoe, 22:**   I took two classes in the years leading up to when I left for college: Psychology 101 and a women's literature class.

**Grace, 19:**   Because I took the California High School Proficiency Exam (CHSPEE) and finished with high school early, I took community college classes in what would have been my senior year.

**Molly S., 20:**   I started taking community college courses when I was thirteen (because my birthday is in December, so I've mostly been a year ahead and that was the year I would have started high school). The first semester I only

---

**Kirby, 26**

I took one semester of community college, that way I can check the box that says I've had "some college." And it is on my resume, but honestly, no one has yet to ask me about it.

---

**Sophie, 19**

I didn't take community college classes in my high school years. I didn't feel ready then.

I am taking classes now and had no trouble getting in. Actually, anyone can sign up as long as the classes aren't full.

took classes in the arts (drama and two dance classes), but after that I jumped right in and was always at the top of my classes.

I love community college for the teachers. For the most part they were all wonderful, and really seem to care about what they are teaching more than, I gather, high school professors do.

I got involved in the dance department a lot more than I had expected to, as someone who wasn't really a dancer. By the end, I found myself president of a dance team and going swing dancing multiple nights a week.

I stayed at community college for six years. I genuinely hate it there now. Six years is just way too long. I still think the professors are mostly wonderful, but the students are very grating because a lot of them really don't care about learning what is being taught. They do not put in, sometimes any work, and it is really tiring to be the only person actually trying in the whole class. For six years.

Why was I there six years? Partially because I was only taking the classes I thought sounded fun for the first few years I was there. I would suggest this for the first semester, or maybe two, but then it would be smart to get a plan in motion. Moving towards an associate degree even if your child does not go on to University. I started working towards my transfer credits late in the game. By the time I graduated homeschool high school, I had been at Pierce Community College for four years, with enough classes left to take that I could have done them in one semester. Since I wanted to transfer in Fall, I spread them out.

My biggest regret was that I was never informed how early the transfer application deadlines are. My older sister had just transferred to art school and she had applied in the summer before she started, so how could I have known that most applications are due November of the previous year. I probably never would have figured it out accept a friend of mine who also attended Pierce Community College was transferring in 2011 and applied and was talking about it. I knew I wanted to do it right and really write my essays the way I wanted to write them, so I eventually decided to postpone another year. I took a few more dance classes, filled time with shows, dance competitions, and applications, which lead to auditions at various schools around the country.

Now I am at a university, still a year ahead, but if I get the BFA in Musical Theatre, it will definitely take three years and I will graduate at age 22, back in the normal year I would have if I had started kindergarten the year I was supposed to and gone up through the school system. I do not know why that bothers me so much, but it does.

Additionally, if I had done the whole process (application, audition) a year prior to when I did, I don't think I would have gotten in because I learned a lot that year with private voice lessons, doing community theatre, and dancing on my own. Perhaps I would have had that experience and waited anyway, and tried again the next year to get in to the school I really wanted to go to, which was University of Michigan.

*Roxana, Rose S., Roya with Jim Hormel - their community college musical theatre and acting instructor, vocal coach and production director*

*Homeschooled teens hanging out together!*
*Mike S., James, Austin, Ari, Kaci, Raphael, Sunny, and Kesley*

CHAPTER 7

## Did You Find Enough Friends?

Parents worry about their teenagers' social lives. That's just a given. Sometimes parents whose teens are enrolled in high school assume that all is well and the thought of removing them from that environment will condemn their teen to a lonely life with no friends and no fun. The homeschooled teens and young adults that answered our survey send that myth crashing to the ground. They, often with their parents' help, found an enormous array of options for meeting other teenagers and experiencing a full and rich social life.

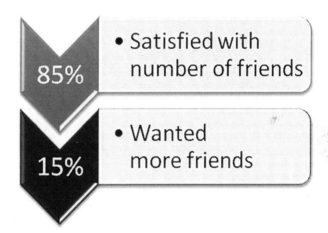

In fact, it may be easier to have a fulfilling social life as a homeschooler because their schedules are flexible and they are not trying to cram everything into those precious after-school hours. We all know how hard it was to squeeze in homework, dinnertime, possibly work and simply some down time into the hours between dinner and bed. Homeschooling enables teens to plug into all kinds of "extracurricular" activities without being limited to that small window of after-school time.

Many families are lucky enough to live in communities that have thriving social networks already in place. These homeschool support groups often offer activities specifically for teenagers. With the ease of social media, finding other teens interested in similar activities is easier now. Additionally, teenagers simply went out into the community and participated in activities with other teens. Just as teens in school have access to community resources, so do homeschooled teens. Many times, families have a difficult time visualizing just where their teens are going to find activities that will allow them to pursue passions, socialize or make friends. This graph-

## Homeschool Support Group Offers...

- Soccer Day (weekly /sometimes more often)
- Destination Imagination
- Odyssey of the Mind
- Small learning groups
- Park Day
- Dances
- Pony Club
- Homeschool Choir
- Debate Club
- Game Day
- Camping Trips
- Homeschool Conferences
  (usually regional or statewide)

## Community Offers...

- Community College: ceramics, dance, film, art
- Club Sports: soccer, fencing, tennis, cheerleading
- Summer Camps: sport, music, special interest, Not-Back-to-School Camp
- Community theatre
- Homeschool Co-Ops
- Religious programs or Church ativities
- Volunteer Work
- Neighborhood Friends
- Friends of friends
- Online friends
- Scouts
- 4H clubs
- Poetry slams
- Work

ic shows some of the ways the surveyed teens and young adults have found friends in their communities.

## Plenty of Friends!

The majority of those surveyed were completely satisfied with the numbers of teens/friends in their lives and the richness of the relationships. Because they weren't limited to the age-mates sitting beside them in school classrooms, they made friends the way adults do—by meeting people with similar interests. These kinds of friendships have a stronger chance of lasting beyond a semester of classes.

**Brenna, 22:**   I had several social circles as a teenager that I found by getting involved in the community. I did Odyssey of the Mind, so I had a great group of friends of my own age through that organization. I also did community theatre, and that netted me friends of all different ages! Finally, I joined a local political campaign, where I gained friends that were mostly in their forties, fifties, and beyond. Being outside of a classroom meant that I was able to make friends of all different ages from all different walks of life.

**Cameron PT., 20:**   I've met loads—through park days, Not-Back-To-School Camp, volunteer work, soccer, and life happening.

**Katie P., 20:**   My mother always encouraged us to participate in local homeschool groups. We went to lots of park days when I was younger. Our homeschool groups often offered field trips and smaller group activities—whatever we were interested in. So I met a lot of others that way. As a younger teen, I met other homeschooled teens as well as teens who went to school through Girl Scouts. But later, I was really more focused on theater instead of just gathering up a bunch of teen friends. I have a couple of friends, that's enough for me.

**Laura, 24:**   I met other teens in all of the extracurricular activities I was involved in. I was a part of several different clubs/memberships/organizations. I also knew people from church/library events.

---

### Aiden R., 17

Yes, I met enough other teens just by being out all the time!

---

### Kirby, 26

I met tons and tons of people, but it wasn't just teenagers. I prided myself for having a variety of ages within my several circles of friends. We had weekly park meetings with other homeschoolers. I met kids and adults from the gaming shop, both the youth/adult classes at the Dojo. You name it. Additionally, the gaming shop was adjacent to a local high school, so I got to know a good crowd from there.

**Mike S., 16:** I would say that I have met enough other teens, but obviously the definition of 'enough' will be different for different teens. I met a lot of my friends through Austin Area Homeschoolers events, and other groups like it. I met a good number of my recent friends through the Austin homeschool soccer group that meets weekly.

**Aiden W., 23:** I met plenty of other teens through my church, the neighborhood, volunteer work, etc.

**Chant, 15:** I went to a home school co-op and that's where I met all my friends.

**Katie F., 24:** I found friends through our statewide homeschool conference, in our local homeschool group, and online. Sometimes it was hard to find other teens nearby, but I never lacked for friends or someone to hang out with.

**Alaetheia, 16:** I meet others through youth group, dance, music, camp, and our homeschooling group.

**Sarah D., 19:** I got to know a lot of other teens through a yearly summer retreat that our church youth group would attend. I only get to see these kids four days out of the year, but those are the sorts of friendships that last a lifetime.

**Alyssa A., 18:** I have met teens through my homeschool group, co-ops, my internship, religious programs, and meeting people in the local college

**Grace, 19:** I met other teens through co-op groups, homeschool choirs, club sports, neighborhood friends. As I got older, I took choir at the "public" school and participated in plays, took science classes, and met really cool people, but for the most part I got to avoid a lot of the unhappiness and drama that can come from "friends" at that age.

**Caitlin, 27:** I met teens through the homeschooling community. There were many events put on for homeschoolers to spend time together. A few of the people I met are still my close friends now.

---

### Alaina, 25

Through Taekwondo, homeschooling roller skating, Destination Imagination and community college. By the time I was a teen I was developing a good small circle of friends that lasted me through college. I never felt the need to have a hundred friends, six or seven was plenty.

---

### Nathan, 22

I can't even count how many teens I met. I was in a religious youth group called United Synagogue Youth (USY) so I met hundreds. More locally though, I ran a teen group in the Albuquerque area where about 5–10 teens would get together once or twice a week and just do "normal" things.

**Sarah B., 20:**   I met tons of other teens. I participated in a teen homeschool group, was part of the local robotics team and was an active member of my church's youth group.

**Emily, 16:**   There are tons of classes for homeschool kids! Plus, church!

**Crystal, 15:**   I met people through volunteering at a local theater for their summer camps. There were homeschool dances several times a year and I was able to meet a lot of friends there. And at my church I met several friends through my youth group.

**Elizabeth, 19:**   Before I started attending public schools, most of my friends were though the sports that I played. After I started attending public school part time I made friends at school as well.

**Hailey, 18:**   I hope so! I have so many friends all over the country and the world from my year abroad and also from the high school, community college, and Parelli Natural Horsemanship.

**Alyssa H., 17:**   Yes, I think I met enough other teens, but of course I'm no social butterfly. Homeschool teens have their social circles just like public school kids. These groups get developed at young ages and once they are there it's hard to break in. I was one of those kids who just didn't quite make it into a group. So I'm a bit of an outsider, which is fine with me.

**Emma, 18:**   I have a lot of friends through things like park day and pony club. I also have lifelong friends because of people I met when my older brother was younger and they had something called play group.

**Hannah J., 22:**   Yes (for my preferred level of socializing, anyway!), primarily through park get-togethers and church activities.

**Sophie, 19:**   I feel like I met enough other teens. I went on field trips and was involved in youth group. I rode horses

---

**Hannah, 18**

My friend base was always very diverse with friends from the ages of 10–92, and I never really had problems finding people to connect with. As for teens I found my most lasting relationships with other teens through un-schooling conferences.

---

**Roxana, 25**

I never felt that I lacked for friends or peers, but I also never wanted more than a small number of close friends at a time. I had a couple of best friends of my age through homeschooling groups, and later had mostly non-homeschooled friends, usually a little older than me, whom I met in the-atre, community college, and online communities like role-playing games (I'm still very close to a group of friends from one game in particular, whom I met about 10 years ago).

and met other girls through that. The co-ops had lots of other kids my age.

**Jackson, 20:**    No, I spent the entirety of my teenage years as a socially inept recluse! Ha! I've met a bazillion other teens in my time, and even became friends with adults, young adults, preteens, and younger kids. I met a lot of my long-term friends through Austin Area Homeschoolers (AAH), a bunch more through Zach Scott community theatre classes, and a few through random happenstances, some of whom were "schoolers." All I really had to do was show up (to AAH park days, Zach classes, soccer, what-have-you) and be my quirky, personable self—a self which I was able to develop pretty quickly through interactions in the local homeschooling community. I've developed some mad friend-acquiring skills over the years, and continued to make friends throughout my college career.

**Jared, 22:**    I had plenty of homeschooled friends, but I also had friends who went to school and the Davis School for Independent Study (DSIS). I met kids when I joined the tennis team, and I had a number of friends who went to school even before joining the team. It was really a mixed bag. The homeschooling community in Davis when I was younger was very extensive. At one point, I heard numbers in excess of 120 homeschooled families. As I got older, some filtered into the independent study program and others went to the high school. But I never had any problems finding friends or kids my age.

**Kaci, 18:**    I met others through theater programs, sports, co-ops.

**Joseph, 19:**    My classes with other homeschoolers were definitely helpful, and I also connected with a couple teens through various homeschooling newsletters. My largest friend base definitely came from the "nerd camp" I attended in the summer, Johns Hopkins' CTY summer program. I met a lot of like-minded individuals who, even given the distance between where we lived, I did get to see often. That summer camp was an amazing experience for me, and I made some lifelong friends through it.

---

**Sunny, 17**

I went to a lot of homeschool events and met other teens there. I'm also a super social person, so I've never faced difficulty meeting new people, ever!

---

**Rose, 30**

Oh, gosh. Some lived on my block. Some went to the same art studio where I took a class. Some I met at the poetry slam. A couple I met in the woods! There are people everywhere. I was friendly. I would strike up a conversation and sometimes it would lead to friendship. (Isn't that just how life is?)

**Alaetheia, 16:** I meet others through youth group, dance, music, camp, and our homeschooling group.

**Kevin, 20:** I met other teens through football and other activities offered through our local homeschool co-op.

**Laurel, 21:** I was an incredibly introverted teen, but I still had lots of friends. I went to a queer youth group, a homeschool teen group, dance class, art class, Not Back to School Camp, and had quite a few online friends. There were no shortages of teens in my life.

**Trina, 16:** I met friends through church, small groups that get together and hang out once a week, a monthly ballroom dance class and through places I go to just for fun.

**Molly N., 19:** I found plenty of other teens. I knew a lot of people through the homeschool group in my hometown, and upon moving to a bigger city at age 14, I met a great deal of my friends through volunteer work I did with teen organizations.

**Nancy, 15:** At my library once a month, the teen librarian hosts a "Friday frenzy." Teens can come in after school to talk and play games.

**Skylar, 26:** Between my youth group, homeschooling group, diving, and community college, I was never at a loss for friends.

**Nicholas, 26:** I met plenty of other teens. I assume that the reason to ask this is about socializing and friends. As to that aspect I had friends in the neighborhood, friends at church, and still maintained a friendship from school. I also went to a church camp (in New York) in one of my last years of homeschooling, I made a couple of temporary friends while there, and after returning a couple of times I became good friends with two of the counselors who were pretty young also. The three of us maintained a pretty good friendship for years.

**Rose, 20:** I had a large group of friends as a teen. This group, for the most part, was the same group that had been

> ### Micah, 16
> I am a people person and love meeting other teens. I meet them at church youth group, co-op, area homeschool functions and now public school sports.

> ### Dakota, 20
> Sure, I met enough other teens. There were numerous groups that met a few times a month where teens would hang out and play games.

my friends from the age of about 4, and, at age 20, is still my group of friends. I met my close friends primarily through homeschool park days. I also had a few schooled friends, who I met through soccer and classes at my martial arts studio. As a slightly older teen, I also made friends through my college classes. However, my closest friends are still the friends I made many, many years ago, as a young tyke at park day.

**Skye, 22:**   I absolutely found enough teens! The homeschool community in Austin (as far as I know) is one of the largest in the country. We collectively planned several events and made the effort to travel together and take the same theater classes and so forth.

**Rosie, 24:**   I met lots of people of all ages through being a part of the world and interacting with the people in it.

**Rowan, 18:**   I met other teens from volunteer work and I met other teens in the Austin Area Homeschool group.

**Sarah H., 24:**   My family was involved in a home school group called HEAT (Home Educators Around Texoma) and I met a lot of my friends through that. I did 4-H for several years, and was involved a co-op that met twice a week for classes. I also attended a youth group where I met a lot of friends, went to retreats, volunteered, and had a really great time.

**Kelli, 21:**   I met teens through co-ops and a homeschool youth program at Zachary Scott Theatre.

**Alsatia, 18:**   I most certainly had enough teens in my life. Mostly through the church (which my family is VERY involved in) but in my later high school years I managed to join a network of other homeschooled people of my own age which was VERY enjoyable.

**Simcha, 17:**   I've met plenty of other teens through family other friends, the internet and summer clubs.

**Teagan, 20:**   Largely through children's and community theatre. My two best friends of nearly ten years are ones I

> ### *Risa, 21*
>
> Isolation may be one of society's greatest myths about homeschooling.
>
> Who knows? I could see us being some of the most socialized kids out there.

met when we all performed in a production of *Alice in Wonderland* together. Also, I have always known that I fit in well with people considerably older than me, so I had just as much luck finding dear, close friends at community college. During that time, between the ages of fourteen to seventeen, some of my dearest friends were between nineteen and twenty-five.

**Sarah P., 17:**   As a teen I have met many teens through weekly soccer, homeschool dances, and Zach Scott theatre classes. But I mostly met people when I was young and continued to be friends with them into teen-hood.

**Carver, 18:**   I met other teens through musical theatre, mainly.

**Cameron L., 24:**   I kept the handful of friends I'd made at school. So once they left the same school I left, to join different public schools in town, it was easy for me to meet their new friends and neighbors. I also made friends at the State Fair, movie theaters, volunteer positions, unschooling conferences, work, camp, and musical events. Some were teens, sure, but I also made a lot of friends who were older as well as younger.

*Jared with his homeschooled friends Andrew and David*

**Trina, 16:**   I met friends through church, small groups that get together and hang out once a week, a monthly ballroom dance class and through places I go to just for fun.

**Zach, 24:**   I met enough other teens though homeschool groups and friends of friends.

**Rebecca, 39:**    I kept my best friend from when I was in middle school as well as friends from church and related activities. I feel like I had more varied friendships than what I would have had if I'd attended school. I was close to the librarian, the vets and other staff I worked with. I enjoyed the company of people from their teens into their 30's and was not limited to the friendships of other people exactly my age. When I homeschooled (from 1988–1991) there were not a lot of homeschool socialization options in our area. This was not something that really affected me but I do believe it was hard on my very social younger sister (5 years younger).

**Molly S., 20:**    My friend group was/is very close knit because we are so small. I wasn't spoiled for choice in who to be friends with. It was a finite number, so we were basically all friends, but I love all of those people and wouldn't trade them.

**Zoe, 22:**    I had plenty of friends. I will say that I was very lucky that the homeschool group I was a part of had lots of families with kids roughly my own age. I also have always been good at making friends with people older than I am. Doing theater is a great way to meet people; I am still very close with people that I did shows with when I was a teenager.

**Risa, 21:**    "Do you have any friends?" As a homeschooled student I must have heard this question hundreds of times, and I would always laugh a bit. When *didn't* I meet other teens?! There are so many opportunities in the homeschool community to meet teens, socialize, and fellowship together. Just in my hometown, there were over 500 homeschool families and we were always doing things together.

Personally, I was involved in a nationally-recognized homeschool choir with over 200 participating teens. Because of my school flexibility, I worked part-time and many of my coworkers became close friends. I competed in a nationally competitive speech and debate league (NCFCA) and at least every month would join many hundreds, sometimes thousands, of homeschool students at tournaments across the state and country.

## Some Wanted More Friends

It's hard to say why some kids have a harder time making friends than others. Adolescence can be a rough time. Most of the teens or young adults reporting that they wish they had more friends admit that they were not isolated in the truest sense of the word. Instead, they simply wished for more than what they had. And, that's not all that uncommon among many American teenagers, homeschooled or otherwise.

Sometimes, the problem is location or family situations. For example, teens whose families move frequently sometimes have a difficult time forming long-term local friendships. On the other hand, they often have the unique opportunity to have friends all over the world.

Again, the answer is for families of homeschooled teens to stay in communication about what's happening in their teen's social world, and how adults might be of help. Of those who occasionally were unsatisfied with the numbers of teens in their lives, here's what they have to share.

**Kristin, 19:** Sometimes I didn't have enough socializing, but those times were the exception. The majority of my friends were from dance, but there were some from homeschooling groups, church, and my neighborhood. I was also involved in a student-run theater organization during my senior year, and I met a lot of interesting people through that. All the teens in that group, whether homeschooled or not, were highly dedicated and intelligent. They had to be, to put on successful plays without any adult supervision. I learned a lot about leadership and innovation from those teens, which I wouldn't have learned at school, where most projects are overseen by adults.

**Caroline, 24:** I had friends at church and one or two in the homeschooling umbrella group. Both of these groups I saw, at most, once a week. Admittedly, I was pretty lonely for a few years. However, the internet was starting to take off around this time and I ended up joining an e-mail list serv for high school teens in my religious denomination. That made up for all my lack-of-friends problems.

**Alyssa P., 18:** I met lots of teens through soccer days, dances, community service projects, or any other fun group activity we planned. But I have to admit that, for a while, I didn't think this was so. That was one of the reasons I chose to go to high school for a year and half. I learned that while

> **Beth, 20**
>
> I met a good number, but wish I had a few more to talk to at the time.

> **Kate, 15**
>
> We have homeschool park days, classes, and socials, but it's always the same fifty kids. Most of the time that's enough for me, but sometimes I wish there were more friends to choose from.

there might be a lot more kids there, it's not that great. And a good group of friends to hang out with is all a person really needs.

**Tori, 18:**    Because I was in public school off and on, I did have a pretty good number of friends from there. I think without school it would have been hard.

**Michael, 22:**    I met my fair share of other teens through Boy Scouts, 4-H, Judo, community service projects, a Film Club (offered through the Dallas PBS station), annual un-schooling conferences and the local homeschool groups. I did run into a little bit of a problem from time to time because while I was a teen, we lived in a small Texas town. My blatant political sentiments and the fact that I didn't go to, not just church, but their church, kept me from getting close to those circles of local teens. Looking back I'm so glad I didn't cave to peer pressure to conform. If I became one of them, I'd having nothing close to the amazing life I have now. I simply looked for other friends in the community. And then at 17, we moved, I went to college, and I had plenty of friends.

**Steen, 15:**    I have constantly struggled with meeting and finding other teens with similar interests as mine but I continue to try with limited success. It has definitely been one of the drawbacks.

**Roya, 27:**    Yes and no. I had a huge, huge, huge number of other teenagers I was friends with—mostly through HSC conferences. A few lived nearby, and I also spent hours online talking and emailing and live journaling. In my day to day life I never felt like I had enough of my homeschooling friends. I had a lot of friends through ceramics, theater, and other local things, but they tended to be older than I was. It got difficult occasionally when they wanted to go to places I wasn't old enough to go.

> ### *Anastasia, 19*
> How many is "enough"?

*Friends off to an informal dance: Katie P., Molly, Kaci, Alyssa P., Centaine*

*Kaci, Ari, Aiden R., Rowan, Kelli*

CHAPTER 8

## Peer Pressure

Drugs, risk-taking behavior, teen pregnancy fill the headlines and top many people's lists of concerns about teens today. Much of this behavior is driven by peer pressure, and peer pressure seems synonymous with school. Parents are scrambling to figure out how to help their teens.

> *How do we help them?*
>
> *What's too much help?*
>
> *What if they need help and we don't know they're struggling?*
>
> *What if they don't trust me or listen?*

When a teen suffers day in and day out with bullying and pressure, it's not surprising to learn that their outlook, personality and temper is often neg-

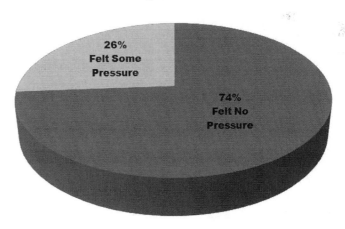

**Feeling Peer Pressure?**

26% Felt Some Pressure

74% Felt No Pressure

atively affected. Developmentally, adolescents are so vulnerable to outside pressures; negative peer input can really affect a teen's ability to discover who they are.

When we first started homeschooling in the mid-90s, a lot of discussion centered on the idea of "hot house" homeschoolers, or the idea that if children didn't have the daily harassment, humiliation, and conflict that schools provide, they would not be able to function in the real world. But homeschoolers—including teenagers who managed to avoid the pressure cooker of high schools – are turning out just fine. They've been able to deal with whatever demands surface in their young adult lives.

As it turns out, homeschooled teens haven't been isolated and kept from any struggle. They have issues with friends or acquaintances, at parkdays and Sunday schools, in dance classes and on soccer fields. They learn to cope and find solutions. The difference is that they can deal with these conflicts in smaller doses. They haven't had to endure the stress day in and day out, with no hope for reprieve. They have the altercation, manage as best they can, chat with a parent in the car on the way home, and do better next time. They weren't trapped with the bully all day long, for weeks, months, and sometimes even years.

The responses from the homeschooled teens and young adults reflect resilience and confidence. While they certainly were exposed to peer pressure over the years, its effect seems to have been minimized.

## Peer Pressure Had No Effect

Some homeschooled teens and young adults felt little to no peer pressure growing up. Or, if they experienced peers attempting to pressure them, their self-confidence was strong enough that it didn't impact their choices or behavior.

**Hailey, 18:**   I was never the kind of girl that ran and jumped off cliffs because her friends were doing it. Anything that I have done that society may deem inappropriate I did because I wanted to experience it myself. I think I've

---

### Ari, 21

It didn't affect me. I've always had an easy time saying no to things I wasn't comfortable with.

always liked to go against the grain, defy the norm, and so forth. I always hated seeing how easily some of my friends were influenced by peers. I hope to be a positive, shining influence on every person I meet.

**Aiden W., 23:**   Because I had the freedom to choose who I allowed in my social sphere, I was able to make friends who encouraged me in good directions. My best friend was also homeschooled, and we belong to the same church. We both committed to certain standards of living, and tried to encourage each other in our efforts to live those standards. Because of this I was able to make good decisions that ultimately led to me being where I am now, happy. I have nothing to regret, and I had a lot of really great experiences growing up because my friend and I pushed each other towards good activities and good attitudes.

**Nathan, 22:**   Peer pressure didn't bother me. I have never done anything I didn't want to.

**Kate, 15:**   Peer pressure doesn't affect me really. I don't feel the need to wear revealing clothes to gain attention, or talk about the latest TV show. I don't read popular teen romance novels just because everyone else is.

**Rose S., 20:**   I don't feel as though I've experienced a lot of peer pressure in my life, especially not when compared to the schooled people I know. None of my friends are huge smokers or drinkers, and not once have any of them ever tried to pressure me into trying anything I didn't want to. Another aspect of peer pressure involves teasing. I've had experiences with teasing, both on the receiving and giving end. I'm not going to say that teasing doesn't take place in homeschooling groups. However, I do strongly believe that homeschoolers, and more specifically, unschoolers, have much less teasing going on than public schools. This just seems like a fact to me. I feel as though I am much more able to stand up for myself, and tell people when I don't want to do something than I would have been if I had gone to school. I rarely "go along" with something just to keep from rocking the boat.

> ### *Brenna, 22*
>
> I'm stubborn as a mule, and any peer pressure I experienced as a teenager served only to make me less likely to do the thing I was being pressured to do.
>
> That may have been a product of being homeschooled, or it may be a product of my personality—it's hard to say.

> ### *Joseph, 19*
>
> Peer pressure affected me very minimally. Considering that I grew up with two younger brothers and many other homeschooled children/teens to socialize with, I rapidly learned how to avoid social traps like peer pressure.

**Anastasia, 19:** Peer pressure didn't have an effect on me. I admit I've always been on the antisocial end of the negative-homeschooler-stereotype scale.

**Kristin, 19:** When I was homeschooled, it barely affected me at all. I was aware of the things that I was doing that were different from other teens, but I didn't really care, and my friends almost never pressured me to be different. Even at dance, where I wasn't built the same way as most other dancers, my teachers and peers never made me feel bad about this, or like I couldn't dance because of it. They just tried to help me improve on things that I could change and would make me a better dancer, like flexibility or turnout.

**Alyssa A., 18:** I'm not sure actually, I would like to think my friends wouldn't pressure me so much. Most of my friends don't try to pressure me into anything. I just have good friends I guess.

**Emily, 16:** I don't feel like I need to be "cool" or like I need other kids to accept me. My mother always says to "Remember who and whose you are!" I want to stand out and be different! I don't want to blend in with the majority of teenage kids! I want to be a light!

**Hannah J., 22:** Not very much—it has tended to bounce off of me as long as I can remember, though internally I bristle when others' poor behavior reaches a certain point.

**Molly N., 19:** I've always been independent and made my own decisions. I surrounded myself with people who aligned with my beliefs.

**Kevin, 20:** Peer pressure didn't affect me. I'm pretty strong-willed with good morals and ethics. I was able to make decent choices, (I think), regardless of what "the crowd" was doing.

**Steen, 15:** I have never been heavily affected by peer pressure and I have always gone my own way about things. I'm never one to be in the mainstream of things. I always seek out interesting and unique people to be around. I

---

### Trina, 16

Peer pressure didn't bother me too much. Some people would make comments about me being homeschooled in a derogatory sense, some would say that's really cool.

Some people wouldn't talk to me after they found that out, but it didn't affect me too much.

---

### Hannah T., 18

I haven't ever really had a problem with peer pressure. I don't feel the need to do something I dislike or don't want to do simply to "fit in" with a group who probably aren't the best people to be around in the first place..

make my own choices on what I do and don't do and take pride not being influenced by the latest fad. I'm able to take advice though.

**Alsatia, 18:**  It didn't really affect me at all. I was mostly removed from it.

**Roya, 27:**  I don't recall significant moments of peer pressure as a teenager. I know that within our local homeschooling groups there were relationship conflicts and cliques occasionally, but I honestly can't pinpoint a time when I felt pressured by my peers. It's harder for me the older I get and I have the frequent decision of informing the groups I am in about my differences in educational philosophies, or keeping quiet and letting them assume I have a similar background as them.

**Rose, 30:**  I'm not sure. My "peers" have always been interest peers. I hang out with writers, with people who are interested in sustainability, you know, folks who are into the things I'm into. My best friend is my age, but that was a coincidence. I do value my friends' opinions. I keep track of societal memes and try to be respectful of the culture in which I live. :::shrug::::

**Sarah D., 19:**  I don't understand the question. Being homeschooled my whole life, peer pressure hasn't really affected me a whole lot, except from my siblings, and that's much less problematic than it would be in a school setting.

**Michael, 22:**  Not at all. I never really felt the need to prove myself to others. Even when we were in a Christian homeschool group in Texas, people tried to pressure me to be like them. But I had a strong self image, so it didn't impact me. Sure, I wanted them to like me, but not at the expense of changing who I was. In some cases I felt a little pressured to drink with the others in college and even try pot – but I was probably 19 years old by then. I was confident enough to try what I wanted and skip what I didn't want. Peer pressure during high school years didn't really exist in my mind.

---

**Nathan, 22**

Peer pressure didn't bother me. I have never done anything I didn't want to.

---

**Teagan, 20**

I don't believe I was any more affected by peer pressure as a homeschooler than I would have been if I had attended traditional school. I did occasionally get an incredulous, "What do you MEAN you've never done/heard/seen that? It must be because you're homeschooled," but I don't think I ever really felt pressured, per se, to conform to those standards. If I ever did, I was able to hold it at bay.

> ### *Micah, 16*
>
> It really doesn't affect me. Since I play on a public school football team I see and hear all the things public school kids feel as pressure. But in many ways, I think I have matured past the stage where I need their approval.

> ### *Laura, 24*
>
> I definitely felt peer pressure, but I was also quite capable of making up my own mind. And I also had a lot of confidence and wanted to do things my own way.

**Cameron P.T., 20:**   Peer pressure doesn't affect me! Mua-hahaha. In all honesty though, very little, and my peers mostly pressure me to hug/cuddle people and other such useful things I want to do anyway.

**Emma, 18:**   When I was of middle school age and high school freshman age I probably wouldn't have been able to stand up to the peer pressure well. I didn't have a lot of self worth. Now I have realized how much I'm missing and how much time I've wasted hating myself. I've realized that some people aren't going to like me, and they aren't worth my time. I have real friends and they are all I need.

**Dakota, 20:**   I'm not really sure if it's a problem. I try to ignore peer pressure.

**Simcha, 17:**   What's peer pressure?

### *Felt a little Peer Pressure*

The teens and young adults responded to this question in a few different ways. Some talked about their experiences with peers trying to get them to try various risk-taking activities. Others talked of the pressure they felt to go to school instead of continuing to homeschool.

Interestingly, several spoke of other parents making them feel this pressure to change. Still, this group shared how they were able to rise above any pressure they experienced, and make choices they're happy with.

**Nicholas, 26:**   Any peer pressure I had didn't have to do with homeschooling or not. I had neighborhood friends that gave peer pressure. But for the most part, I was "the good kid" that resisted.

**Crystal, 15:**   I'm not going to say that it didn't affect me at all but the pressure I felt was not very strong. Most of it was from people I didn't really consider to be friends, so it was much easier to deal with.

**Alyssa H., 17:**   Peer pressure, you would think there wouldn't be much peer pressure if you're homeschooled, but there is. From the other kids and other parents. Some is good peer pressure and some is bad peer pressure. The one thing I have going for me is that my parents have helped me learn to discern what is good and what is bad as far as peer pressure goes.

**Sophie, 19:**  I was raised around good friends and they never peer pressured me. As I got older I would interact more with public schoolers and they would pressure me to try drugs or drink or have sex. I was able to say no because I had such good influences all my life. I was always around my parents and very good kids that stayed away from those kinds of habits.

**Sunny, 17:**  Sometimes I felt that I was missing out on a "high school" experience, but then I was like "Or you guys are missing out on a homeschool experience." It's all about perspective.

**Caroline, 24:**  My clothing changed somewhat because of peer pressure. I went from wearing plain jeans to a tighter boot-cut style because I felt very out of place with the other jeans I had. This is the only real instance I can think of where not looking similar to other high schoolers really bugged me.

**Katie P., 20:**  If I had gone to school, I think peer pressure would have had a great effect on me. From what I've heard, it might have made me more self-conscious, or more hesitant about jumping into things I wanted to do. But since I didn't go, it never really bothered me all too much.

**Sarah H., 24:**  I think peer pressure was not as bad for me as it was for my friends in public school. I never had drugs or alcohol or sex pushed at me. Most of my friends were Christian homeschoolers. I think there was pressure to fit in, for sure, and pressure to act a certain way because my dad was a pastor. So maybe it was a kind of opposite pressure, the pressure to be good, instead of rebel, I guess.

**Jackson, 20:**  I did feel a little bit of pressure to go the community college route, as that was what most of my

---

### Katie F., 24

I didn't have much peer pressure at all. Having more time away from peer pressure left me very well equipped to handle it, and brush it off, when I went to college and got a job.

---

### Katie P., 20

In theatre, where I spent a lot of time, but also in dance classes, there was often a meanness or competitiveness that would happen. Often that came from the kids from school. They didn't like if someone got more attention than them. I was mainly competitive with myself—just trying to push myself to do a better job. They were into tearing people down. So when I didn't hang out with them, or act like them, they turned on me. Thank goodness I didn't have to be cooped up with them for 8 hours a day! That would have been awful! I was able to shake it off and just focus on my own stuff.

friends were doing and they had set themselves up well for colleges that way. In general, the only pressures I felt were those that compelled me to achieve success on par with my peers. Most everything I did or did not do socially was met with acceptance.

**Skylar, 26:**   I had it like everyone else. I belonged to a youth group, B'nai B'rith Youth. I smoked weed. I drank. My teenage years were pretty "normal." I also had time to step away from it and make my own decisions, so I was able to keep it under control.

**Roxana, 25:**   I started wearing skinny jeans because everyone else was…

**Sarah P., 17:**   Peer pressure, even for homeschoolers, is always and will always be a problem for young people. I have been pressured my whole life to be things, do things, and say things. The pressure to act a certain way has definitely affected me in the past, but I feel that through my parenting and more supportive friends, I have been able to stand up to peer pressure more often than not. Generally, homeschoolers face less peer pressure than school children, maybe because there are fewer of us, or maybe because of the environment of each individual group, but it still exists.

**Alaina, 25:**   I felt a peer pressure but I mostly ignored it. I think the worst came from adults who thought that something was wrong because I was not in school. Individuals were quick to judge that I was abused or something akin to this because I wasn't in school. Also, adults took it as a personal judgment on their parenting because my mother was willing to stay home with us. I frequently heard the comment "Oh, I could never spend that much time with my kids." This negativity made me more defensive about being homeschooled. I felt as if I had something to prove because I didn't go to school.

**Mike S., 16:**   Peer pressure affected me in a couple of different ways. There were times when I felt like I was possibly being left behind, like I wasn't learning enough. But then there have been many times where my fellow

---

### Zoe, 22

I think I had pretty much the normal amount of peer pressure. If you are talking about pressure to go to school, that came mostly from adults, not my peers, they were interested certainly but I never felt much pressure to go to school from people my age.

---

### Molly S., 20

When I was a pre-teen I was very affected by the actions, likes, dislikes of my group of homeschooled friends. I wouldn't have admitted it then, but the reason I dressed in black and listened to Linkin Park was because they did those things. That was about the worst of it.

teens complained nonstop about their boring schoolwork, and while it makes me feel a bit guilty, I'm glad that I'm homeschooled/unschooled.

## Peer Pressure in School Settings

Some of the teens and young adults shared their experiences with peer pressure from their friends who attended middle school and high school. Some of these respondents attended school for a little while as teenagers and wrote about what they saw, heard or how it impacted them.

**Kelli, 21:**   Peer pressure was never a prominent issue while I was attending public school but it did affect the way I presented myself at times. Luckily, I left before it became my priority to fit it. Otherwise, I think I would have let it dictate much of my life decisions. Fortunately for me, that did not happen.

**Elizabeth, 19:**   I have always been very independent (probably partly due to homeschooling!) and so I have never been too affected by peer pressure. Since Davis High is such a competitive high school, the only pressure that I felt was the pressure to get good grades in classes and to get into a good college.

**Grace, 19:**   I felt a little of it in high school, but not from my homeschooled peers, and not very often because I didn't have a lot of friends around who would try to negatively influence me.

**Tori, 18:**   I think peer pressure has both hurt my grades and helped them. Sometimes my motivation helps other people, sometimes I slack off with them. My school friends were all very supportive of my homeschooling though.

**Chant, 15:**   When I went to public school kids were always trying to get me to do things, now that's not a problem because there are hardly any peers to pressure me!

**Laurel, 21:**   Some peer pressure does occur within the unschooling community, although it is usually unintentional. I can only think of a few instances when I was personally

> ### Jared, 22
>
> I never felt peer pressure within the homeschool community.
>
> But my friends who went to school were pushier.

> ### Caitlin, 27
>
> Peer pressure and bullying were the main reasons I left school. After I started homeschooling I encountered very little peer pressure, which was a much better environment for me.

affected by peer pressure, and they were mostly from the three years I spent in elementary school.

**Alyssa P., 18:** I felt no peer pressure while I was a homeschooled teenager. I always felt free to be myself. I mainly saw peer pressure when I went to high school. One main reason I went was to see what average teenagers deal with on a day-to-day basis. Since I've seen both worlds—homeschooled and public schooled—I can say that the world teens live in at school is not good. They feel so trapped. And that probably explains why they bite at each other all the time, always trying to put someone down, so they can move up the food chain a little more. How can that be good for someone? Peer pressure never really affected me, in my mind, I was there for me. I'm pretty independent.

**Kaci, 18:** It affected me mostly in my middle school years, when I was young and kind of vulnerable. It got me into some trouble and bad situations. But they weren't things I couldn't get myself out of on my own.

*Alyssa P., Sarah P., and Katie P., at a party together.*

*Kaci and Ari*

CHAPTER 9

## Dating

While most parents are in no rush to have their teens start dating, no one wants them to have limits on their options. Dating in the teenage years can be a great growth experience, a horrible drama, or anywhere in between. Just as teens who go to a high school have a wide range of experiences, so did the homeschooled teens and young adults from our survey.

Of those who responded, about half went on dates during their adolescence while the other half didn't date or develop romantic relationships until later.

### Did They Date During the High School Years?

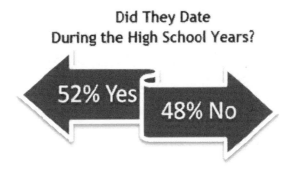

52% Yes  48% No

A variety of reasons were given to explain whether or not they dated. As you can see, these factors are very similar to those affecting the "dating world" of teens who attend a high school. It's difficult to distinguish the true impact from the perception of the impact. I'm not even sure it's necessary to differentiate between the two. It's not unusual for most of us to have a "grass would have been greener" theory when we have faced problems or we're looking back at some struggle we had. It's also a little tricky to determine whether many of these teens/young adults would consider these issues the size of speed bumps or true hurdles. The comments that they candidly share will give parents a glimpse into their lives, though, and perhaps you'll be able to see where you could help your own teen. Some need a little boost of confidence, some might need help widening their circle of friends, and others may simply need to be reassured that they don't have to date just because it appears to be "The Thing To Do."

## Homeschooling Did Not Affect Dating

A little more than half of the teens we talked to dated as homeschooled teenagers. Some had long-term relationships while others simply went on a few "dates." Their experiences sound somewhat similar to those of teens in high school, except they appear to be shrouded in a little less drama. Here is what they said about their dating experiences.

**Tori, 18:**   I don't think homeschooling had any effect on my dating life. I only had one boyfriend throughout high school, and I met him through dog-mushing.

**Aiden R., 17:**   Homeschooling didn't affect my dating at all. I've had several girlfriends; one relationship lasted over 2 years.

**Sarah P., 17:**   I am currently dating a homeschooler and have been for over 2 years, so you could say it's been good! The groups of friends, though, are often so small that the "picking" can be... sparse.

**Hannah, 18:**   I don't think my dating habits were affected all that much by my homeschooling. I dated a few worthwhile guys during my teen years. Other than that first conversation where I was explaining what unschooling was, it never really came up again.

**Tess, 27:**   Homeschooling had no effect. Dating was normal.

**Simcha, 17:**   I have far more dating options than I know what to do with! There are ten little old ladies that have their eye on young men for me and I have met some already.

> ### Sunny, 17
>
> Dating for me was just as normal as any other teen! I've dated homeschooled guys and public-schooled guys, homeschooling never had an effect on this.

**Katie P., 20:** It was a little tough, because if you were dating someone who went to school, you couldn't really talk to them until they got out of school. But otherwise, it was like any other kind of relationship. I didn't have a problem with dating.

**Molly N., 19:** My dating experience was unique because I was a bisexual teen, and I went through some emotional issues causing me to be disinterested in dating for some time. I did have relationships, though, and I do not think being homeschooled had an impact on me or any of my friends.

**Jackson 20:** I didn't really "date" in the traditional sense, instead having my first relationship blossom out of a long-standing friendship. I never felt the pressure to go out with assorted ladies or anything, and I've generally looked for relationships that were more long-term.

**Laurel, 21:** Well I just got out of a year and a half relationship with someone I've known for years because we grew up in the same homeschool group. And even though the relationship just ended, I have no regrets. So, being a homeschooler has definitely had a positive effect on my love life.

**Rose, 30:** Umm… well, I had the same girlfriend for my entire adolescence, and I met her before I was homeschooled, but online. I don't think our schooling situations affected us much. I had a lot of free time to spend without her. I think that helped me keep a sense of self when I was absorbed in what was really a pretty intense relationship.

**Rowan, 18:** I think dating was a lot more pleasant being a homeschooler. There has been little to no drama around relationships or break-ups. I am currently in a relationship with a 18-year-old boy who is also a homeschooler. We never fight about anything more serious than simple miscommunication, we have never broken up/got back together again, and we have been together happily for 2 years.

> ### Kaci, 18
> Dating is good for me. I met a guy who is also homeschooled and we've been dating for almost 2½ years! It hasn't had any kind of effect because we come from the same lifestyle.

> ### Jared, 22
> I don't feel like homeschooling put me at any disadvantage for these types of things. I actually went to senior ball twice, once junior year and once senior year. I had a girlfriend my senior year as well. I never felt like I was missing out in any way.

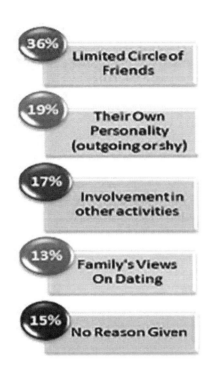

36%    **Limited Circle of Friends**

19%    **Their Own Personality (outgoing or shy)**

17%    **Involvement in other activities**

13%    **Family's Views On Dating**

15%    **No Reason Given**

---

**Sarah P., 17**

Dating is certainly possible within the homeschool community, and happens constantly, but eventually many must venture out of their respective friends groups, and sometimes out of the homeschool community in general.

---

## Homeschooling Had Some Impact

Many of the teens and young adults encountered a few obstacles to dating. Some didn't date at all. Realistically, some teens who go to school have trouble with dating. It's an unfortunate part of adolescence, or so it seems. The homeschooling world is not that much different in this regard. Some made this decision not to date deliberately, some were pursuing other interests, and others weren't as pleased with their situation. We'll look at some of the reasons they think this occurred. But first, we'll start with one who found the impact to be a good thing.

**Nicholas, 26:**    Considering I met my wife because of homeschooling, I think it had a strong effect! My parents never allowed me to do the traditional dating. They were pretty adamant about courting, and doing family activities with another girl. I can't say I blame them, too many teen pregnancies are a result of kids being allowed to go do whatever they want and having too much alone time. Without going into too much detail I met my wife who was from Indiana at a homeschooling event. From then on we both anxiously looked forward to the next homeschool field trip that our three-state group was taking.

### Too Busy for Dating

These respondents shared that their dating life was directly affected by how busy they were as a homeschooled teen. Some teenagers simply have other priorities for their time during adolescence. One benefit of homeschooling is that there's no pressure to conform to what's happening at the local high school. Teens are able to prioritize their time and energy based on what's truly important to them.

**Risa, 21:**    I didn't date very much in high school, not due to restrictions or the fact that I was a homeschooler, but because I was so focused on my interests. I was very involved with what I loved and didn't really have time for a committed relationship then.

**Sophie, 19:**    I never dated until sophomore year. I just was never into boys until I started hanging out with the neighbors that went to school. The guy I did date went to public school and I met him through a very good friend. I've been very focused on horses though so my focus on boys and dating is a bit distracted.

**Alaina, 25:**    I dated very little as a teenager. I was more interested in other things. I never felt the pressure to date.

**Alyssa H., 17:**    Dating, I never dated in high school. When you're homeschooled there aren't really that many guys to choose from and I was really too busy for a boyfriend.

**Micah, 16:**    I am not really into that much yet, but do have many girls who call or text me. I will get around to it when I get some time. Ha!

### Limited Circle of Friends

The majority of this group of teens and young adults attributed their lack of dating to the fact that their homeschooling circle of friends was too small. Some families have remedied this by helping their teens expand their circles of friends by participating in local, state and regional homeschooling events. Homeschooling groups around the country are offering more options for teens to socialize. Local communities are embracing homeschoolers more, and this also creates more opportunities for teens with common interests to meet.

Even as situations are improving for homeschooled teens, I'm not sure this idea that "my circle is too small" is limited to homeschoolers though. Teens that come from smaller schools where the kids have known each other for many years, or even teens in larger high schools can often feel that their "dating prospects," for a variety of reasons, are also limited.

Still, these homeschooled teens and young adults share how they believe that their smaller circle of friends had somewhat of a negative impact on their ability to date as a teenager.

> *Laura, 24*
>
> I didn't date in high school—I was too busy.

> *Zoe, 22*
>
> Yes, I would say there was a distinct lack of eligible boys. To be honest though, if I had gone to high school I may have just met MORE boys not necessarily BETTER boys.

---

**Skye, 22**

The only strains on dating came from being very close with everyone, almost feeling like family (despite the fact that there were over 200 families in the homeschooling community I grew up in), so it was matter of finding people you didn't perceive as a sort of chosen sibling.

---

**Wendelyn, 34**

I only dated one man and I married him. Not sure that I will encourage this with my own children, but it did work out for me. :-)

---

**Ari, 21:**   When we moved to Atlanta from Austin when I was 13 years old, socializing was more difficult. There were far fewer homeschoolers in such a large area.

**Dakota, 20:**   Negative effects, indeed. Most of those I hung out with were younger than me.

**Steen, 15:**   I have just begun to enter the dating arena and so far have had limited success. Being a homeschooler has limited my choices in women my age but I'm sure there are plenty out there and it just takes more time to find them and more planning than being around them at school.

**Beth, 20:**   It never affected me too much. Sometimes, the fact that the guy would go to public school, he seemed to have a different life with me and in school.

**Alsatia 18:**   I have to this day never been asked out on a date. I doubt it was because of being homeschooled and more to do with the fact that all the friends I had were dating each other or people at their schools.

**Sarah D., 19:**   I didn't date at all in high school, and I haven't really dated since I got to college. I didn't really miss it so much, because I didn't know anyone else who was dating.

**Rose S., 20:**   I met my first real boyfriend through my martial arts studio. He was very traditionally public schooled. He was a nice guy, and we went out for two years. But I did tend to feel a little defensive about the way I was raised and educated. He did not really agree with the methods. Like many schooled people who find out after the fact that I was homeschooled, he tended to think of me as the exception to the "all homeschoolers are maladjusted freaks" rule.

My current boyfriend Daniel was homeschooled, though fairly traditionally, as opposed to my very, very relaxed unschooling. He was one of the instructors at my martial arts studio, and the best friend of one of my old friends. We met and became friends almost immediately. He's five years older than I am. We were friends for about five years before we started dating. We've been together for three years now. Daniel was very intrigued by the way I was raised, and over the last three years has learned a tremendous amount about unschooling, having been to and spoken at many different conferences now. He is completely sold on the concept, the whole concept, of radical unschooling. I can't imagine being with someone who didn't respect the way I was raised. My first boyfriend and I were never particularly serious, primarily because I could not see myself being with him for very long, because of his opinions about homeschooling in general, and unschooling in particular.

**Roya, 27:**  My first boyfriend I met at an HSC [HomeSchool Association of California] conference—so yes, being homeschooled was an important factor! He lived a few hours away, and we'd get together with another homeschooling family frequently. The only other serious relationships I've had, up until I met the man who became my husband, were also with homeschoolers. One lived just a few hours away, and one lived across the country and I ended up living out there for about six months. I always assumed I would end up with another homeschooler, so it amuses me that I married someone who wasn't!

In terms of how homeschooling affected my dating life, I don't think I ever really dated. Groups of us would hang out at conferences and camp outs, you'd be attracted to someone, say something, and try out the relationship for the duration of that trip. Sometimes that kept going, sometimes not. I never went on a "date date" until college, and even then I didn't take it seriously or do it traditionally.

**Alyssa P., 18:**  Sometimes homeschooling affected my ability to date as much as I wanted, and other times, it was fine. But dating in the homeschooling circles is very different from high school dating. In my eyes, homeschool dating is a little harder than high school, simply because there weren't that many guys to choose from. And everyone REALLY knows each other. So sometimes dating within your circle of friends is a problem. My hobbies (cheerleading, dance) didn't bring me in contact with a lot of guys either. Although, after being in high school for a year and half, it was clear that people played a lot of games with

> **Rose, 20**
>
> I believe being a homeschooler had a pretty drastic effect on my dating, for a few reasons. First of all, my dating pool was a little different than kids that went to school. I had a fairly small group of friends that were basically my friends for my whole life. So dating any of them would have been slightly more complicated, I believe, than dating one out of five thousand students in a high school.

> **Hailey, 18**
>
> The pickings are slim in my town. I do not blame homeschooling for my lack of ever having a serious boyfriend. But hey, I'm still young. Plenty o' time for that later—after I experience the world a bit.

other people's feelings, there was a lot of peer pressure and dishonesty. This was not something we saw in the homeschool community too much at all.

**Molly S., 20:**  The one thing that was unfortunate in having a smaller number of peers than I would in a public school setting, was the lack of boys. There were the boys who didn't pay attention to us at all—or bathe—and were always playing *Magic: the Gathering* in their small group by the playground. Then there was the group of girls, with two boys who hung out with us. One of them was like my brother, and the other boy was fought over by literally all of the girls as he made his way through us one by one. It's pretty comical looking back at it now, because I know that when it was my turn with him, I think we may have held hands once or twice, and that was the extent of it.

Sometimes I do feel like being a homeschooler made me miss out on some practice relationships that everyone else has had before coming to early adulthood. I can't decide if this is a good thing or a bad thing. Besides, several of my friends had more than one relationship during our shared teen years, and so some of that is down to me not looking for something like that. They met at conferences or at events attended by multiple homeschooling groups, such as dances.

### Personality Traits

Other teens and young adults found their difficulties in the dating arena to be due to their own personality. These teens might have overcome the same issues—feeling shy or self-conscious—had they attended school. Or they might have had the unfortunate experience of being pushed into dating when they weren't ready or left to feel somehow inadequate because they weren't dating. Homeschooling allowed their personality to unfold at the rate and speed that was most natural to them.

**Caitlin, 27:**  I dated a little bit, although I only dated another homeschooler once. I think I would have had a larger dating pool in school, because there would have been more

> ### *Caroline, 20*
>
> I didn't date.
>
> Homeschooling probably affected that, but, honestly, I wasn't too interested in the reality of boys in high school. I "wanted" a boyfriend, but it was more of a dreamy thing than based in reality. If I had wanted to date, I believe my parents would have let me, with rules in place.

people of a similar age, but I don't think I would have dated any more than I did, because I am a very shy person.

**Emma, 18:**  I think homeschooling has had a bit of an effect. Since I didn't go to high school I was never really forced into a situation where I had to talk to boys much. So I got really awkward around them. Now not as much, just because I've stopped caring what everybody thinks of me, but I also don't want to date at the moment.

**Nathan, 22:**  I never dated in high school. Yes, being homeschooled made this very difficult. I was asked out a couple of times, and I asked a girl out more than once. I think it was more me not really looking for that at the time, than anything else.

**Teagan, 20:**  I have never been much for dating. I wouldn't say that homeschooling really had too much to do with it, as much as my own precociousness and independence. I have always identified as being older than I actually am, and this made dating difficult in itself—when you're fifteen and YOU are certain that you would be mature enough to date someone in their twenties, that doesn't really make it appropriate. Also, once I was in community college, I was spending less time with people my own age and more time with people older than myself, so dating never really became a part of my life.

**Anastasia, 19:**  In a roundabout way, homeschooling had an effect. It has allowed me to be completely non-sexual without stigma and I quite appreciate it.

**Kelli, 21:**  I was never really interested in dating in high school but it never put a damper on my sister's dating life or my friends that were homeschooled.

**Skylar, 26:**  I'm bad at dating. I would occasionally make out with guys in high school, but that was about it. I think I would be screwed up regardless if I had attended high school or not.

**Katie F., 24:**  I didn't have much of an interest, and I don't think it had anything to do with my schooling situation. I

> ### *Zach, 24*
> I didn't date much until my senior year when I played soccer at the high school.
>
> I was probably more shy than most.

> ### *Sarah H., 24*
> I did not date anyone until I was 19. I really do not think I would have dated before then if I had gone to a public school. It was just the way I was.

briefly dated in a long-distance situation, but I didn't want to start dating until I was ready to start looking for a husband.

**Cameron P.T., 20:**   Well, being me had the effect of me not dating—at all—until I was 18. Heck, I hadn't had a crush on someone (that I noticed) until I attended Not-Back-to-School Camp (NBTSC) at age 17. Finally, I went to meet up with friends from NBTSC (all unschoolers), and I ended up in my first relationship all of a sudden. So homeschooling was pretty related to my dating life so far in that sense.

### Dating Didn't Start Until Later

Several of the respondents didn't begin to date until they were a little older. They've shared what they think kept them from dating as a homeschooled teen, and how they had no problems with dating after their "high school years."

**Kristin, 19:**   Dating was practically nonexistent, for me. I went on one "kind-of" date with another homeschooler friend when I was 16 years old. But that was it, as far as dating went. This bothered me at times, but by senior year I realized that I didn't really like any of the teenage boys I knew well enough to date them. Once I did start dating when I was in college, I didn't really have any problems because I hadn't dated before.

**Aiden W., 23:**   Eh… dating wasn't so great as a teenager, but that had more to do with moving around and a lack of datable people than my schooling. Once I was little older and more settled I was able to date a bit, and I had a lot of fun. I'm married now, and my husband and I had a really nice courtship. I remember my schooled friends talking about their dating and relationship experiences, and I remember I thought it sounded really artificial and counterproductive. Most of the dates I went on were really cheap, and we did things that allowed us to get to know each other. I was also really clear on my boundaries physically. Maybe a little too clear…only one person attempted to kiss me before I met my husband…but that's okay by me. I am

---

**Joseph, 19**

I had a few relationships through high school, and it's worth noting that those relationships started as friendships that grew into something more. That is, I never really learned how "normal" dating works in high school, and I had to pick up those skills later in college. If there's one negative element of my homeschooling experience, my lack of "normal" dating experience would definitely be it, though I know some homeschooled friends with different experiences here.

allowed to say, with perfect truth, that he's the best kisser I ever kissed! :-)

**Michael, 22:**   Homeschooling really had no effect. I felt like the only thing I might have been missing out on was more open-minded girls. I was certainly interested in girls but we lived in a very small town while I was 13–17 years old. It was ultra-conservative and the exact ideological opposite from me. That kinda limited my options. I remember liking this one girl and her mom saying she would only let her date if the family was with us the whole time. She didn't like me anyway so it worked out for the better. Ha! I did do some long-distance dating by meeting girls from a film club I worked with and from the unschooling conferences we attended, and I went to the local public school prom with a girl who lived nearby and needed a date. Once I left for college, I had no problems meeting or dating.

### Parental or Religious Reasons Not to Date

Teenage dating isn't acceptable in all families, whether they homeschool or not. Some of the homeschooled parents set parameters on their teen's dating and some of the teens decided to set some of their own. These homeschooled teens and young adults share what it was like to be a teen not dating because of personal, parental or religious reasons.

**Hannah J., 22:**   My parents didn't allow me to date until I transferred to a four-year university. They were a relatively large part of my first relationship, which I appreciated. Other than that, the fact that I was homeschooled versus public-schooled has been irrelevant.

**Grace, 19:**   I wasn't allowed to date till I was 16 years old, so homeschooling wouldn't have changed much of that. By age 16, I was pretty unimpressed by the way relationships were handled by my age group and didn't have much interest in a boyfriend. I kinda stayed away from it until college. I've never felt like homeschooling made any difference.

**Emily, 16:**   I personally do not believe in dating! I do believe God has a plan for me. I don't have to ride the dating

> ### Kevin, 20
> 
> Haha, I don't really date many people. I believe dating should be preparation for marriage, so I don't really date.
> 
> I'm waiting for God to bring me and the person he has for me together. Gotta have faith.

> ### Trina, 16
> 
> My parents and I decided no dating until I'm out of high school. Some kids I know think that crazy and weird, but dating is just a bunch of drama and that's not my thing.

roller-coaster to find that person either. When the time is right God will bring us together. I don't have to worry about impressing people or showing myself off. I don't have to worry about whether or not this or that person likes me. When it is time I will know. I'm giving it to God!

**Alyssa A., 18:**    My parents are the strict parents in this area, I wasn't allowed to date till I turned 18. I am honestly kind of scared about dating now because people ask about past dating experiences. I think the fact that my parents had more control about where I was most of the time had a greater effect on this no dating policy. So yes, homeschooling did probably affect this.

*Rose S. with her (homeschooled) boyfriend, Daniel*

*Risa at her Homeschool Senior Prom*

*Sarah P. and Mike S.off to prom!*

*Do people ask you about missing Prom? Did you care or go to something similar?*

## CHAPTER 10

## Going to Prom

Prom falls into the category of being somewhat of an iconic high school event. Movies and television glamorize it. And, because most adults attended high school themselves, they often worry if homeschooled teens are "missing out" by not attending a high school prom. It's interesting, to me anyway, that this fairly specific question comes up almost as frequently as the broader "What about socialization?" Perhaps they are really the same question. Or perhaps adults have simply fallen prey to the billions of dollars in marketing that makes "going to Prom," such a big deal. Maybe they still carry around their own anxieties about popularity and being asked to prom or not.

### Did They Go to Prom?

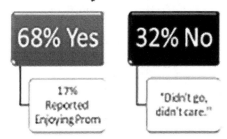

When asked if they are questioned much about not getting to attend a high school prom, many were fairly tired of hearing that from adults in their lives.

According to those who took our survey, only one (out of 75!) expressed regret about not going to a prom. Many local homeschool groups offer proms or dances and several respondents attended prom at the nearby high school with friends. Most of those that went to a prom report that it wasn't all it was hyped up to be.

But if you, as a parent are thinking about your teenager and proms, notice that the majority of these homeschoolers actually attended a prom. And the number goes up when you take into consideration the dances and similar events the "prom-deprived" were able to attend. The percentage of those who went, but reported not having a good time, is probably close to what teens in school would report.

## Attending A Homeschool Prom

Some of the homeschooled teens and young adults lived in an area that offered a homeschool prom. All fifty states have homeschool groups and many of the larger groups host proms now. Sometimes proms are offered as a teen activity at regional homeschooling conferences.

Any homeschooled teen who feels like they'd like to have this experience, should round up a few friends and buy their tickets. No one needs to feel that homeschooling prevented them from going to prom, if that's important to them.

**Mike S., 16:**  My parents never brought it up. I've never felt like I'm missing out. I have been to a homeschool prom, and really liked it.

**Beth, 20:**  There was a Homeschool Prom for all the homeschoolers in the area. And I went to a few public school proms.

**Kate, 15:**  Actually, our homeschool hosts a prom each year. I am going to the prom for the first time this year, and I'm looking forward to it! (And our proms don't have police escorts like the ones at public schools.)

**Sarah P., 17:**  Many people, young and old, have asked me about homecoming and prom. No, I generally do not care, because I have had plenty of homeschool dances and will have a graduation in the near future. I have been to a homeschool prom at a Dallas Convention Center and it was

---

### Joseph, 19

Actually, for a number of years I did attend a prom run by homeschooling parents, for homeschooling teens. Located in New Jersey and hosted annually, the NJ Spring Prom is a lot of fun. Hearing some of my schooled friends' experiences at their respective proms, I might actually say that our homeschooled prom was far superior. The atmosphere was very free-form and fun, no social pressure coming on from anywhere. And since a good 100+ teens would attend each year, it was definitely a fun, social experience. I can't say I know of any other homeschooling proms, but I also haven't looked.

They exist, though, I can definitely say that.

awful. Not to say that school proms can't be great, I'm sure they are, but I think I'll stick to Lindy Hop.

**Sarah B., 20:**    I went to the homeschool prom held yearly down by the New Jersey shore. Not many adults ask me about it, but my public school friends did.

**Crystal, 15:**    I was able to go to a homeschool prom.

**Molly S., 20:**    I actually did attend a homeschool prom, and I don't see what the big deal is. I didn't really enjoy it that much. It was kind of fancy, but it wasn't any more fun than the dances my mom set up for homeschoolers in our area, which were more low key and smaller than this huge prom. I also got there late because I was coming from rehearsal for some play I was in, I believe.

**Alaetheia G., 16:**    Yes—I'm asked this all the time. For a few years, I had a grand plan of throwing a "homeschool prom" at the aforementioned museum. Ironically, as soon as I stopped caring, I went to one, but I'm not much of a dancer.

**Tess, 27:**    I had a prom planned for my local homeschool group, but had to cancel it and refund tickets because the term 'prom' scared the parents of homeschooled kids. This was frustrating, as I had gone to great lengths to make a fun, supervised occasion all at the age of 16. I should have called it something like "The Homeschool Fling" rather than OMG IT IS AN UNGODLY PROM!!! I went to two proms, enjoyed dressing up but found them highly overrated.

**Zach, 24:**    Yes people do ask me about prom. I actually went to my senior prom with my girlfriend at the time.

**Micah, 16:**    We have large homeschool proms in this area and I am also eligible because I play football for a public school so I can attend all their functions too. I have the best of both worlds.

> ### Risa, 21
>
> Adults would sometimes ask what it was like not having a prom, and I would surprise them each time with "we do!!"
>
> Throughout high school years, we had formals and my graduating class had a senior banquet, a prom, and a trip.

## Public School Proms, Homeschooling Dances & Formals

Many knew other teens outside their homeschooling circles who often invited the homeschooled teen to their prom or homecoming at the local high school. While a few commented on having fun, many were bored or "underwhelmed." Still, if going to prom is a significant event, this is a good option.

**Jared, 22:**    I actually went to senior ball twice, once junior year and once senior year.

**Teagan, 20:**    I don't think anyone has ever asked me about missing prom, to be honest. Though I did go to several high school dances when I was a teenager.

**Tori, 18:**    I attended my school prom. My prom let in homeschooled students if someone invited them, so I do know several people who were able to attend prom even though they were not attending public school.

**Rose S., 20:**    Actually, I've never had anyone mention missing the prom when I tell them I'm a homeschooler, though I have heard of this happening to other people. I went to winter formal at a nearby high school. It was pretty boring. It did not make me have the desire to go to prom.

**Michael, 22:**    Sometimes they ask, not that often though. I mainly tell them, that I went as a date to someone else's prom, which was ok, I guess. I really thought it was much ado about nothing. There were dances when we moved to Austin and I participated in the Austin Area Homeschooler's group. And I went to a couple of dances at conferences we went to (Live and Learn, Rethinking Education)

**Elizabeth, 19:**    I was able to go to prom since I went to public school part-time or full time all throughout high school.

**Hailey, 18:**    I went to a prom as a sophomore. It was awful. I didn't miss anything not going to the senior prom.

**Sophie, 19:**    With easily accessible social networking sites, I found teen clubs and I had friends that went to school. I

---

### Brenna, 22

I dated a local high school student, so we went to prom together. It was probably one of the most unpleasant experiences I've ever had, actually! I'm glad I got to find out what it was like—it made me realize that I hadn't missed anything by forgoing traditional high school.

---

### Alyssa A., 18

I'm asked this all the time, by both adults and teenagers. Whether or not I care depends on my mood, considering we have a homeschool prom in my area. I'm still not sure if I'm going or not. But if I don't, it's not going to be something that is going to affect me for the rest of my life. It's not that big of a deal in my opinion.

would get invited to proms and I would get to go dancing with friends at the teen clubs. Once I started realizing how much I liked dancing, I always tried to go to dances when my public school friends went. I did get involved with Smith Flat Charter School and they had dances and a senior prom that I was able to go to.

**Grace, 19:**    I went to dances, and ended up getting a ticket to the "Senior Ball" after I skipped my senior year for community college. It would've been "my" prom had I stayed in high school, so I ended up going with friends. To be honest, it was underwhelming. It was just a dance that people got really excited for, and then got over. It's not something I look back on and wish I could do again. I've had people ask me about missing graduation and prom, etc. and I'm not bothered by it. Some people have had awful proms because they weren't planned well, or the DJ came late, and it hasn't altered the course of their life. I guess I'm not a fan of people putting so much importance on one night of my life. What about going to college early? Isn't that cool? Won't that have more of an impact on my life than going to a high school graduation? It's a question that's always seemed kind of purposefully obtuse to me. I guess it's just something people think should be important.

## Something Similar to Prom

Sometimes putting on a Homeschool Prom is too big of an endeavor for a local group. Or maybe logic is prevailing and teens and their families have chosen to avoid the outrageous costs associated with prom. Often, local groups opt for dances, formal or informal. Occasionally, teens create events for themselves where they have the opportunity to get dressed up in "prom clothes" and enjoy a party, sometimes commemorating a rite of passage. It all depends on how resourceful you are and what the interest level is in your community of teens.

**Aiden R., 17:**    I went to something like it and my girlfriend still went to school dances with her friends.

> **Teagan, 20**
>
> One of my best friends went to a very cool progressive high school in my hometown, and she brought me along to her homecoming dance two years in a row.
>
> It was incredibly fun, and I'm so glad I got to experience it, but it certainly wasn't enough to make me wish that I had gone to high school!

> **Laurel, 21**
>
> First of all, no adult I've ever talked to actually enjoyed their senior prom. The town I live in actually has an 'Alternative Prom', which I attended for 3 years, and chaperoned once.

**Kaci, 18:**   I didn't miss prom at all. Austin, Texas, has a big homeschooling community. So they have set up several proms around town for people to go to so they didn't miss out on it. I didn't really care for it much, but it was still fun.

**Aiden W., 23:**   I didn't care. Prom sounded pretty lame actually. I'm picky about the music I listen to, and I knew they played songs that would make me uncomfortable. I liked going to church dances, and I went to a couple alternative proms my church put on. Those were pretty fun. I kind of had a date for one of them, but it wasn't really a date and he spent the whole time in the room with the cookies and punch, which was fine by me. I went and danced with my friends.

**Alsatia, 18:**   Sure, people ask me if I "missed" Prom. I wouldn't have cared if I had. But lucky for me I found a group of homeschooled high school seniors to graduate with and we had a prom. It was officially a "Junior/Senior Banquet" but we all knew what it actually was.

**Skylar, 26:**   I went to my youth group formal. That was enough for me.

**Alyssa H., 17:**   Yes, they do ask about prom! I tell them that I really don't mind missing it. Our homeschool group had a "Spring Formal", but I never went. It was about $40, not including a dress and all the extra stuff. I was saving to go to college and every little bit helped. I think college was a much better choice than a night of fun.

**Sunny, 17:**   Meh, I was never heartbroken not to go to an official prom or any other school dances. Austin Area Homeschoolers and some of the teenagers in the group throw an annual homeschool prom! They've been doing it two years in a row.

**Cameron PT., 20:**   I really never gave a crap. I have attended prom-like events, and my sister, who is unschooled, has attended actual school proms and balls. It's not like you can't go if you don't attend the school.

---

### Alaina, 25

Oh my goodness, it was impossible to not have these questions asked. Do your child a favor, don't bring it up. Yes, I never had a prom. Yes, there was a homeschooling prom that was cobbled together but it was actually pretty lame. Prom wasn't a 'thing.' I wanted to go to a dance, and one of my friends invited me. That was enough for me. In my experience, growing up not thinking about popularity, dances, and boys, prom just didn't seem that important.

**Roxana, 25:** Some ask about prom, but not many anymore since homeschooling has become more mainstream. I never had any interest in it. I had the opportunity to go to a homeschoolers' prom once or twice, and the HSC annual conference usually has teen dances—but again, I didn't have much interest in going to them, though I could have if I'd wanted to. I did end up going to several formal dances as a college student, in my sorority, and I loved every second of those (because I was there with close friends). I never have regretted missing a high school prom.

**Chant, 15:** Our homeschool co-op has a dance every year that's like a prom. So I don't miss it really.

**Trina, 16:** People ask me frequently about missing prom. But my monthly dance class has a prom every spring.

**Jackson, 20:** Hah, I think I've been asked one or two times about it. I did attend the "UnProm" at the Rethinking Education Conference, which was pretty fun, and Austin Area Homeschoolers has semi-regular dances for those over 10 years of age.

**Katie P., 20:** A lot of people ask me if I was sad that I was missing prom. But in truth, I don't miss it at all. Ever since I was ten and I started acting, I became completely focused on that, and that alone. In my old homeschool group, however, we had an end of the year dance that could be considered a prom. It was a causal event that honored the "graduates." But I never really had too much fun at those. I was too busy trying to figure out what shows I should audition for!

**Kristin, 19:** Some people ask me that, but it doesn't come up very often. Most adults I talk to didn't really care much about prom when they were in high school. I did go to prom, though, senior year. I went to two proms, in fact. One was Queer Prom, which was for anyone and everyone, and the other was Joy Prom, a prom for special needs teens and adults held by a Baptist Church. They were both a lot of fun, and both were attended by other homeschoolers. I even met my current best friend and roommate at Queer Prom.

> **Kelli, 21**
>
> Yes, people asked me about prom and it was annoying. I never cared about prom but our homeschool group always has many dances during the school year including a prom.

> **Zoe, 22**
>
> That is one of my most frequent questions. We had a birthday party where we all dressed up in fancy prom clothes. But if I had to balance out missing out on one night of prom vs. having a totally kick ass childhood I think that I come out ahead!

**Roya, 27:**    I am so glad to be old enough now that people have mostly stopped asking me that. I did not go to a school prom, but Not-Back-to-School Camp had the Un-Prom, which I attended once. It was fun, I like dressing up, and I like dancing. But I also liked the crazy costumes other people were dressing up in (a dress made out of towels, for example) which I am pretty sure are frowned upon at school proms. I went to a few dances at conferences. I hosted a few when I got older and ran events for adults with disabilities as part of my job. Never missed having that "perfect prom night"—I've seen enough movies.

**Molly N., 19:**    I did not miss prom. I enjoyed going to my girlfriend's school dances with her, and I also enjoyed dances at my sexual minority youth resource center and at the unschooling summer camp I went to.

**Rowan, 18:**    I went to Un-Prom a few times with the Austin Area Homeschoolers. I did not enjoy it very much. I am not disappointed that I did not get to go to "Prom."

## No Prom for Me!

For the respondents who were "non-attendees" most had no interest and even expressed a little irritation that so much focus is placed on whether or not a teen goes to a prom. Here, they share their thoughts.

**Hannah T., 18:**    Any homeschooler who gets asked this question knows how annoying it can be. I always thought it was pretty ridiculous idea to base my entire education and life around one night in a gymnasium with awkward dance moves and expectations. I never went to anything like a prom, but I did learn to salsa dance and have gone to many fun and entertaining dances through that.

**Rose, 30:**    I really didn't care. Maybe it's a matter of not knowing what you're missing.

**Anastasia, 19:**    I didn't actually figure out what proms were until my mid-teens. I've never attended one and no

---

### Laura, 24

People always asked me if I had any regrets and I never did. Honestly, I thought prom was pretty stupid and I didn't like it when homeschool groups "conformed" to the public school mentality and hosted things like "Homeschool Prom." I wouldn't have gone even if one was offered near me.

---

### Sarah H., 24

Yes, I have been asked about missing prom. There was a homeschool prom in Dallas that my brother and some of his friends attended, but I really did not have an interest in going my junior or senior year. I did not really care. Getting all dressed up did not really sound appealing to me at the time.

one has brought it up, but then I don't think they're big affair in most of Canada.

**Simcha M., 17:**   ugh!

**Caitlin P., 27:**   I was asked regularly about missing prom. I had never cared about going to prom and told that to anyone who asked me.

**Ari, 21:**   I had opportunities to go to several, but never had interest to go to them.

**Steen, 15:**   Yes, adults and my friends (almost all of whom are adults) have discussed those types of things. While it's an opportunity I have missed, I am not terribly upset over it. I have done plenty of other exciting things in my life most youth have been unable to do.

**Alyssa P., 18:**   Yes, they ask me if I care. Considering that I left high school a couple months before prom kicked in, obviously it wasn't as big of a deal as people seem to think!

No, I don't miss it. How can you miss something you never even went to or know about? And no, I didn't go to any of the Un-Proms. But I did go to dances that our support group put on. Those were fun, not really as big as "prom" though.

**Nicholas, 26:**   They say the only stupid question is one not asked. So I will only be sarcastic for a moment: "Really!? No, I didn't go to prom and now I am homeless and stupid." On a less cynical note, lots of adults did and still do ask me about prom when they find out I was homeschooled. I never went to prom. I did go to a school dance when I was in the seventh grade and liked it, but also got my heart broken. I honestly don't see what is so important about prom! I already had a special someone and we had opportunities to go to dances separate from "prom." I didn't care then and especially don't care now. Prom is trivial compared to the important things in life.

**Sarah D., 19:**   I never had any sort of prom, and sometimes I feel bad that I never got to get a pretty dress and go to a dance with a cute boy. But if that's all I missed out on by being homeschooled, I think homeschooling is better.

> *Jackson, 20*
>
> I don't really care about proms as life events, though. If prom is/was really that important to you, you might want to reexamine your priorities a bit.

> *Skye, 22*
>
> I personally did not care about prom.
>
> If any of us really wanted one, though, we could have made it happen.

**Wendelyn, 34:**   At the time, I was disappointed that I missed out on all the "fun" that happened at schools. Looking back now, I wouldn't have traded my experiences for their "fun."

**Dakota, 20:**   I feel like it would have been a cool experience, but it's not a big deal that I missed having a prom.

**Emma, 18:**   If I had wanted to go I could have gone to the local high school's but they never really had any draw for me. I hate dresses.

**Katie F., 24:**   Yes, I was asked to go to prom. No, I did not care. I don't like loud music and wouldn't have gone even if I had the chance.

**Hannah J., 22:**   No one has asked; I did not go to any kind of dance in high school, since none were available. In college, though, I found a ballroom dance club.

**Nathan, 22:**   Never once did I care about prom or dances. I got that in USY and I'm not really into that scene.

**Julia, 15:**   I used to care when I was little. Honestly as I got older and started to learn about school, feminism and stable relationships, the idea of prom no longer has any appeal.

**Rebecca, 39:**   I didn't care about prom, but people ask. There are options for prom now. My oldest daughter has gone to a homeschool prom recently and I have to say it was super exciting. I enjoyed sharing that experience with her. But I would have hated it.

**Emily, 16:**   I can't count how many times kids and adults have asked me if I wish I could go to prom and "don't I feel like I'm missing out on all the high school stuff?" The truth is, I couldn't care less about prom!

**Caroline, 24:**   I have been asked about prom—more so when I was in high school. I did not, and still do not, care. It wasn't my type of thing. I had multiple chances to attend a homeschooling prom through the umbrella group and passed up the opportunity every time.

---

### Hailey, 18

Let's put this into a bit of perspective here:

If the only thing that adults have to argue against homeschooling is missing out on prom, or senior night, or senioritis, what kinds of lives are they living?

If their own prom was that big of a highlight in their lives I must assume that they're living pretty mundane lives.

What about falling in love? What about sky diving?

What about dancing in a club in France or Italy?

Is prom REALLY going to beat those?

*Kate and her date at the Homeschool Prom*

*Local homeschool football team – the Cougars!*
*Ari and Kevin played for this team*

*Were you involved in Sports?*

## CHAPTER 11

## Sports

Participating in sports gives teens the chance for many kinds of growth beyond the physical abilities: the psychological skill of persistence, the social practice of winning and losing graciously, the job skills of working with teammates and listening to coaches. Sports can also instill habits for a healthy active lifestyle.

American school kids spend much of their time sitting in classrooms. According to a 2011 Center for Disease Control report on the physical activity of teenagers, only 29% of teens in high school participate in daily exercise outside of school, and while in school only 53% are offered PE classes. Homeschooling provides an opportunity to improve on those statistics, and the teens surveyed appeared to be taking advantage of their less constrained daytime hours.

While we cannot determine if the homeschooled teens' exercise was daily, 69% of the respondents report participating in sports during their teen years. That's significantly more than the national average. Finding opportunities for team sports or facilities for individual ones can be a challenge for teens not in school. They may need

### Team Sports

- Intramural Sports: Soccer, Basketball
- City League: Basketball, Softball, Baseball
- Community-based Soccer (AYSO)
- Martial Arts Teams
- Homeschool Leagues: Soccer, Volleyball
- Charter School Leagues: Football, Golf
- Club Teams: Swim, Dive, Water Polo
- Local High School: Tennis
- 4H Clubs: Horseback Riding & Competition
- Dance Classes/Groups Performance
- Competitive Cheerleading
- Junior Olympic Archery
- "Pick up" Soccer & Football with friends

help finding resources in the community. Sometimes teenagers can find sports opportunities that interest them through friends, local advertising or even the Internet. Your local support group may provide team activities.

Our family had a unique opportunity to see how a homeschooling group can step up to the plate when it comes to offering athletic opportunities. Parental involvement played a big part when we lived in Wichita Falls, Texas, where a parent with an affinity for a sport coached and inspired our young athletes. The support group there had one athletic mother who set up an entire league of homeschool, co-ed volleyball teams. She encouraged other parents to help with coaching; older kids learned to referee. The teams held practices throughout the week and played during school hours at the local Boys & Girls Clubs. Participating in the teen volleyball league was something that the younger homeschoolers all eagerly anticipated.

Then we moved to Austin, Texas, where we found that the local support group had been consistently holding soccer games every Tuesday and Thursday morning since 1994! In a completely different fashion than the Wichita Falls group, all ages, including parents, were allowed and encouraged to play. Younger kids came and played earlier in the mornings, and as the day progressed, the teens arrived and the pace picked up. Parents sat around the fields in lawn chairs chatting (chatting can be aerobic!), while the kids organized the teams based on who was there. Soccer at Zilker Park became a great opportunity for teens to get to know each other, and for parents to find out what was going on with the homeschooling community.

## Individual Sports

- Tennis
- Martial Arts
- Squash
- Fencing
- Bowling
- Golf
- Figure Skating
- Ultimate Frisbee
- Gymnastics/Acrobatics
- Competitive Dance
- Ride & Show Horses
- Dog Mushing

## Soccer

Whether the homeschooled teens and young adults played in leagues and organized tournaments or simply regular "pick-up" games at local parks, soccer is a favorite of many.

**Rose S., 20:**    I played soccer for fifteen years, through AYSO (American Youth Soccer Organization) My family was involved in AYSO before I can remember. I don't remember not playing on an AYSO team. I love soccer, and I love AYSO, which is why, now that I can't play due to age restrictions, I coach. Most of the girls I played with were public schooled,

*Rose S. waits to do a throw-in*

and even the few homeschoolers participating were very traditionally homeschooled—definitely no unschoolers other than me. Sometimes it was difficult—the other girls spent a lot more time together, as they all went to school together (my city is very small, with only two real options for middle school and just the one high school). I felt left out a lot, because I was having different life experiences than the other girls I was playing with. But overall it was a terrific experience. I feel as though half the reason I am so close to my father today is because of AYSO, and soccer in general.

> ### *Elizabeth, 19*
>
> I have played soccer since I was 8 years old, and I did gymnastics from ages 7–14. I also started playing tennis in ninth grade.

And I have formed friendships with some of those girls that continue to this day.

**Cameron P.T., 20:**   I played soccer. My mom told me about it; I'm not sure how she found out. It was a lot of fun, although our town has basically the worst soccer team for a hundred miles. We lost 95% of our games over 4 years.

**Rowan, 18:**   I played some soccer with the Austin Area Homeschool group. It was a short but sweet experience.

**Carver, 18:**   I played soccer until I was 13; I stopped because it was conflicting with theatre.

**Caitlin, 27:**   I played soccer for a few years in a community league and did martial arts for several years. Both were very good experiences.

**Beth, 20:**   I played soccer and ran track. It was great to just get out there with the other kids my age.

## Multiple Team Sports Options

Some of the homeschooled teens participated in a variety of team sports throughout adolescence. Different communities offer their own ways of connecting teens to sports teams. With a little searching, the families of these teens and young adults found recreation centers and city leagues, while others tapped into the sports offered by local homeschooling support groups. If families are concerned that homeschooling would prevent their teens from participating in sports, these young adults sharing their experiences will undoubtedly lay those fears to rest.

**Laurel, 21:**   I played softball when I was younger, and was on a swim team for a few years. I eventually got tired of the competitiveness, though. Since then, the only sport I've really enjoyed besides dancing is ultimate frisbee. I suck at it, but heck if I care! I also had homeschooled friends who were able to join high school sports teams even though they didn't go to school there.

---

> ### *Kaci, 18*
>
> I played basketball for a local homeschool team here in Austin. It was a fun experience and showed me my own personal strength. I did gymnastics until I got hurt at age 14. And I've only recently gone back to it.

> ### *Zach, 24*
>
> Yes, I played intramural soccer and basketball. My parents found them and often coached or helped run leagues. I loved my sports experiences and still do. I feel they help with many aspects of life and make for more well-rounded and achieving people.

**Kevin, 20:** As a teen, I participated in sports in public schools and through the homeschool co-ops. I found them by looking around. The experience was great, I am a very athletic person, and love sports. Still miss playing them.

**Sarah P., 17:** YES! Sports! Sports have always been an interest of mine. I found some through my homeschool friends but the sports themselves were not through a homeschool group. I have only been involved in a few sports through the Austin Area Homeschoolers association directly. Sports in general have been a great experience for me, though I do wish there were more opportunities for homeschoolers with football, etc.

**Kate, 15:** I've participated in Junior Olympic Archery, soccer, and swimming.

**Michael, 22:** When I was younger there was probably more of a variety of sports available than during my teen years. But later, sports involvement became huge in my life. Moving around as often as we did exposed me to even more since different communities offered different sports. In Alaska I played hockey for 3 years. I remember playing in the pitch black afternoons of Alaska winters when it was 10 degrees outside. And I'll never forget having my birthday fall during the state championship game. After scoring ZERO goals all year, I scored the go-ahead-goal that game. The whole team piled on top of me on the ice. It was great to be part of a team like that. Later I dabbled in volleyball, because it was what the local homeschool group offered. There were enough teens to create 14 teams! But I never really loved it. I also rode horses as a teen, but not really as a sport.

**Jared, 22:** I did gymnastics for two years when I was about six. My interest in that faded away, and I found tennis when I was nine years old. I played a few tournaments when I was about twelve years old. I joined the Davis High Tennis team when I was a freshman and played for all 4 years of high school. It was a great experience! I still am playing to this day.

---

**Sarah H., 24**

I played volleyball all four years of high school through a homeschool league. I was terrible at it, but I did have a lot of fun. My favorite was going to tournaments.

---

**Ari, 21**

I played football for 5 years, one year in Atlanta and 4 years in Austin, Texas. Three weeks into my senior year of playing I injured my knee. I was able to play the next year because I was homeschooled and it was a homeschool league. I found our team, the Cougars, while looking for homeschool activities online. My experience was good. It gave me confidence and strength in many different ways.

Nathan, 22:   I played baseball and basketball. Both were through my town. I loved it.

Katie P., 20:   When I was a really young homeschooler, I played ice hockey in Alaska. I got into it because my brother was doing it, and I wanted to do cool stuff like him. I did it for one season, and I found it extremely fun. Good thing too. Because in the winter, that is all we do: play hockey or go skating. Then, when I was 12, I played volleyball through my homeschool league. Once again, I did it because I wanted to do what my brother did. We were even placed on the same team. As a teen, I started taking dance classes. Most of these ended with a group dance performance or two—which I loved. And now I teach dance as a part-time job.

Nicholas, 26:   The local city basketball team let me play on their team. I tried it out and didn't like it. The thing I enjoyed about basketball in school was playing with my friends. With the city team it was a bunch of strangers who already knew each other, but not me. Karate was an excellent alternative!

Micah, 16:   I was in Karate, Jujitsu, and other martial arts. I play football for a public school team. That was a culture shock at first because I was not accustomed to friends being so self-centered and cutthroat! I have learned to just accept that as the way they have had to be to survive in public school sports. I am not that way because I believe if I do my best, I will either be good enough or not and to me that is not a big deal. Many on my team believe their future lives depend on their sports ability and I don't see it that way.

Alyssa P., 18:   I took Hip Hop dance classes at a couple of different dance studios. That was fun. I learned to be pretty good at it. I enjoyed these classes. Then when I was 14 years old, I did competitive cheerleading for one year. My mom found the organization online, so I went and tried out. I loved it! We travelled around the state performing. There was a lot of choreography as well as stunts. I had so much fun! I did go to the local high school for a year and a half. I made the dance team there. My experience was…different. I ended up quitting because of the way some (most) of the

---

### Jared, 22

I did gymnastics for two years when I was about six. My interest in that faded away, and I found tennis when I was nine years old. I played a few tournaments when I was about twelve years old. I joined the Davis High Tennis team when I was a freshman and played for all 4 years of high school. It was a great experience! I still am playing to this day.

girls acted. I am a tough person and I don't like to hear people complain about every little thing. Also they were very mean girls, and I didn't want to be associated with them. But I loved the training, the performing, and being part of the team.

**Hannah J., 22:**   I played sports informally, as a weekly get-together with other homeschooled families at a public park. There was good variety (including many climbing trees, which I still enjoy when I can find them) and little pressure to do any particular activity each week, so I was free to "float" and participate in a lot of things.

## Martial Arts

Martial arts have become increasingly popular, and homeschooled teens are having a lot of fun with a variety of styles. Often, entire families participate together, learning skills, improving their abilities, connecting with each other in an entirely different way.

**Michael, 22:**   I found Judo after going to Japan when I was 16 years old. I fell in love with the sport and trained for four hours a week and then an additional four hours of other martial arts as well. In the three years I played I won my share of matches and lost probably a lot more. But everything about the sport and the players was such a positive experience I'll never forget.

**Laura, 24:**   I did martial arts and we joined a studio to practice. I enjoyed the exercise and learning something new.

**Zoe, 22:**   I was really into Tae-Kwon-Do, which had classes at my local YMCA. I loved my Tae-Kwon-Do class. But I was never that into sports. We did have a gym class available to my homeschool group, but I never really enjoyed it.

**Rose S., 20:**   I've done martial arts for eight years. I went to martial arts classes with two different groups—one was entirely homeschooled families, while the other was mostly schooled kids about my age (teens). However, these people

> **Caroline, 24**
>
> I was involved with karate and swimming. I did karate at a nearby place that I passed every day. Competitive swimming came out of swimming lessons. I swam during the winter season one year and summer seasons for four or five years. I didn't really enjoy it as my nature is competitive but I was a slow swimmer. I enjoyed and performed much better at karate.

*Risa and her (all homeschooled) Beach Volleyball Team*

---

**Alaina, 25**

I was really into Taekwon-do. I taught it and earned my Black Belt. It was a lot of fun and gave me a real sense of accomplishment.

---

did not all know each other from school, and therefore I definitely felt less left out. My educational background was similar to a lot of the other students, including one of my best friends, who started classes at the same time as me. It was a more relaxing environment in a lot of ways, because I never felt like I had to justify my lifestyle. My involvement with martial arts started at my local park day. We had a new family come to the park one day, and the moms found out that the new mom was the owner of a martial arts studio. They suggested a homeschool class and :::poof:::, a homeschool class was born (that class has now lasted for over eight years and got so big that it had to be split into two groups). I started hanging out at the studio with my friends, not taking classes, just playing games. My mom kept suggesting I try the class, but I was hesitant about starting something new, especially when all my friends already were fairly advanced. Eventually I did give it a try, and the rest, as they say, is history.

## Water Sports

Swim teams, diving, water polo are also fun ways homeschooled teens have participated in local sports. Communities frequently offer club teams or recreational leagues for teenagers as well as young adults.

**Grace, 19:**   I tried a lot of different sports when I was younger. I really got into water polo for a while and was on the club team in my town for a while; I even did one season on the high school team. I loved the sport, but it wasn't important enough to me to devote as much time as was required. It was the one place that I had a bad experience with other girls.

**Alsatia, 18:**   I swam for a semester of high school. It was hard work. I played soccer in elementary school. Soccer was fun and swimming was hard but I learned and didn't give up on any of it.

**Roya, 27:**   I played soccer before we started homeschooling and then after, I started swimming. I found my first swim team through my cousin, and when that team had to disband, I did team-shopping and found one that I liked. At various times my sisters were also on the teams. I liked it—but I was so heartbroken after the first team disbanded that I never felt connected to the other. I know I was more invested in that team than the rest because they were all looking forward to swimming on their high school swim teams, and for me, the USS team was all I had.

> **Skylar, 26**
>
> I started diving (springboard and tower) when I was 7. I continued off and on throughout high school and competed in the community college circuit—I even made it to State Champs when I was 16!

## Horseback Riding

If their teen was interested, parents found opportunities for them to gain exposure to horses by networking online or exploring the local area to find horse communities nearby. Teenagers who don't own horses seem to have more access to borrowed horses because of being homeschooled, since they are more available on weekdays. Homeschooled teens are often valuable volunteers in places where horseback riding is offered to special needs children and adults. They brush, clean stalls, and exercise the horses, gaining not only access to horses, but also providing a community service and benefiting from helping others.

Some of the teens and young adults in the survey rode horses on their own for pleasure, while others participated in group events, 4-H, and/or showing horses.

**Rose S., 20:**   In addition to my other sports, I rode horses, in both private and group lessons, as well as through 4-H. With horseback riding, the girls I was riding with were very different from me in a lot of ways. They had a different outlook on life. And they all did tend to know one another from school, and saw one another more often. But I loved horseback riding. I was really into the idea of riding horses, and one year for my birthday my mom and dad got me lessons as my gift. I guess my mom must have done research into which stable to go to. After that started to get too expensive, my mom found out about a fairly local 4-H club that had an active riding group. I stopped riding when my 4-H club fell apart, and I got more involved with martial arts and ran out of time. But it was an extremely satisfying experience, and I know that I will continue to ride again someday.

**Emma, 18:**   Riding was my sport. I've done it since I was born because it's in my family's blood.

**Michael, 22:**   I rode horses for several years. Occasionally I rode in small competitions, but it was really just for fun.

**Molly N., 19:**   As a pre-teen, I swam on a swim team through the city parks and recreation center. I rode and showed horses from age 8 onward. I found them independently and enjoyed the experience.

## Individual Sports

Team sports can be rewarding, but often, teams stop being an option when a teen grows up. Not so with individual sports. These sports are often carried into adulthood bringing exercise, camaraderie and fun.

---

### Sophie, 19

I did track and field and horseback riding. We found these sports because emails would go out to the homeschool group my mom was in, and so she would sign us up for P.E. Horseback riding is the kind of thing you find by driving by a barn and stopping in to talk to the people. I still ride and love horses.

**Mike, 16:**  I've played ultimate frisbee, soccer, and football, all very casually with my friends, meeting on a regular basis. I found them mostly through my friends, and I've enjoyed them all a great deal.

**Rosie, 24:**  For a while I took fencing. And for most of my life I enjoyed juggling, and acrobatics.

**Anastasia, 19:**  I have never played team sports, but I enjoy occasional Squash and Arnis [Filipino martial arts].

**Chant, 15:**  I don't play sports but I do dance in competitions around Colorado.

**Hannah T., 18:**  I figure skated for about six years. My brother, who was also homeschooled, skated as well, and we found most of the ice rinks and coaches locally. It was a pretty great experience to be able to explore that passion without having to fit it into a busy school schedule like many of my other figure skating friends had to.

**Dakota, 20:**  I played soccer on a homeschool team when I was younger. Now I bike.

> ### Steen, 15
>
> Yes, I play tennis and golf and have an interest in coaching football. I found out about tennis from watching it on T.V. and then playing the sport with my parents. I found out about golf by taking homeschool golf lessons and now I am an active golfer for 4 years now.

*Jared hanging out with tennis buddies*

> **Tori, 18**
>
> I would say dog mushing was my main sport, but I also have been taking dance classes since I was 4.

> **Rebecca, 39**
>
> No sports for me.
> My focus was entirely on animals, music and theater.

**Molly S., 20:**   The only sports I played were homeschool classes through my homeschooling group, unless you count dance.

**Jackson, 20:**   I played soccer with Austin Area Homeschoolers (AAH) a few times, which was pretty fun, but I'm not really a particularly sporty individual. I do love that I would often have time to drop everything and go bowling with my dad, and I still do that as often as possible. I suppose that's my main sport, and it's certainly the one I'm best at.

## No thanks, to Sports

Some believe that the school systems are overly focused on sports. And, certainly, a large number of people have interests elsewhere. By homeschooling, teens are given the choice to participate or not – based upon their skill and interest instead of whether it's the "popular" thing to do. Here respondents share a little about why they chose not to participate in sports during their homeschooled teen years.

**Sunny, 17:**   I am awful at sports, when I tried soccer, I dislocated my knee. When I tried longboarding, I sprained my ankle. I try to find other occupying things.

**Simcha, 17:**   I have never had much interest in sports.

**Alyssa A., 18:**   I didn't play any sports during high school aside from playing basketball with my brother.

**Trina, 16:**   I played basketball, and the experience seemed good at the time but looking back on it, I see that it caused me more drama and stress than I needed. And it pulled me away from my homework.

**Kristin, 19:**   I never played sports, other than the occasional game of Capture the Flag at parties.

**Joseph, 19:**   I was never really a big sports player, so I can't say much here. Having younger brothers growing up gave me plenty of opportunities to get out and play games.

**Hailey, 18:**   I chose not to participate in school sports as I never really enjoyed them nor am I competitive about games.

**Wendolyn, 34:**   No, I did not participate in sports. Looking back, this was an area that was lacking in my experience. I have helped my son, now seven, get involved in sports. There are more choices available to families now than when I was unschooled.

**Emily, 16:**   When I was younger I played sports through the YMCA, but as a teen I haven't been very interested in sports.

**Alyssa H., 17:**   In my high school years I didn't play any sports, but I did play basketball from fourth to eighth grade. I loved it! It was through a local church.

**Teagan, 20:**   I spent one spring playing on a community soccer team when I was young, but quit immediately after when I realized that I had neither passion nor talent for it.

> *Skye, 22*
>
> There were opportunities to play sports, but I wasn't interested, and I liked having the option not to partake.

*Michael working at the Schlitterbahn Water Park*

*Did you work as a homeschooled teen?*

CHAPTER 12

## Teen Employment

Being employed during adolescence gives teenagers such an opportunity to grow, to expand their circle, testing the waters of adulthood. Teens in schools have the same issues with employment that they have with sports: they can only work after school or on weekends which takes its toll on their ability to do much else—extracurricular activities, hobbies, or homework.

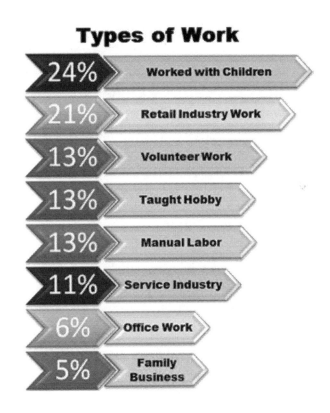

**Types of Work**

| | |
|---|---|
| 24% | Worked with Children |
| 21% | Retail Industry Work |
| 13% | Volunteer Work |
| 13% | Taught Hobby |
| 13% | Manual Labor |
| 11% | Service Industry |
| 6% | Office Work |
| 5% | Family Business |

It's not unusual to find homeschooled teens holding down jobs during their high school years. While some worked in the summer, many were able to take advantage of having a flexible schedule during the school year. Being employed as a homeschooled teenager gave them opportunities to manage their own money, interact with a wider variety of people, learn new skills—all without becoming sleep deprived or interfering with their other activities.

My own children worked in a variety of jobs throughout their teen years, because they had a particular interest in the field or they simply wanted their own spending money. Each of them pursued a different path. One chose a make-up internship and a little retail work. My budding actress and fan fiction writer worked for a bookstore and a movie theatre. And my adventure seeker tried everything in his path!

91% of those who completed the survey held jobs or volunteer positions as teenagers. The graphic on the previous page shows the various areas in which these homeschooled teens and grown homeschoolers worked.

## Child Care

Childcare, working as a nanny, and babysitting were the most frequent jobs homeschooled teens found. Babysitting is a pretty common job for most American teens. Homeschooled teens, however, have greater flexibility so they're available to watch the neighbors' kids during the morning, while mom runs out to the grocery store or indulges in late-night babysitting on a "school night" because they don't have morning classes. Also, because homeschooling parents are often interacting with each other, it's easy to match up teens with parents in need. Because parents, teens, and kids are meeting at park days or attending group field trips, the parents of younger kids are able to see how the homeschooled teens interact with their kids, easing any anxiety about hiring a sitter.

**Skylar, 26:**   I started working as a mother's helper when I was 9 years old. I started a job paying taxes when I was

> ### Caroline, 24
>
> During the school year, I babysat very frequently. At one point I was averaging five nights a week. Because I didn't have to get up early in the morning, I was very flexible with the lateness of my evening hours.

12 years old. And at 16 years old, I had a regular job with official shifts. By age 17, I quit my hostess job and became a nanny. I would never have been able to be a nanny if I had attended high school.

**Emily, 16:**   I used to babysit. Being able to babysit on school days was very helpful. I have also done various other odd jobs that other kids couldn't because it was on a school day. For example, I worked for our minister at his honey plant.

**Skye, 22:**   I worked in child care as a teen and I still do. Having an enormously flexible schedule was very convenient for my employers and me.

**Joseph, 19:**   I babysat starting around the age of 13. My open hours were definitely a plus for the families that hired me. With my other jobs throughout high school, it was definitely helpful that I was available when my supervisors were working.

**Sarah P., 17:**   I do not work yet. But I have had a number of babysitting jobs that were easier to do because of my free time.

**Rose, 30:**   I did work for a time as a mother's helper. Her child was homeschooled but she worked. She needed someone to be around during the day. I wouldn't have been able to take that job if I hadn't been homeschooled.

**Alsatia, 18:**   I do/did work. I was a nanny for 20 hours per week during my senior year of high school, from 12 p.m. – 5 p.m. four days per week. This would NOT have been possible had I had a public school schedule.

## Retail/Service Oriented Jobs

Shops and theatres are also big employers of homeschooled teens. Retail and service-oriented jobs are options that appeal to teens who enjoy socializing and interacting with the public. They also learn about inventory, operating cash registers, and various skills based on the particular industry.

> **Sarah B., 20**
>
> I would help my neighbors with their daughter in the morning because they both worked. I helped her get ready for school, then drove her to the bus stop or to school. Sometimes I picked her up and watched her after school. I was able to do this because of my flexible schedule.

Caroline, 24:    Yes, in high school, I worked as a cashier during the summer. Because I was homeschooled, I was able to work more months because my school year finished earlier than the public school year. Because I was always one of the first "seasonal" cashiers, I normally had my pick of the hours—I rarely had to work nights or weekends.

Molly S., 20:    I worked a lot last summer at my first conventional, salaried job at a movie theater. School was not a factor. I have worked, not for pay, at various theaters as well. Rehearsals are always in the evenings and they would not conflict with school anyway.

Rosie, 24:    I worked in a theater for many years. It was convenient that I had flexible hours.

Teagan, 20:    I had my first real job when I was seventeen—I worked at a used book store during the spring and summer before I left for Chicago. During that summer, of course, my availability wasn't changed by my school status, but during the spring it was helpful. Even though I was going to community college full-time, I had some days off from class, and some days when I got out early. My boss definitely appreciated that!

Risa, 21:    I have worked continuously since I was sixteen years old. In order to fund my speech and debate tournaments, I worked part-time at Jamba Juice for three years. I believe working is a fantastic opportunity for young people to gain valuable experience and build leadership skills (something college desperately want to see!). One of the reasons I was hired at Jamba Juice, and consecutive jobs, was my availability during weekday hours, a time student employees are needed, but rarely available. Being homeschooled definitely gave me an advantage and allowed me employment options that might have been otherwise impossible.

Cameron L., 24:    I was hired for my first legitimate job at age 14 at a deli in my hometown. I had already left school, so there was nothing to hold me back from going to work at 8:00 or 10:00 a.m. every morning. Clearly it wouldn't have been possible to attend school and work. I learned very much

---

### Nicholas, 26

I did work during the week and even though school was still my primary focus, I had flexible hours that helped make me more appealing to my employer. At 15 or 16 years old, my job at Sears helped me learn early what the adult work world was like.

---

### Anastasia, 19

Being homeschooled was somewhat appreciated when I worked retail. Although when I say I was available during "weekday hours," I mean "as late as 3:00 a.m."

there—from customer service to fractions to running the cash register to cooking. At first, they paid me under the table, but eventually I was treated like everyone else—taxes were withdrawn from my paycheck.

## Family Business

Some homeschooled families run businesses where their teens can step into and find work. Real world application of economics can't be avoided. Sometimes, these teens are exposed to some of the management aspects of employment that they may later use in life.

**Sunny, 17:**   My family bought a coffee shop (almost) two years ago. As a graduation project, they put me and my siblings in charge of it for a few months. It was a great experience, but we still got our school done!

**Micah, 16:**   I work for my dad and learned mechanical things because of my flexible school time.

## Office Work

Entry level office work is a possibility for some of the homeschooled teenagers. Learning how the business world works, office organization skills, interacting with clients and other professionals are all some of the life skills that office work can provide.

**Tori, 18:**   I worked as an office filer in the morning, which I could only have done as a homeschooler.

## Teaching in their Hobby

Many of the homeschooled teens became quite proficient in one or more of their hobbies. Noticing their skill & interest level, along with their daytime flexibility, employers often offered the chance for them to teach younger, less experienced students in their field. Opportunities like this contribute to the teen's skill set for future employment and gives them a sense of accomplishment and confidence.

> **Kate, 15**
>
> I do data entry work for my dad's advertising business.

> **Brenna, 22**
>
> When I was a teenager I got a job as a receptionist and an event leader at a franchise called *Young Chef's Academy*. I worked on weekends and afternoons. Being available during the day on weekdays didn't matter.

*Rose S. – Martial Arts instructor*

**Kirby, 26**

The gaming store, Active Imagination, hired me because I was the only person willing to run the weekly Pokèmon event, which had 70+ children attending. I taught the youth class at my Dojo, which was primarily due to my being the senior student/turned "adult."

**Roya, 27:**   I started working as a henna artist with a homeschooling mom a few hours a week. It was definitely helpful that I didn't go to school. Then I went on to work at Laguna Clay Company, a major ceramic supply store, when I was about 16 years old. I couldn't have had this job if I was in school, since it was only open during the day. I loved working at the ceramics store and learned a lot about the field. I went on to work in the Cypress College Ceramics Lab—a job I would never have been offered if I hadn't had my prior experience with the Laguna Clay Company.

**Kaci, 18:**   I worked at a summer camp for 3 summers as a camp counselor. It was a fun, but tiring job.

**Katie P., 20:**   When my dance teacher opened her own studio, she took me with her. I added 'teaching dance class' and 'teaching acting class' to my list of jobs. Being available in the mornings to teach the little kids was really a big advantage.

**Rose S., 20:**   I have held a job at my martial arts studio for over five years. I originally started helping out with the homeschool classes, which were on weekdays in the early afternoon. Most of the instructors at the studio were also home-schooled (the owner of the studio is a homeschooling mom).

When I was originally hired, the owner of the studio was in a bind, as one of her instructors had quit unexpectedly and she had no one to cover. I was not a black belt yet, and could not be an official instructor, but I helped out at the homeschool classes for a few months. After I received my black belt, I became an official instructor.

## Variety of Jobs as a Teen

Some homeschooled teens attacked the work opportunities with gusto. They've tried out a variety of options, jumping in, learning new skills, and earning their own money. Being flexible opened up a lot of options for these homeschooled teens. More and more employers saw the benefits of hiring them.

**Jackson, 20:**   I've had many more opportunities than most doing odd jobs earning cash here and there. Having the free time in which to do so was invaluable.

**Sarah H., 24:**   I worked as a janitor and childcare worker at my church from when I was 13 years old until I moved away from my hometown ten years later. I worked at a movie theater when I was sixteen. Being available in the mornings while others were in school was really helpful, especially working at my church.

**Katie P., 20:**   I had several jobs before I left home. I loved to read, so a job as a bookseller at Barnes and Noble was perfect. I dealt with customers and worked the cash register. Later in my teens, I got a job at the movie theatre.

**Hannah T., 18:**   Yes, I worked a lot! When I decided to go to Mexico when I was fifteen I wanted to earn the money myself, and started a babysitting and house cleaning service that turned a good profit. Without the freedom of unschooling I would never have been able to do that. The independence and work ethic required to be successful have followed me into my adult life and have been an invaluable

---

> *Hannah J., 22*
>
> I taught violin, tutored middle and high school subjects, and babysat. I had a lot more opportunities because of my flexible schedule.

> *Michael, 22*
>
> When it comes to working, I think I've had a lot more jobs than others my age who went to school. I've worked on farms, paper routes, supermarkets, bookstores, restaurants, scout camps, cafes all before going to college. And in college, I worked at the campus newspaper and radio station as well as a lifeguard in a local water park. One of the reasons I worked in so many places as a younger teen was because I was trying to earn enough money to go to Japan as an exchange student at 16.
>
> And, yes, I did make enough and spent the summer in Japan.

asset. I've had a wide range of jobs and gained some really diverse experiences from basic emergency medical work to concrete pouring.

**Cameron P.T., 20:**   I've worked at a fruit stand, and as a PC repair man (word of mouth under the counter only). I learned all the skills for repairing PC's as a result of all my free time from unschooling.

**Nathan, 22:**   I worked two jobs in high school. I was a religious school aide on Sundays and Mondays but not during school hours. My other job was at a grocery store. They specifically told me in the interview I was picked because of the hours I could work.

**Katie F., 24:**   I've worked a lot! I had a paper route, which didn't matter whether or not I was available during school hours. I cashiered at a fast food restaurant, and they loved that I could work any time they needed. I even had the freedom to nanny in a different state for several months. It was a wonderful experience and one I would not have been able to do if I had been attending a regular school. I just took my schoolwork with me.

**Wendelyn, 34:**   As a teenager, I worked at a vet clinic, a library, a drive-in, a childcare ministry, and as a nanny.

## Summer Only or Not Much Work

Sometimes working isn't a big priority for homeschooled teens and their families. These families might prefer that their teen considers their educational time as "their job." Picking up occasional jobs for extra spending money was common for these homeschoolers.

**Sarah D., 19:**   I've never really worked, except occasionally subbing for musicians at local churches. I think it's really something from which I would have benefited.

**Elizabeth, 19:**   I worked junior and senior year. However both years I was taking 5 classes at the high school so I never had any hours open during the day.

---

### Molly N., 19

When I graduated early, I was able to spend a year working in my field. This gave me a head start in my career.

**Grace, 19:** I worked in the summer, not during the school year.

**Sophie, 19:** I never had a real job in high school. Most of my jobs were pet sitting for the neighbors which is already a flexible position.

## Volunteer/Internships

Several of our survey respondents had the opportunity to work in internships that interested them or volunteer in fields they enjoyed. While most of these positions are unpaid, the teens gained professional experience that helped them explore different industries and become more involved in their communities. Some of these experiences turned into employment later for these teens, while others simply gained exposure in a wide variety of areas.

**Caitlin, 27:** I did a summer apprenticeship at age 17. I worked as both an administrative assistant at an office and as a receptionist at a vet clinic for what was the equivalent of my senior year. I would not have been able to do either of those jobs (let alone have time to hold two jobs) if I had not been available during the day.

**Alaetheia, 16:** I have worked several volunteer jobs, including my current training to be a fire fighter. This summer, I worked on a construction crew building a geodesic dome.

**Alyssa A., 18:** I don't have an actual job, but I do a lot of volunteering work. I am an intern at a museum in my area, but it's not a weekly thing.

**Nancy, 15:** I volunteer at our local library on Mondays from 9 a.m.–11 a.m.

**Alyssa P., 18:** I worked at a natural make-up company in Austin as an intern for what would have been considered my entire "freshman year." My flexible hours made it possible to go in several times each week during the day. During what would have been my "senior year," I enrolled in Cosmetology school. I made tips from clients there.

> ### Katie P., 20
>
> When I took theater classes, I worked as an intern to get price reductions on my theatre classes. I wanted to take EVERY class!
>
> So I worked the desk, cleaned up the rooms and did inventory.

## Flexible Hours Made All the Difference

Throughout this chapter, the homeschooled teens and young adults shared how homeschooling offered flexibility in their employment opportunities. Most of the jobs they were able to find and keep came because of their availability in the daytime and/or unusual times of day.

### 96% Identified Flexible Hours As Major Homeschooling Benefit

Several addressed this idea a little more, sharing how they believe their flexibility was their biggest advantage as a homeschooled teen searching for a job.

**Zoe, 22:**   I have had a job since I was 14 years old. I started washing dishes in a cafe. Having more freedom with my hours helped immensely in getting a job. I feel very ahead in the job market in some ways because I have started working at a young age. I have held on to my current job for over three years now.

**Beth, 20:**   Yes, I've worked since I was 15 years old. It was great to be able to work weekdays because then I could have the weekends off.

**Rebecca, 39:**   I worked at a local library and veterinary clinic. My schedule and flexibility were huge factors I believe in my getting hired.

**Laura, 24:**   I did have a couple of jobs in high school. I had some good opportunities because I was available during the day.

**Katie P., 20:**   When I was still a teen, I was cast in commercials and an independent film through an acting agency. I needed a flexible schedule for all the auditions and shoots. It was definitely an advantage on my end that I was available during the day and could move things around in my schedule. Juggling the time between all of it was another story, but it all worked out in the end.

---

### Kelli, 21

I did not work but I did volunteer. I was able to do that because of my flexible schedule. My parents considered it vital that we learn in as many different ways as possible and volunteering achieved that.

---

### Kristin, 19

I had a job at the University of North Carolina at Chapel Hill and I worked during school hours. That was an opportunity that I wouldn't have had if I had been in school. The job taught me as much as my schoolwork ever did. I learned how to navigate a university library, website, and administrative system, as well as how to write reports.

**Tess, 27:**   Being available to work hours on weekdays gave me more work opportunities. This enabled me to take college courses during high school years. I have worked since the age of fifteen.

**Hailey, 18:**   I am currently working for a lady in town, a friend of the family. I work about 15 hours a week on Mondays and Wednesdays 9 a.m. – 4 p.m. It certainly helps that I am available during school hours.

**Chant, 15:**   Because I have a great resume and can work just about any time in the week, I don't have too much trouble getting a job.

**Alyssa H., 17:**   I have three jobs, two are during the day. If I wasn't homeschooled there would be absolutely no way I could do these jobs and save enough money for college.

**Julia, 15:**   I am starting a job this year that I wouldn't be able to do if I was in school.

**Zach, 24:**   Yes, I was able to be more flexible with my hours.

**Laurel, 21:**   Yes, and almost all of my jobs would have been hard to keep if I didn't have a flexible schedule.

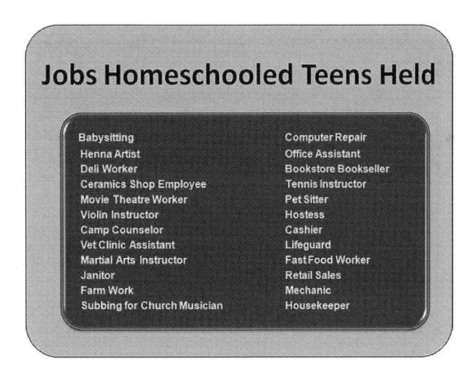

## Jobs Homeschooled Teens Held

| | |
|---|---|
| Babysitting | Computer Repair |
| Henna Artist | Office Assistant |
| Deli Worker | Bookstore Bookseller |
| Ceramics Shop Employee | Tennis Instructor |
| Movie Theatre Worker | Pet Sitter |
| Violin Instructor | Hostess |
| Camp Counselor | Cashier |
| Vet Clinic Assistant | Lifeguard |
| Martial Arts Instructor | Fast Food Worker |
| Janitor | Retail Sales |
| Farm Work | Mechanic |
| Subbing for Church Musician | Housekeeper |

*Brenna at the pottery wheel*

*What hobbies have you enjoyed as a homeschooled teen?*

## CHAPTER 13

## Enjoying Hobbies

This chapter is so full of passion! The homeschooled teens and young adults describe what they love doing and how they're able to fill their lives with joy. It's inspiring to read the enormous array of options they have indulged in.

Homeschooling gives kids, teens, and parents the time and the focus to discover an enthusiasm or hobby. Maybe the parents expose their teens to a field that becomes a consuming interest; maybe the kids expose the parents. Because time is less of an issue, curiosity can be satisfied and fostered; some teens might just dip their toes into a particular activity, others might discover a new passion, and still others might go on into adulthood with that hobby turning into a career.

### 100% Enjoyed at least one hobby throughout their adolescence

### 31% Grown homeschoolers are still enjoying hobbies they discovered as teens

When you read about the hobbies that these teens and young adults are pursuing, notice the diversity. When a teen goes to high school or middle school, they are often limited—by time, availability, and peers—to what that particular school has the money to offer. Usually, their "extra-curriculars" are primarily sport-related. Parents of school kids must satisfy their kid's interest in the arts or science or community involvement on their own. While some parents try to do this, they still have to fit any hobby in the small window after school and before homework, or on the weekend.

Teens' schedules are often so packed, they are too exhausted to enjoy pursuing any passion—let alone explore new ones.

Homeschooling offers a completely different situation. Many of the grown respondents shared that they continue to pursue the hobbies they found in their teen years. They definitely felt that their lives, then and now, are much richer because of their opportunity to delve into their interests to such a degree. And most attribute this opportunity to being homeschooled.

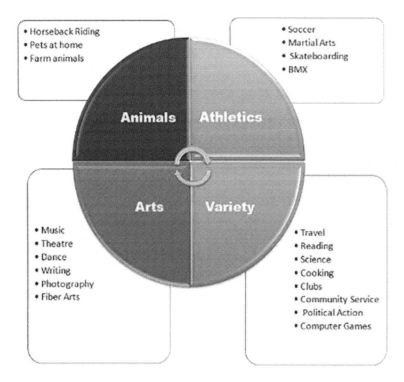

Of the homeschooled teens and young adults we interviewed, three common categories emerged for hobbies: The Arts, Animal Interests, and Athletics.

## The Homeschooled Teens' Hobbies

First, let's examine the responses of those teens who are considered still in their high school years. They're too young to know if they will maintain their current interests. But even if they stop pursuing a particular passion, the traits that hobbies develop—competence, confidence, focus, and depth—will remain. Also, hobbies connect teens to others who share similar interests, sometimes leading to long friendships, deeper learning, and often a richer life. These teens describe what they're doing and how they're envisioning their future. What an exciting time for them!

## The Athletes

The survey respondents offered much more insights about their sports involvement in Chapter 11. But these teens identified their athletic endeavors as one of their favorite hobbies.

**Trina, 16:** Wakeboarding, skateboarding, snowboarding and writing.

**Aiden R., 17:** I have a lot of hobbies: primarily BMX, skateboarding, music and my love for animals.

**Alyssa P., 18:** I did competition cheerleading. I played backyard hockey, soccer, gymnastics, dance classes. I could sleep in if I was tired, and go to practices that were in the daytime with no problem.

## The Animal Enthusiasts

Teens can continue their love of animals whether they live in the city or the country. While many families include pets, these teens shared how important animals are in their lives.

**Emily, 16:** I work with and ride our horses. Riding is my favorite "sport!" I have raised tons of chickens, as well as other animals. I have been able to study art and photography. I hope to become a professional photographer and I am currently training my first colt.

**Tori, 18:** I would say mushing was my main hobby. Mushing can take a whole entire day or longer, one of the main reasons I homeschooled during high school.

**Emma, 18:** My horses take up a lot of time, showing especially. Most of my school friends have to miss school days when showing, but not me! I bring my school with

> ### Crystal, 15
> I love Kung-Fu. I became a black belt at the age of ten and that would not have happened if I had been in school.

> ### Sophie, 18
> I am still considering a career in the horse industry. I've gotten good enough and I have met enough "big-time" people that it could easily become a career path for me. I could go for riding lessons in the middle of the week and in the middle of the day. This gave me more one-on-one time. I was able to work at barns during the times most kids couldn't, which improved my reputation and work ethic.

me! I mainly just ride and compete for fun. I rode English and competed in "Three-day Eventing". I'm not looking to make a career out of it. However I have always wanted to be a vet, now an animal pathologist, and because of Pony Club I probably have greater chance of that.

**Alyssa P., 18:**   Animals have played a HUGE part of my life—we even lived on a ranch for five years. I had dogs and horses and we participated in a variety of 4-H projects. We also had 3 cats that we bottle-fed when coyotes got the mother, a couple parakeets, two cockatiels—which actually turned into a business where we raised and sold the babies. We had goats, cows, chickens, ducks, as well as guinea pigs and a red-eared slider turtle. I know—that's a lot!

> ### *Hailey, 18*
> My main hobby includes training my horses and attending group events and clinics. I couldn't have missed traditional school this much to do this.

*Alyssa P., applying monster make-up for a
Halloween Haunted House*

**The Artists**

Homeschooled teens are often involved with a variety of art forms: music, fiber arts, photography, theatre arts, dance, or creative writing—just to name a few!

**Alyssa H., 17:**  I love theater, writing, history and reading…just to name a few! I started acting in our town's children's acting group. Then I was placed on the costume crew one show and I fell in love with it! I'm currently costumer of my first show and this is my second paying position for a theatrical production. I hope this will continue, because I love doing it!

**Julia, 15:**  My hobby is dance.

**Sarah P., 17:**  I have been involved with the Zach Scott theater center, which helped me meet friends, and parents, and gave me many skills for growing up. (or at least taught me how to act grown up when I didn't want to :P ) I have also had more time to pursue and travel for dance. Although I do not plan to be a professional actress, dance will hopefully always be an activity of mine.

**Alyssa A., 18:**  When I was little, I loved to sew. Later this turned to knitting, crochet and needlepoint. I also play piano and sing a lot as well as make jewelry. My musical side has definitely geared me towards something more. I am actually planning on getting an associate degree in music, perhaps one day I will teach piano.

**Mike S., 16:**  Right now I'm also currently doing the National Novel Writing Month 50,000 word challenge, and I'm on track to reach my goal. I've been in the SCA (Society for Creative Anachronism) for four years now, and hope to continue to participate in and learn from such a great community. I'm planning on being in a production of a play this coming spring with my friends and some directors I've known for a while.

**Chant, 15:**  I am able to pursue my dancing and interest in botany on my own time, those are my favorite pastimes. I hope to get a job studying plants at a lab somewhere, and

> **Mike S., 16**
>
> Music, acting, historical recreational fencing with the Society for Creative Anachronism (SCA), electronic music production, piano, game design, programming, writing novels, and probably a few more that I can't recall at the moment. I've been producing electronica for less than six months, but I've loved every minute of it and I can easily see it as being one of my main career paths.

> **Tony, 15**
>
> My hobby is music, specifically piano and guitar.

I hope I can have a part-time job teaching dance at a studio near there.

## The Travelers

Several of the teens mentioned traveling with their families throughout the year. Having the freedom to leave when it suits the family best – often when crowds are lighter and fares are lower—instead of working around a school schedule is a wonderful benefit of homeschooling. Travelling to see some of the things many American children only read about, is another great advantage of homeschooling.

**Alyssa H., 17:**    Take history for example, my family takes a lot of trips to historical places and if I was going to school outside the home then I wouldn't be able to go and see all the sights that I have. And, I love theater.

**Hannah T., 18:**    I was also able to travel and gain work experience from a young age. I learned invaluable information from traveling quite a bit in the U.S. and funding my own trips to Mexico and Japan. When I was around 13 years old, I got really into forensic anthropology and because of my free time and ability to go off traditional coursework I was able to fully engage in my interest.

## The Activists

A few of the teens noted participating in community service or local politics. Realizing that your efforts can make a difference is very helpful to these young people. Participating in their local communities can help them feel more connected and identify ways they can change the world and themselves.

**Steen, 15:**    Politics, human rights and political activism, sports, social media, military related activities, stock trading, investing and economics, history. I am the political director for the high school Democrats of Georgia and a local precinct captain for the Gwinnett County Democratic party. I am an activist and have been heavily involved in the Arab Spring and Occupy Wall Street move-

> ### Hailey, 18
>
> World travel is my hobby! I am currently in the planning process of writing a book that involves traveling and interviewing elderly folk from all over the world to ask for their words of wisdom.

> ### Alaetheia, 16
>
> I've participated in protests with the local Occupy movement.

ments, among other things. I have my own activism group that did many high level activities in Libya and Syria.

## The Dabblers

Lots of teens try out a variety of different hobbies throughout their teens. Some are consecutive hobbies—one following another—and others are clearly overlapping.

**Rowan, 18:**  I've completed over 300 hours of volunteer work for a charity haunted adventure that last year donated $25,000 to the Breast Cancer Resource Center. I create art to sell and teach others about the crafts I create, including but not limited to sewing, knitting, and crocheting. I have been able to spend time with horses. The list of activities and projects that I am involved with is endless. I do not think I would be able to enjoy a quarter of what I do if I was in school.

**Grace, 19:**  I played piano, read a lot, sang, did a couple of plays in junior high, and started keeping fish at age 12. I even kept a 55-gallon salt water fish tank. It was a hobby that I would not have had time to do, if I hadn't been homeschooled.

**Simcha, 17:**  Sewing, cooking, laundry, cleaning, money handling, horseback riding, gardening, reading, art.

**Tori, 18:**  Homeschooling also let me learn things like cooking or sewing or whatever else my mom was doing that day.

**Micah, 16:**  Karate, the arts, guitar, traveling, culinary arts.

**Alaetheia, 16:**  I've enjoyed extensive music education, sewing, raising livestock, and world traveling. I hope my hobbies will blossom in the future. My songwriting started out as a hobby, and I intend to pursue it as a career.

**Alyssa P., 18:**  I really enjoyed hanging out with friends, having mid-week sleepovers, watching a lot of T.V. Also, I loved having pets. We lived in the country for a few years and my hobbies were mainly horses, dogs, cats, goats, chickens, birds, turtle, guinea pigs. In my mid-teens, I worked as an intern at a natural/organic make-up store called MYKA

---

*Sunny, 17*

I explored many different things. When I was/am interested in something, it's very easy to pursue because of my flexible schedule.

---

*Sarah B., 20*

I horseback rode all through my high school years. I also was on the local robotics team. I spent a lot of time playing with electronics and taking stuff apart. My mom would incorporate what I was interested in to make my classes more fun.

> **Caroline, 24**
>
> I liked to read and had an immense book collection by the time I was in high school that consisted of both "kid friendly books" (Nancy Drew) and "heavy" reads such as *Beowulf* and *The Count of Monte Cristo*. I played piano extensively through most of middle and high school and earned a second degree black belt in karate during the same period. I could have pursued these while in the public school, but being homeschooled, I had a much larger amount of time to devote to them.

> **Kaci, 18**
>
> My hobbies have included:
> - Photography
> - Dance
> - Sports
> - Gymnastics
> - Going to Concerts
> - Having time to meet other homeschoolers
>
> I've done "normal" teenage things—but I was able to do it my own way.

in Austin, Texas. I learned so much there! I worked behind the scenes at fashion shows, assisted with make-up classes when groups were scheduled, learned about customer service, inventory, running a store, even how to make the make-up products. I eventually supervised other interns and became the assistant store manager. Because I had weekday availability, I was able dive in so much deeper than if I had been in a classroom Monday through Friday.

**Kate, 15:** I programmed lights at our local community theater, pursued junior Olympic archery for a while, and read a lot.

### The Readers

Many of the teens mentioned a passion for reading along with some of the other interests they're exploring.

**Alsatia B., 18:** I read. All the time. I love books. When I was younger I would go to the library on Tuesdays and come home with a stack of books at least 2 foot tall. I would have them read by Friday and be bored out of my skull all weekend.

## Looking Back at Hobbies

Some of the young adults shared their thoughts about pursuing hobbies during their teen years. Those experiences during formative years helped them discover more about themselves, identifying interests that later enriched their adult lives. Sometimes hobbies gave them opportunities for building leadership and developing life skills. Often, as homeschooled teens, they were able to give themselves to a passion simply because there was time available to explore. Many had the freedom to try out different hobbies without a lot of pressure. Many of the grown homeschoolers shared a variety of hobbies they were able to enjoy as a teenager.

**Brenna, 22:** My hobbies were gardening, theatre, classical voice, composting, ceramics, poetry, formal logic.

**Teagan, 20:** Being homeschooled has allowed me to pursue theatre in ways that never would have been possible had I attended traditional school. I started doing children's theatre when I was five years old, and have barely stopped to breathe between shows since. Being a homeschooler allowed me to devote my time and energy to auditioning and performing, and attending community college early in my teens put me at the forefront of bigger and better performance opportunities immediately.

**Risa, 21:**  One of the benefits of homeschooling is the level of freedom students are given to explore their interests. Homeschooling personalizes education and develops individual passions or hobbies. One of my interests has always been global politics and public speaking. During my sophomore year of high school, my family and I became involved with a nationally competitive homeschool speech and debate league (NCFCA). I loved how fun, educational, and intense it was and would travel across the state and country competing in tournaments against thousands of other homeschooled students. As participants, we debated controversial topics such as medical malpractice, immigration reform, and U.S. foreign relations. It was a hobby that simultaneously sharpened my communication skills, research and writing abilities, and heightened my awareness of global politics and complexity.

Not all was competitive and intense however! Homeschooling also allowed me to explore my interests in photography, nature journaling, and travel.

**Michael, 22:**  As for hobbies, homeschooling certainly didn't limit me in any way. I was always involved in some new club, project, team or something that kept my schedule full. I love history. When we lived in California, I participated in a Civil War reenactment group of homeschoolers. We were all wearing either south or north uniforms each week, learning about the history of the Civil War and what life was like during those times. We had some incredible hands-on activities associated with it all. We even spent the night on Angel Island in an old fort that was built in that time but never saw combat. This sparked my love of history and other cultures. Community service was a hobby of

> ***Joseph, 19***
>
> My primary interest was computing. Thanks to my education, I took on a project to build my own computer at the age of 14, ultimately shaping all of my academics from that point on.

> ***Jared, 22***
>
> I think when you have large blocks of time with nothing scheduled, you naturally guide yourself toward things you really want to be doing. It's an intuitive process that is greatly aided by having freedom and no constraints. Homeschooling definitely gave me the time and freedom to experiment with anything and everything.

mine throughout my teens. I organized a group of kids to take on a different project each month—making blankets, collecting food, cleaning up the highway, building with Habitat for Humanity, serving in soup kitchens. I loved to camp and hike, primarily with my dad, but also with my Boy Scout troop. I did some community theatre, and even competed in a state level 4-H poetry presentation contest.

**Skylar, 26:** My hobbies included: diving, youth group, and volunteering at a grief support center.

**Beth, 20:** I loved piano, dance, Spanish, and was able to travel at a moment's notice. I was able to get a job and work around my schedule around my jobs. I became more involved in writing and literature, kayaking, swimming.

**Zoe, 22:** I was interested in, Tae-Kwon-Do, dinosaurs, reading, reading, and more reading. For two weeks I thought I wanted to be an ice skater. Homeschooling gave me the freedom to pursue all of my interests.

**Molly S., 20:** I enjoyed musical theatre, dance, swing dance, music composition, writing fiction, playing the piano, singing, crafty things, knitting, sewing, journaling, cooking, video editing, photography, make up, graphic arts, drawing.

**Rose S., 20:** Some of my teenage hobbies: soccer, horseback riding, martial arts, gaming, watching T.V., and writing.

**Katie P., 20:** I was able to audition for so many productions and pursue any opportunity to act. I didn't have to worry about something getting in the way. I was also able to write without having a time limit or having to write about a scenario that didn't completely interest me.

**Nathan, 22:** I liked knitting, reading for pleasure, photography and volunteering with animals.

**Kelli, 21:** I was able to take a Renaissance painting class for 2 years in high school. Also, I was able to be in countless theatrical productions every year in high school.

---

### Skye, 22

Some of my hobbies included:

- Photography
- Theater
- Creative Writing
- Hiking
- Canoeing

---

### Roya, 27

Oh my gosh, where do I start? The hobbies that I was able to spend a lot of time on were… swimming, Girl Scouts, theater, fiber arts, heritage arts, dressing up, ceramics, camping, poetry, hair dying, traveling… just to name a very few.

**Caitlin, 27:**   There is no way I would have had time for all of those things if I had been in school. I participated in Odyssey of the Mind, eventually taking first place at the international competition. I took community college classes in my areas of interest. I did a lot of artwork, knitting, and other crafts. I took piano lessons, played soccer, and learned martial arts. I volunteered at the zoo several days per week which helped me rebuild my confidence after all the bullying I experienced. Without that, I would not have been as successful as I have been throughout the rest of my life.

**Jared, 22:**   Filmmaking caught my interest when I was 8 and has stayed with me to this day. My time was really protected so I could play with it a lot. Filmmaking just happens to be something that needs a lot of time to experiment with. I am pretty certain that without homeschooling, I would not be where I am today. I'm very grateful for my homeschooling experience.

**Molly N., 19:**   I was interested in horse riding, dance, art, any college class I had interest in, and theatre arts—which became my career.

**Sarah D., 19:**   I could read or write as many novels as I wanted, and I took up crocheting and knitting. I also got to keep bugs in jars and watch their life-cycles, which might sound like school to you, but it's always been one of my biggest passions.

**Hannah J., 22:**   Math team, adult choir, and homeschool orchestra/chamber quartet.

**Kevin, 20:**   I always did outdoors stuff as a hobby.

**Rosie, 24:**   My hobbies included: juggling, theater work, keeping animals, playing musical instruments, philosophy, reading, politics, travel, hand crafts.

**Dakota, 20:**   I liked biking and Parkour as hobbies… still do today!

> ### *Cameron L., 24*
>
> I loved everything. First it was magic, then skateboarding, filmmaking, drumming, cooking, traveling, writing, farming. School gets in the way of all those hobbies... or passions as they were for me. School took away all my time. But unschooling offered all the time I needed to focus on anything I found passion in. Once I find something I enjoy doing, I dive completely in and spend all my time on it. That's impossible while in school.

**Alaina, 25:**  My hobbies included flute, Taekwondo, Destination Imagination, drawing.

**Ari, 21:**  My hobbies were Bonsai, aquariums, Kung-fu, football and photography.

**Sarah H., 24:**  I guess I would have to say traveling and photography. I was able to go places I wouldn't have been able to if I had gone to public school.

**Nicholas, 26:**  I took Karate and trumpet/piano lessons. All these could have been done without homeschooling but it would have been difficult to find the time. With homeschooling I got a better education with more free time. I didn't have to spend hours after school doing homework any longer. Karate was a little different for me. My class was mostly adults, but that worked well because I was pretty mature for a teenager.

**Kristin, 19:**  I was able to learn how to bake and knit pretty well, since I had a lot of freedom. The two hobbies that I got to pursue to a greater extent than most people were reading and dance. I read voraciously, whether for fun or school. I loved history, so I read a lot of historical fiction and learned a lot of my history that way. I could also take a lot more dance classes than most high schoolers, and got to take them at unusual times, like during the mornings. This meant that I got to dance with more dedicated and unusual students and that I got a lot more time one-on-one with the teachers.

**Kirby, 26:**  I did martial arts for ten years, specifically the style called Shorin ryu. I actually stopped after being burned out for several months, and then being more interested in raiding within World of Warcraft. I did a lot of board/card gaming and video games.

**Katie F., 24:**  I was the editor of a monthly e-mail newsletter and volunteered extensively at a riding stable for the handicapped.

**Roxana, 25:**  I was able to get MUCH more thoroughly engaged in theatre. I loved performing in musicals. I could

---

### Laura, 24

I was interested in writing in high school. My parents encouraged me to pursue it and so I attended writing conferences, read books about writing, joined writing clubs, joined writing critiques, entered contests, spent hours writing every day, and researched the publishing industry.

---

### Cameron PT., 20

My hobbies included programming, robotics, building model airplanes (the invented from scratch version that either fly or crash spectacularly), reading. Actually, lots more, but those meant the most to me.

be part of productions that rehearsed late at night or during typical school hours, meaning I wasn't limited to auditioning for 'youth' companies. I was also able to spend more time on every new hobby that came up for me, because I wasn't told, "Okay, you've spent an hour on your English lesson, it's time to move on to biology now"—I could spend ten hours a day reading, working on a story, playing a video game, whatever I wanted. I've always been someone who gets completely passionate about one thing for a few months and then moves on to the next passion. Homeschooling enabled me to dedicate my time in this particular temporal structure that was better suited to how I work.

**Rebecca, 39:** I worked at our local library and vet clinic. I had a passion for nature and animals—rescuing, rehabilitation and breeding—I bred hamsters for a while and sold them to local pet stores. I took drama classes and workshops, auditioned for and participated in plays and musicals (my backside is in a movie that was filmed locally!). I also traveled and sang with my family.

**Laurel, 21:** I liked visual arts (painting, drawing, photography, henna, beading, etc.), dancing, swimming, cooking and baking, gardening, journalism, blogging, and so many other things. Had I stayed in school, I probably still would have explored some of these hobbies, but not to the extent that I was able to, because I was homeschooled.

**Wendelyn, 34:** I baked, cross-stitched, read, sang, developed newsletters for our small church's children's program and performed in musical theatre.

**Rose S., 20:** I have been an avid soccer player and watcher since I was born. It is something that my father and I have shared. I played in a league that was almost 100% school kids. I watched a lot of soccer too, going to see many more games, simply due to my more flexible and open schedule. I could watch a game on a Tuesday morning (and my dad could take off work for it) and other kids simply could not. For many years, I took weekly, private horseback riding lessons during the day. Eventually I started riding through a 4-H club in my area. Many schooled kids do this too. How-

---

> ### Rose S., 20
>
> I am a writer. The main push for my writing came from National Novel Writing Month (NaNoWriMo). This is a self-challenge put on every November, inviting people around the globe to write a 50,000 word novel in one month. I did this for the first time at the age of 12, and I am currently working on my eighth novel. This challenge can be difficult for many schooled kids, partially because they don't have the time, but also because they do not have the support of their parents, who think writing something that long, that fast, not for school is a waste of time.

ever, I feel like I was more able to fully utilize this resource because I could attend classes without being fully exhausted from a full day of school. I was able to spend many more hours at the stable. I was fully responsible for the morning feedings, because I didn't have to worry about getting to school on time.

I have done martial arts since I was 12 years old, and it has been one of the most amazing experiences of my life. It has truly shaped the person I am today. I started because I was at the studio anyway, hanging out with my friends all day. I started taking the homeschool classes, and then very quickly I started taking all the classes I could. I was at the studio up to four times a week, taking sometimes eight classes a week. Schooled kids simply did not have that kind of schedule.

Television is a huge passion of mine. I watch some shows that are on now and some that have been off the air for many years through DVD, the Internet, or streaming on Netflix. Because of my schedule and my mother's support, I was able to fully enjoy television in a way different from many other people. Most kids simply do not have the time to sit and watch an entire season of *DS9* all in one go, or catch up on four hours worth of television in one night. They don't have the parental support to watch hours and HOURS of *Roseanne* and *The Cosby Show* night after night for months. My parents were willing to sit down, watch and talk about the show—really get into it and care about what I was thinking.

I've been an avid game player for many years. Sometimes I play video games, but mostly I'm into pen and paper role playing games, card games and board games. I enjoy the traditional games, but my passion lies mostly in the realm of *Magic: The Gathering*, and board games such as *Betrayal at House on the Hill, Zombies, Pandemic, Vegas Showdown* and *Munchkin*. I've been playing *Magic*, and *Dungeons and Dragons* for over ten years. Our gaming group has met weekly for about that long. We have moved from *D&D* to *GURPS* and other types of games. We play role playing games via the internet sometimes, since we have members of our group that have moved out of state. I had other hobbies, naturally, but my freedom and time to explore these was because of unschooling.

*Michael climbing the Guadalupe Mountains*

*Brenna shooting photos*

*Kate and her Passport*

*Did you travel much as a homeschooled teen?*

## CHAPTER 14

## Travel

It's not unusual to find homeschooling families who travel a lot. Flexible schedules allow them to break free, fitting trips between semesters or in the summer when rates are high, lines are long, and the weather is stifling, too! The majority of those we surveyed report that their family was able to travel more because they homeschooled.

Homeschooled teens certainly benefit from traveling. Instead of reading about national landmarks and cultural events, how about going to Washington D.C. as my family did? We took a week off to go explore the museums, the Metro, the monuments, the government buildings, and the surrounding areas one autumn while the rest of the country was settling into back-to-

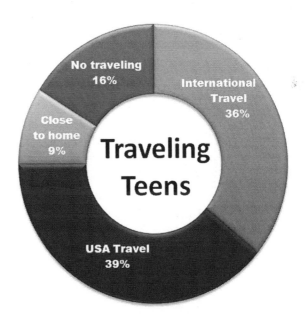

*Roxana figuring out the
New York subway system*

school routines. Or maybe your teens would be more interested in exploring the Everglades? Or Comic-Con? The Oregon Trail? The Sundance Film Festival? Whether it's the fiestas in San Antonio, fish markets in Seattle, or battlefields in Virginia, there are so many places to explore!

Travel adventures with the family can strengthen the bond that comes from shared experiences. Overcoming the obstacles that inevitably arise is a wonderful life skill teaching confidence, problem-solving, and deep-breathing. Several homeschoolers mention learning to travel alone, which provides additional opportunities for growing self-confidence. Figuring out the complexities of the route and finally arriving at the destination is a fabulous feeling! Across the state, the country, the world, every trip enriches one's education.

Most listed travel as one of their happiest memories! These homeschooled teens and their families have created fantastic memories of learning and exploring near and far.

## *International Travel*

I was surprised to see how many homeschoolers had the opportunity to travel to foreign countries as teenagers. Not only are they able to visit fabulous historic sites, but they're also able to mingle with the locals in other cultures, exposing themselves to a much larger picture of the world. Searching for similarities and enjoying the difference of other countries, these homeschooled teens and young adults share some of their international adventures.

**Tony, 15:** I went on a six week trip with my family to Israel; we stayed with my mom's family there, and went on a whirlwind tour of the country.

**Elizabeth, 19:** Being able to travel was one of my favorite parts of being homeschooled. My family was able to go on a lot of trips during the least busy time for traveling. We went to Sweden, Florida, Washington D.C., Hawaii, and New York. I think because I have been able to travel a lot, I have developed a wider perspective on the world and have developed an interest for international relations.

**Molly N., 19:** I visited my best friend on the east coast several times, and visited friends in Canada several times.

**Alaina, 25:** I traveled all over the United States. I also went to Japan. My brother was stationed there, which made it a lot of fun. We also traveled for educational purposes. It was great to learn about history in a hands-on way.

**Tori, 18:** Homeschooling didn't really affect my traveling, but I have traveled to Germany, and have driven across Canada twice.

**Micah, 16:** I have traveled to almost every state and many foreign countries because my mother was a flight attendant before she retired. I love experiencing the different cultures, but it always makes me very appreciative of the U.S. after visiting these other countries.

---

### *Hailey, 18*

I spent my junior year in Germany on the Congress Bundestag Youth Exchange Scholarship. It was the highlight of my life, to date. I also visited The Czech Republic, Denmark (where I saved a baby seal), Sweden, and Austria. All of my traveling only made me realize how much more of the world there is left to see! So that's my current passion and goal—simply to travel. I wish to go anywhere and everywhere, and every penny that I save is going to that pursuit.

---

### *Skylar, 26*

I saved all of my money from my jobs and Bat Mitzvah and backpacked through Europe with three of my friends (all homeschoolers) when I was 17, the summer before college. I have also been to China, Australia, and Canada.

### Grace, 19

I've been to Germany, with stops in Belgium and Amsterdam, and I've been to Brazil. Both were amazing. I went with my sister, who is 6 years older and we stayed with her friends.

### Cameron L., 24

Travel was, and is, my life!
- ▲ Born in Germany, 1988
- ▲ Australia, 2000
- ▲ Germany, 2001 & 2011
- ▲ Scotland, 2005
- ▲ England, 2005
- ▲ Mexico, 2008
- ▲ Canada, 2008
- ▲ Italy, 2011
- ▲ The Netherlands, 2011
- ▲ France, 2011
- ▲ Austria, 2011
- ▲ Peru, 2011

I've also been to 36 states in the USA, multiple times by plane, train, bus, car, boat, and my favorite, hitchhiking.

I blog about my travels at onewanderingpoet. wordpress.com

**Sarah B., 20:**   I traveled around the U.S. and to Canada. We were able to go away when most other children would be in school.

**Michael, 22:**   Oh, yes! I have traveled. First of all, I've lived in Texas (Austin, Wichita Falls, San Antonio, Dallas and San Marcos), North Carolina (Greensboro), Alaska (Eagle River & Anchorage) and California (Dixon). We always drove to these new locations, so we would take a few weeks (sometimes a month) and explore interesting places along the way. For instance, when we moved to Alaska, we drove from San Antonio up to Yellowstone National Park. After a few days, we went on up to Montana, saw Little Big Horn Battleground, talked about how different all the geography was. Then we drove over through Washington, explored Seattle, before we hopped on board the ferry in Bellingham and took 3 days up the Inside Passage. From there, we took more days of driving and talking about all of the history and landscape we were seeing on our way into Anchorage. I think we even had a flat tire along the way, but the view was a glacier! The point is—it was always an adventure! I've visited Hawaii, Washington D.C., St. Louis, Albuquerque, and NYC as well. Being a military brat introduced me to travel and then I started going places on my own. I went to Japan as part of a foreign exchange program at age 16, and then to Belize to work on an archaeology site for a semester through Texas State University. Now I'm in Nicaragua with the Peace Corps, teaching English. I absolutely love travel and it's definitely my dream to see as much of the world as I can before I die. It's become a requirement of any future wife that she love travel as much as me.

**Risa, 21:**   I traveled so much! Because school was possible on the road, my family traveled domestically throughout the academic year. We road-tripped through the Southwest visiting the Grand Canyon, Mesa Verde, Navajo reservations, and more. The history, cultures, and geography were no longer confined to our textbooks, but a tangible part of our lives.

**Rose, 30:**   When I worked as a mother's helper for a family, they took me overseas with them. I made loose with a Grey-

*Kate and her sister Claire at the Parthenon, Greece*

hound pass! I got to visit friends and relatives all over the country. Traveling gave me a sense of confidence and competence and made me curious about a thousand new things.

**Rosie, 24:**   As a child I traveled extensively with my family. In the U.S. we went to all of the states except for Alaska and Hawaii (so I've got to go back one day) We saw just about all of Israel, a good portion of Canada, and visited Mexico, Austria, and England for shorter periods. When I was 20, I hitchhiked around the Europe for a year on my own.

**Laura, 24:**   We got to travel whenever we wanted because we never had to worry about school. One time, my dad had a business trip to London and we went with him. It was awesome. We definitely took advantage of our availability and took many family trips.

**Alaetheia, 16:**   I have traveled extensively. I've been to China, Australia, Hong Kong, The Netherlands, Austria, Germany, France, Ireland, England, Canada, and Switzerland.

**Simcha, 17:**   Did I ever stop traveling?? My family went up and down the east coast for a year. We went from New York to Canada and then from New York to Israel.

> ***Teagan, 20***
>
> When I was fifteen, my mom and I went on a two-week trip to London and Paris, just for the heck of it. That visit did wonders as far as opening my eyes to the vastness of the world and the things I hoped to one day experience in it.

**Laurel, 21:**   We've taken many trips along the west coast, from Canada to Mexico and everything in between. In 2008, I traveled around Argentina for six weeks with eight other teens through a fabulous program called "Unschool Adventures." In 2011, I traveled alone to North Carolina and New York; with my sister to New Orleans; and flew to Puebla, Mexico to visit my girlfriend who was an exchange student there.

**Beth, 20:**   We visited almost every state, plus Mexico, Puerto Rico and Canada.

**Roxana, 25:**   While I was a child and teenager, my family traveled a lot throughout California, and homeschooling meant we never had to worry about fitting our adventures into a school schedule. When I was 20, I spent three months studying abroad in Paris, France, through my community college. I didn't speak much French at that time (though I learned a LOT by the end of the 90 days!) and I had never lived on my own at all, much less in a foreign country. So I was terrified and sort of homesick for a while. The first couple of days, I seriously thought I was going to starve to death because just buying groceries was so stressful. I got over that. I also didn't starve—far from it, I had some AMAZING French meals. I wasn't a teenager at this point, and technically maybe I wasn't homeschooled anymore, since I was past high school age and took the trip through a college, with other college students. But I do credit my having been homeschooled with giving me the confidence to take off for an adventure like that.

**Hannah T., 18:**   I've been all over the U.S., sometimes with family and more recently on my own. Internationally, I've been to Mexico, Japan, and Canada. Traveling gave me so much in the way of experience and learning. I'm forever grateful that my homeschooling allowed me that freedom.

## Traveling Around the USA

Going out to explore the Midwest, or the Boston Harbor, or the Appalachian Trail is exactly what these homeschooled teens and young adults' families did. Immersed

---

### Risa, 21

During the summer/fall of my senior year, I spent two months in Europe travelling and visiting close family friends in Germany, Belgium, the Netherlands, and Spain. Unlike the common tourist, I was able to immerse myself in the customs and lifestyle of these countries, giving me a fresh perspective on global politics and outside view of the United States for the first time.

in the varying geography, dialects, architecture, food, and culture that exists in different parts of the United States, these families considered travel to be rich and vital parts of their educational path.

**Sophie, 19:**  I would travel around the country to visit relatives on the east coast, no European vacation for me though! Anytime I went anywhere with my family, my parents would make it a teaching opportunity. We would tour Civil War battlefields, the Wright Brother's flying discovery setting, and all kinds of museums in the different states I went to.

**Katie P., 20:**  My parents loved to take family road trips or vacations, and trips to the museums as often as possible. We saw it as another way about learning something. For example, we didn't just learn about American history, we actually went to D.C. to visit the monuments and see other historical sites. Also, we went to quite a few homeschool conferences around the country, namely Live & Learn and the HSC Conference in California. So, yes, we traveled around the country a lot.

**Aiden W., 23:**  We traveled around the U.S. a bit. It was a lot of fun. We never did the theme parks or anything like that; it was all Ellis Island, Mesa Verde, the Smithsonian. To tell you the truth, I did go to a theme park once with a couple friends, and I think the things my family did were way cooler.

**Jackson, 20:**  We travel all the time! My dad works in the movie business, and has to go on location for months at a time. Before my sister and I got really busy with "extra-curriculars" (theatre, my drum lessons, her gymnastics and dance, etc.) we would travel around with him: LA, Chicago, even Paris when I was a wee lad. I've made friends all over the place, and my family has strong ties with a homeschooling group in Long Beach, California.

**Trina, 16:**  I moved from Oklahoma to Georgia and have traveled to Colorado, Texas, Tennessee, and New Mexico.

> ### Sarah H., 22
> In May, 2003, when I was sixteen, my aunt took me on a thirty-day train trip. We went to the west coast, national parks, and Canada. It was one of the greatest trips of my life. I saw so much and learned a lot. For my 20th birthday, that same aunt flew me over to visit her in Japan for two weeks. I would recommend to anyone to travel outside the U.S. if you can. It is such an eye-opener to see things from a different perspective.

> ### Katie P., 20
>
> We were a military family, so we moved a lot. And in between each move, we visited lots of places along the way. We turned those trips, that could have been done in a day, into more like a couple of weeks of sightseeing and learning!

> ### Nathan, 22
>
> I traveled all the time with my family. When we studied Gettysburg, we actually traveled there. We also saw sights like Niagara Falls. I loved it because instead of just reading about it in a book, we were actually seeing the places. This made it more real and easier to comprehend.

**Alyssa P., 18:** My dad was in the U.S. Air Force. So we moved A LOT!! Every time we moved it wasn't just a new state it was a new home, new friends, new everything. I enjoyed it at the time. Each place we moved to, we'd go exploring the area, seeing all the tourist sights and then all the stuff only locals know about. We saw a Volcano in Lassen State park, glaciers in Alaska, all of the national monuments and attractions in Washington D.C. And we went to homeschool conventions that were in other parts of the country, which were really fun. We went to St. Louis, Albuquerque, North Carolina, and Sacramento. We made friends all over the country from those conferences! But now, I am so done with moving and packing boxes! Travel is fun, but I'm staying put for a while!

**Sarah P., 17:** When I was very young, I traveled with my family all over the country—mainly California, where we met a wonderful homeschool community that we are still close to. In fact, that was the main reason we homeschooled. We wanted to be able to travel with my father for work reasons. As my brother and I found new interests and began taking recreational classes, we were no longer able to travel with him as much. Now, though, I travel around the country for competitive Lindy Hop, and plan to leave the country for a small time during my college years.

**Sarah H., 24:** Oh I love traveling! I went on trips with my family around Texas, including Fredricksburg, and different places around the Dallas/Fort Worth area. We also took many trips to the Wichita Mountains in Lawton, OK. I also visited Austin with my aunt and two friends in high school.

**Aiden R., 17:** I have been to Mexico, Florida, New York City, California and more.

**Emma, 18:** I traveled an average amount during vacation times, not outside of the U.S. yet though.

**Anastasia, 19:** I've only traveled around the country – lots and lots of highways. Canola and flax crops can look mighty impressive. I've also visited major museums in three

Canadian provinces—all amazing! The Manitoba Museum does have a ship in it, though, so it gets extra points.

**Rowan, 19:**   Yes, my family and I would drive up to Wisconsin every year for an annual event with friends. We would also drive to Dallas and Houston and stay there for two months each while my parents sold their incense and soap at Renaissance festivals.

**Alsatia, 18:**   I went to Ohio at some point as a teen. I went with my dad on a trip to San Diego, California, for a work conference the summer before my sophomore year of high school. Halfway through the fall semester of that same year my whole family took a week-long trip through Oregon with a stop in Washington to see Mount Saint Helens. That was an exhausting trip because we covered so much in so little time.

**Roya, 27:**   So much traveling! One of the first things I remember as a homeschooling family was going on a lengthy camping trip through northern California. We focused on gold rush sites. It was amazing—I remember my mom and I getting so fast at setting up a tent that we were under a minute. Traveling with my family helped me learn a lot, so when I was a little older and wanted to do it on my own, I had the skills. I did a lot of Greyhound and Amtrak travel up and down California. We went to every homeschooling campout and conference we could, and I visited friends in between. This southern California girl lived for the better part of a year in Madison, Wisconsin, learning how snow-people do it. Later in my life, I became the Access to Adventure Coordinator, where I planned trips and events for adults with developmental disabilities. I don't think I would have been comfortable doing this unless I'd had all that travel experience when I was younger—I was responsible for taking 50 adults all over the world. We went to Alaska, Mexico, and the Bahamas to name a few, and I really credit that travel I did when I was younger to the fact that I brought everyone back in one piece!

**Mike S., 16:**   I have traveled a great deal. The first family vacations I can remember are to Boston, of which I

> ### Nicholas, 26
>
> I did a LOT of traveling as a homeschooler. We went on field trips with our homeschool group. Separate from the group, my mother and I also took a long trip that took weeks. The emphasis was on Civil War. We made a big loop through almost every state on the east half of the United States. Some of the states we visited included Missouri, Arkansas, Alabama, Florida, and Georgia.
>
> We visited MANY historic sites. We mainly stayed with other homeschoolers and were able to form some good friendships. That was an educational experience you could never get in a regular school.

have fond memories. We've been to Colorado once, New Mexico at least twice, and California probably four or five times. I also went to New York City last year, and had an amazing time.

## Traveling with Family

Some homeschooling families made fun excursions out of traveling to visit other family members around holidays or throughout the year. These homeschooled teens and young adults took full advantage of these family vacations and share some of their experiences here.

**Alyssa H., 17:**   My family loves to travel. My dad's co-workers actually call him a "World Traveler." This makes us all laugh, because none of my immediate family has ever been out of the country! I practically grew up in Williamsburg, VA, but my travels also include: Washington, D.C.; Atlanta, GA; Gettysburg, PA. Those are some of the bigger trips, but there's always a day trip planned for some small museum or historical place. I love it!

**Rebecca, 39:**   We traveled locally, singing together as a family.

**Kevin, 20:**   Yes we traveled a lot while I was a teen. We didn't go anywhere really big, but we could go see some family more often with the flexible schedule.

**Chant, 15:**   My family still goes on vacation together, and I go to see my friends that I have back in Maryland every once in a while.

**Kate, 15:**   We travel all the time. We actually live in two places and travel frequently between them, so I've learned to study on the road.

**Zach, 24:**   My family took a few weeks in late spring to go to the beach which we could not have done had we gone to school. I still look back at it as some of my fondest childhood memories.

---

### Ari, 21

My dad traveled a lot for work, and since we had the time to do so, we'd go with him. I was able to spend extended time with my grandparents.

---

### Molly S., 20

I haven't traveled very much, but that is going to change soon!

**Kaci, 18:**   I would go on trips with my boyfriend and his family. My own family isn't very into traveling.

**Crystal, 15:**   I traveled with my family on vacations and such but I have plans for travel by myself in the future.

**Caroline, 24:**   I didn't travel much during high school years. My family was large and traveling consisted of going to my out-of-state grandparents every two or three years. My freshman year in college I spent the winter session in an immersion program in Mexico. It was a huge culture shock that I hated sometimes, but I'd love to do it again. I went to Turkey a year later for one month. A few years after that, I went to Europe for a month with a backpack. That was a great experience. I would have loved to travel in high school and learn other languages, but my family situation really didn't allow it. I'm making up for it now!

**Emily, 16:**   I have done some traveling with my family, but not abroad.

## Staying Close to Home

These families stuck a little closer to home, exploring their own local community. Various sites that are nearer can be incredibly interesting, educational and much less expensive. Interestingly, the majority of these survey respondents share that they plan some extensive traveling in their near future.

**Joseph, 19:**   I traveled on my own from our house in Yonkers to all over NYC for my various classes, since I was 13. I earned my parents' trust to travel on my own, and never abused or lost it. In fact, the ability to travel on my own definitely affected my independence at just the right age. If I did not travel on my own as far or as often as I did, I probably would have had a significantly different experience coming to college.

**Alyssa A., 18:**   When I was little, we traveled a lot more than we do now. But that is mainly because I am taking

> ### Teagan, 20
> My family did a fair amount of traveling when I was a kid (back and forth to Pennsylvania, where my mom's family is, as well as accompanying my dad on business trips when he could spare the frequent flyer miles), and not being restricted by a school schedule certainly helped make that possible.

classes at the local college. I have the same breaks as public school students, so that limits my traveling a lot.

**Skye, 22:** I didn't travel as much as I would have liked due to my financial status. I was, however, able to go to several places in the city—museums, theaters, parks, etc.

**Steen, 15:** I would like too but my parents are not inclined to travel very much. On the other hand I have friends all over the world and have done things all over the world with my activism, especially in the Middle East. Traveling in the future is one of my dreams.

**Cameron PT., 20:** I didn't travel much as a teen, just within America mostly. Homeschooling did make it really convenient at times, but most of my travel happened after starting college.

---

### Kristin, 19

My family and I did travel, but we didn't go very far. We didn't go on planes or to other countries. We mainly went to places close by, often with an educational focus (more because we like learning new things than anything else). Since we could go at times of the year where everyone else was in school, we often had vacation spots to ourselves, and got better rates. We went to a lot of museums, national parks, and ate lots of good food. We didn't do glamorous things, like go to amusement parks or New York City, but we always had a lot of fun and met interesting people at cafes and bookstores.

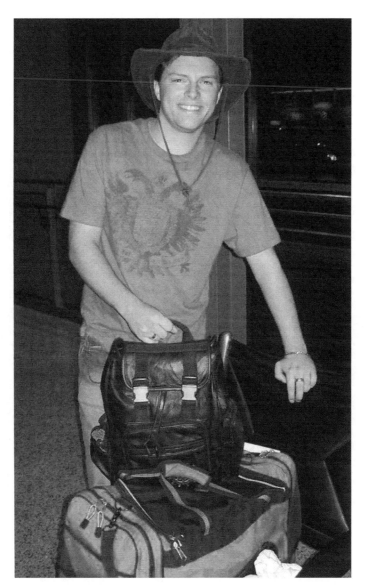

*Michael all packed up for the next adventure*

*Zoe and her brother, Quinn*

*Are you close to your siblings?*

## CHAPTER 15

## Sibling Relationships

It's not unusual for families who send their kids off to school to have children who don't get along that well. Arbitrary age/grade level divisions and excessive competition can easily become obstacles for creating empathy between siblings or developing positive relationships. While homeschooling is not a panacea for all sibling discord, spending more time together allows everyone the opportunity to create the type of environment where these relationships can be nurtured.

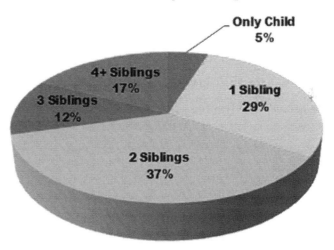

**How Many Siblings?**

Only Child 5%
1 Sibling 29%
2 Siblings 37%
3 Siblings 12%
4+ Siblings 17%

That's not to say that homeschooling families are immune to squabbling or typical sibling disagreements. They are, however, able to have more adult input on solving some of the problems that arise. There is motivation to get along with the people who you spend all day with, so homeschoolers are inspired to work things out. Also, since there is more time for parental attention, there is less impetus for sibling rivalry. Home becomes a safe venue where siblings can practice arguing without falling apart or without undue influence from peers who may not be any better at interpersonal communication than they are!

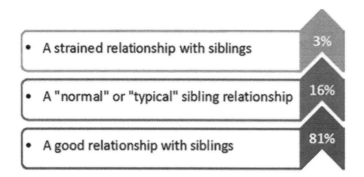

- A strained relationship with siblings — 3%
- A "normal" or "typical" sibling relationship — 16%
- A good relationship with siblings — 81%

The family dynamics in every homeschooling family is unique. Often, siblings spend a lot of time together, whether they're at home or out participating in a community activity. These shared experiences throughout the year—not just limited to one family vacation or an occasional weekend—interweave their lives together in a way that is really unlike any other relationship. Families who spend a lot of time out in the community exploring and discovering together, often create unique friendships between siblings, and wonderful memories.

The homeschooled teens and young adults were asked to tell us about their relationships with their siblings. The vast majority reported being incredibly close, some referring to their siblings as "best friends." While this appears to be the case with many of the survey respondents, others are candid enough to share that it wasn't always an idyllic world as teenagers together. They reported some of the typical arguing and irritation with their siblings. But the grown homeschoolers share that most of the tensions they experienced as teens have resolved. The majority report excellent relationships with their siblings as adults. Only a small number of survey respondents shared that they have relationships that they wish were better. And those who have had siblings grow up and move out of the house, while they were still homeschooling, expressed a little sadness to have them leave.

Additionally, we asked about family size since sometimes people have ideas that certain sized families are best for homeschooling, but families who choose home education come in all shapes and configurations. And from the data we've collected, no one size appears happier than any other!

## Smaller Families (0-1 Sibling)

Families with only one or two children make up nearly one third of all of those who completed the survey. These smaller families are often able to provide more resources for their children, as well as having the time and energy to focus on helping their children explore their passions. They might need to make a little more effort to be sure that their teen has the social interactions they'd like to have, but overall, these families enjoyed their close relationships.

**Zoe, 22:** My brother is one of my best friends and the best boy I know. Yes we fight but I love him very, very much and there is almost nobody I would rather hang out with than him.

**Alaetheia, 16:** I have no siblings, though, when I was little, we had three teenage refugees from Burundi live with us for a few years.

**Anastasia, 19:** I am very fond of my younger sister and I think we get along well. Sometimes I'm a horrible sibling though.

**Aiden R., 17:** I have a brother and our relationship is pretty good. We get along well and are pretty close.

**Nicholas, 26:** I have one older brother he went through all of the regular schooling including high school. I think some of the things he went through influenced my parents into wanting to homeschool me. We have a very good relationship and even though he is older, he seems to follow in my footsteps.

**Sarah P., 17:** I have one older brother. If anyone bullies anyone, it is me to him. But we generally get along great, and do not have many serious relationship issues.

> *Caitlin, 27*
>
> I have an older brother who was also homeschooled. We are good friends and spent a lot of time together as teens. We would likely not have spent so much time together had we been in school, because we wouldn't have been doing so many activities with each other (such as martial arts, Odyssey of the Mind, etc.)

**Teagan, 20:**  I have one brother, who is five and a half years older than I am. We have been incredibly close all my life, though inevitably distance took its toll. I had a very hard time when he first moved out of the house to go to college, largely because I was still so young and he had been my most constant companion. Now that we're both older, our relationship is, naturally, different. We live fairly far apart, see each other rarely, and keep in touch only sporadically, but we know that we can pick up where we leave off. I love to hang out with him, his fiancé, and his friends, now that I'm old enough to be cool!

**Jackson, 20:**  I have a younger sister with whom I get along decently well. Our relationship was better when we were younger. Nowadays we argue a good bit since I have those crazy older-brother protective impulses. I'm excited for her to "graduate from high school" this year!

**Carver, 18:**  We're brotherly.

**Ari, 21:**  I have a younger brother, and we've always had a good relationship.

**Alyssa A., 18:**  I am the youngest of 5 siblings. However, I only grew up with the younger one of my brothers. We were pretty close until he left for college. We keep in touch but it's not really the same.

**Emma, 18:**  I have an older brother and we've had our ups and downs but we're really good friends now.

**Wendelyn, 20:**  I have a sister who is five years older than me. We became fast friends when she got her driver's license and she could take me places. Through the years, she has become my best friend and we depend on each other for many things.

**Laura, 25:**  I have one younger sister. I always felt we got along well and understand each other. Even though we were both really different and didn't always see eye-to-eye we still get along well and have a good relationship.

---

### Rebecca, 39

My sister is absolutely my best friend. I have to say that we weren't terribly close until I got my driver's license at sixteen. At that point, we began spending a lot more time together going out, shopping, etc.

---

### Kate, 15

I have a little sister. Though we are completely different in several aspects, we are very close to each other. She knows that she can turn to me for anything. As her big sister, I've always defended and helped her. We've got each others' backs and know it.

**Laurel, 21:**   I have one younger sibling. She's my best friend. 'Nuff said.

## Mid-Sized Families (2-3 siblings)

Families with three children comprised the largest group of those who took the survey. And if you combine it with families of 4 children, this group makes up 50% of the teens and young adults represented here. Our family falls into this category. One of the benefits of this size is that when each had a different interest, the others pretty much had to tag along. That may seem like a recipe for disaster, but it wasn't for our family with 3 kids. It gave each of my teens a chance to learn to compromise, to see if they could find something positive in a situation that really wasn't one of their top choices. For instance, those with no real interest in auditioning for a play might agree to fill a background role if someone quit. Then they'd get the feeling of being in a play, without a lot of the stress involved. Or the ones that were only moderately interested in community service projects would be the core participants when one wanted to get groups together. Exposure would often lead to more involvement—and it certainly has led to some wonderful childhood memories.

**Kaci, 18:**   I have a brother and a sister. My sister was homeschooled with me, but my brother wasn't. My relationship with both is pretty normal.

**Elizabeth, 19:**   I have an older brother and a younger sister. My sister and I are close and we enjoy doing a lot of activities together. My brother and I are also close. I think our relationship is normal compared to friends who have attended school their whole life.

**Roya, 27:**   We are close. We fought more when we were younger—and sharing a bedroom. I was less respectful about other people's space and things than my sisters would have liked. We spent a lot of time playing make believe and dressing up. Because we were homeschooled I think it was really helpful for my parents to be able to take all three of

---

**Risa, 21**

I have three younger siblings and we are all incredibly close. We have very different talents and personalities, of course, but the homeschooling experience forged a very unique friendship among us. As the oldest, I feel homeschooling was particularly special for me as I got to teach my youngest brother to read, tutor another brother through algebra, and lead my sister's biology dissections. As homeschoolers, siblings teach each other and learn together; we share the same experiences and grow together. The four of us love to hang out together and, honestly, are more like tight-knit friends than siblings.

us places and then let us do our own thing—for example, all three of us would go to park day and be able to do what we wanted. All three of us were in the same Girl Scout troop but doing different activities. All three of us did the swim team, but had different levels of investment. I don't remember ever hating having my sisters around, or ever not thinking that they weren't the most talented people I've ever met. Our relationships have grown closer and closer the older we get! It's been interesting seeing how our interests have overlapped and diverged—for example, all three of us have done something involving theater, but only my middle sister has gone on to pursue it as a career. We've all done a martial arts class or two, but only my youngest has become a black belt and taught karate. I really do think that my sisters are the two most incredibly talented people I've ever met.

**Sunny, 17:**    My sister, who is 18 years old, and I are very close! I love her to death and she's been my best friend since I was old enough to understand what a best friend is! Haha! My brother (age 20) and I are also extremely close. Traveling for 7 years made it easy to get along and be close.

**Hailey, 18:**    I have two little sisters. They are 9 and 14 years old, and I love them both dearly. I can't say if that love is reciprocated all of the time though. ;-) We are all really close and I wouldn't trade them for the world... 75% of the time.

**Sophie, 19:**    I have a 14 year old sister and a 17 year old brother. We have a good relationship. They are going to an actual high school though. They like it and it's fun to hear about their experiences in high school and see how they interact with all the different kids. I'm closer with my sister, I think just because we're girls. But my brother and I have a lot of fun together and we both have similar views on things. We all love talking and joking around together and just goofing off.

**Katie P., 20:**    My brother and I are very close. I did a lot of stuff that he did, like hockey or playing video games. My sister and I have a very good relationship. I turn to her for fashion and style advice, even though she's younger than me. Sure we have our spats, but we always have each others' backs, no question about it.

---

### Julia, 15

I have two brothers—we're triplets! We have great relationships and, for the most part, get along. Although we have noticed that we get along better if all three of us are present—and not hungry!

---

### Sarah, 24

I have a brother who is about two years older than me. We grew up very close, but grew apart some in our teen years, fighting a little then. But after all that was over, we went back to being very close. He is married and, he and his wife are expecting their first child. I also have a brother who is eleven years younger than me. He is still being homeschooled at home by our mom.

**Joseph, 19:**  I have two younger brothers, ages 16 and 11, both also homeschooled. I definitely had some issues with my brothers growing up, the usual sibling rivalry-type issues. I think that only really came from living with them both for so long—now that I'm in college, I think they're both great kids, and I love spending time with them both at home.

**Aiden W., 23:**  I have three siblings. I think I have a really good relationship with them. I'm the oldest and I tend to be a little maternal about them. They're very nice about it. Since leaving home I talk with them once a week or more. My husband and I just went home for a visit and we had a really good time together. When we were younger we had our spats, but they were pretty short and we forgave each other.

**Cameron PT., 20:**  We're pretty close, we're kind of a slapstick comedy trio. I've got two older half brothers, but we don't see each other much. And two full sisters who I'm close to.

**Tess, 27:**  I'm close to all my siblings, homeschooled and public schooled.

**Hannah J., 22:**  I have two older brothers and one younger. Having them around all the time when growing up was stressful for me, but our relationship has gotten better since then, probably due to plain old growing up.

**Trina, 16:**  I have two sisters, one older and one younger. We have a great relationship with one another and talk a lot more than the average public schooled siblings.

**Roxana, 25:**  I'm the middle of three sisters, about three years apart on either side. We're all very close, and we also fight like cats and dogs. Sometimes they drive me absolutely crazy, and I know I do the same to them, but even though one day we might be yelling at each other, there's always an unspoken line we would never cross in fighting, no matter how angry we might get. We've gotten closer since we've gotten older, too. All three of us live in different places now, though not very far, and it's easier to

> **_Alyssa P., 18_**
>
> My brother, sister and I are three EXTREMELY different people. But we get along fine, I mean everyone fights, argues, whatever. I am very very proud of them. My big sister is now living her dream first in New York City and now L.A. going to film school, my big brother is also living his dream of traveling and is off in another country with the Peace Corps.

value someone's friendship and affection when you're not also dealing with the roommate aspect. I know I can always, always count on both of my sisters for anything, and they know the same about me, and that kind of reliance acts as a foundation for our relationship through having fun or fights.

**Alaina, 25:** I have two siblings, both older. We were all homeschooled. My sister is the closest in age. I have a very good relationship with both of them. My sister and I had a rocky teenage phase but we are now friends.

**Tori, 18:** I have two older sisters. I think our relationships our pretty good. My oldest sister went to boarding school for high school, and middle sister went to Germany for a year, then attended college in Minnesota for a year. So there have been long periods without them in my life, but we love each other and can count on one another.

**Kevin, 20:** Good. Not always, but as with anything, you have ups and downs. Our parents helped with that sometimes. We were close though, even if we got on each others' nerves.

**Michael, 22:** Compared to so many people I've met, our family is so much more functional! I have very positive relationships with both of my parents and siblings. Yeah, as the older brother I tend to give my little sisters a lot of trouble and they certainly give it back but there's no animosity between us. We really do love each other. We seem to be much more involved in each others' lives, we're always talking about what is going on with each other and giving opinions in a positive nonjudgmental way.

**Sarah B., 20:** I have three siblings. I am quite close with all of them. We are all really different, but we get along well.

**Alsatia, 18:** I have two siblings, a brother (17) and a sister (13). I can tell you for sure we drive each other NUTS but we also tend to be clingy, hanging around each other at social functions and such. I know I love them and as far as I know they (mostly) don't want me dead.

> ### *Zach, 24*
>
> I have an older sister and a younger brother. They are two of my closest friends. I know that we would not be as close had we not been homeschooled.

> ### *Kelli, 21*
>
> I have 2 siblings, an older brother and a younger sister. Being educated at home with my sister definitely brought us closer together. I have a great relationship with both of them.

**Rose S., 20:**   I have two older sisters. Neither lives at home full time anymore—the oldest is married and lives one street over from us. My other sister lives at school, comes home a few weekends every semester, and lives here during school breaks.

My sisters and I have been close since we were little. We played together a lot, and have remained close. We fought when we were younger. We still fight now (not physically, just verbally). But my sisters are my closest friends and two of the people I like hanging out with the most. Most of my favorite moments have been shared with one or both of them.

**Mike S., 16:**   I have three siblings: an older brother who is eighteen, a younger sister who is fourteen, and a younger brother who is twelve. My relationship with my older brother is much like that of stereotypical brothers, and we get along very well. My relationship with my younger sister is very good, but we don't share as many of the same interests. One nice thing is our appreciation of the other's art forms (she's a great artist and I'm a musician). My relationship with my youngest brother is also very good, and we have a great sense of humor, but obviously with the larger age difference there is more conflict, but not to an unmanageable degree.

## Big Families (4+ siblings)

Families with more kids are sometimes very interesting to watch. You can witness friendships emerge between siblings at a particular age, and then see it change to a different sibling later down the road. They get opportunities to practice leading and following as well as being around to help each other understand things they may have had trouble with. What larger families may lack in monetary resources, they seem to make up in people resources!

**Chant, 15:**   I have seven siblings, most of them are elsewhere in the U.S. and I keep in contact with them as much as possible even though they are very busy. I have a very interesting relationship with my siblings that live with me,

> ### Crystal, 15
>
> Yes, I have eight siblings, three older and five younger, and it's been wonderful. As I was growing up they were my playmates and some of my best friends, and it was never boring!

> **Grace, 19**
>
> I have four siblings: one older sister, two younger sisters and one younger brother. I'd say we're all pretty close. We have the kind of close sibling relationship that I think all parents want their kids to have. We talk about problems with each other, sometimes it feels like we're having a meeting when the 5 of us get together.

> **Sarah D., 19**
>
> I have lots of siblings, and my relationships with them are all really close. Because we all lived together all day long, we learned to deal with people who occasionally drive us crazy. I'm especially close with my two sisters, who are right around my age. I love that they're my sisters, because if I wasn't homeschooled, I wouldn't be friends with girls like them. Yet, this way, I still have them in my life.

I try to be as close as possible but my older brother is pretty busy and my little sister likes to be by herself, I manage to find time to hang out with them though.

**Rosie, 24:**    I have six brothers, and they are, and always have been, my best friends. Growing up we did everything together.

**Molly S., 20:**    Besides my two, much, much older half brothers, I have a younger brother and an older sister. My brother and I were really close pretty much from the beginning, whereas my sister used to hate me when I was little. As I grew up and started going to community college with my sister, and singing and auditioning for musicals with her, and later going swing dancing with her, we have become very close. She is my best friend. We talk frequently, even though we no longer live together. For a lovely little time, I felt very close with both of my siblings. Now my brother is in the throes of puberty that is very difficult. I'm waiting for the day he regains his joy and then hopefully we can be close again.

**Emily, 16:**    I am the oldest of seven children. I love every one of my siblings. They are my best friends! My family is my greatest blessing and they are my favorite people! I don't want it to sound like we have perfect relationships or like we are the perfect family. We are not but, we are much much closer than most families I know. I know my siblings' strengths and weaknesses and they know mine. We have spent every day of our lives together. What a wonderful blessing!

**Caroline, 24:**    I have an older brother and a younger brother and two younger sisters. During high school, I got along best with my younger brother and youngest sister. I was constantly fighting with my older brother and my middle sister disliked me (I think).

**Nathan, 24:**    I have three siblings who were all homeschooled. I was the youngest. I have moved out of my parents' home, they are still there. Our relationship is a little strained, but I think it is because of family dynamics more than having anything to do with homeschooling.

**Simcha, 17:**   I have five siblings and my relationship varies with each one.

**Hannah T., 18:**   I have lots of siblings! I'm the youngest of five, but through marriages I have a total of 7 older siblings. I have good relations with most of them, especially my two older brothers who homeschooled with me.

**Beth, 20:**   I have six older siblings and we are all extremely close.

## Siblings with Big Age Differences

Families that have a large spread of time between children face different dynamics. And it especially depends on the situation. While one may grow up as somewhat of an only child, others may experience it as having these young adults to turn to for advice or guidance.

**Kristin, 19:**   I have two brothers, one older and one younger. There have been times that we haven't gotten along quite as well, because we were going through various stages and got on each others' nerves, but overall, we get along great. We watch a lot of the same movies and television shows, and we all recommend books to each other. Since we're pretty far apart, age-wise, and we all have very different interests and hobbies (other than reading, which we all love), we don't compete much. We have almost as many inside jokes as my friends and I have, and sometimes our conversations sound like utter nonsense to outsiders. It's always fun to go places with them, and when I was younger I could always be assured of good company, even if my friends weren't around.

**Alyssa H., 17:**   I have a brother who is fourteen months younger than me and my parents pretty much raised us like twins. This means that we are really close. I don't really ever think of myself as the eldest. I also have two younger sisters. One is six years younger than me and the other is ten years younger. I'm close to them, but not as close as I probably should be.

> ### Rowan, 18
> 
> I have two older siblings who both went through school and college. My sister has a degree in physics. She stays home and runs the family soap and incense business. My sister is 19 years older than me and my brother is 13 years older than me. We are not close, but there is very little friction between us.

**Steen, 15:**    I have one brother, age 2. I get along with him great and he's a very good boy. I am proud to call him my brother. Since he is just a toddler my experiences with him are somewhat limited but he's great to be around and my relationship with him is excellent. I hope it stays that way in the future.

**Skye, 22:**    My half-sister is about eight years older and lives hundreds of miles away. Our communication isn't as much as we'd like, and our interests share few commonalities. We love each other and have almost always gotten along in spite of our differences. My brother is about three years younger and has attempted to model his education after mine. It is only recently that we have really been civil toward one another.

**Micah, 16:**    My siblings are older and have already graduated college and in their careers. I do have a nephew who has pretty much lived with us since he was born.

**Molly N., 19:**    My siblings are all much older than me and didn't live at home when I was homeschooling.

> **Cameron L., 24**
>
> My brother is eight years younger than I am. I wished for him. We've never been the type of sibling that had a rivalry, mostly because I made the conscious choice to treat him with constant respect and genuine love.

*Roxana, Roya, Rose S.*

*Crystal with her brothers and sisters*

*Sue with Alyssa P., Katie P., and Michael*

CHAPTER 16

## Relationships with Parents

Parents contemplating homeschooling are often concerned that homeschooling their child will negatively affect their relationship. When my kids were very young and I was considering homeschooling, a parent I knew told me that she'd never "do that to her relationship with her child." She believed that the role of mother allowed her to be more nurturing and less strict. She thought that the child needs to come home and vent to their mom about how difficult the teacher was being. Even then, before I had read much about homeschooling, this seemed baffling to me.

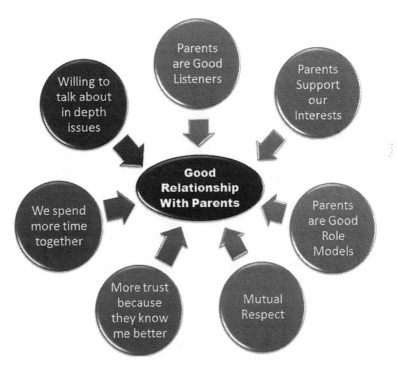

If your impression of learning is that someone has to make you do it, or it won't get done, then I imagine you're right. But what many homeschooling parents have discovered is that learning doesn't have to create an adversarial relationship. That's a remnant of schoolish thinking, and it's an unnecessary dichotomy. Parents were their children's first teachers, and we hear of no resentment about learning to walk or talk! Parents who are consciously prioritizing their relationship with their teen, all the while providing a stimulating learning environment have nothing to fear. The two are not mutually exclusive!

Our respondents are a cross-section of many different homeschooling methods as well as parenting styles. More than three fourths of the grown and teen homeschoolers shared more information about their relationship with their parents.

### 96% report being very happy
### with their parent relationships

These teens and young adults shared some of the reasons they think they have such a good relationship with their parents. Trust, mutual respect, support and communication are some of the main factors. And many of them went out of their way to express their gratitude for their parents taking the time and making some of the sacrifices necessary to homeschool them.

*Rose S. and Roya with their dad, Cyrus*

## *Closeness*

Many of the respondents wrote about being very close with their parents. Some elaborated on why they think their relationship is so good. Several were very candid about some of the troubles they've had, but noted that the family unit was still very close.

*Aiden R. with his mom, Cydney*

**Zoe, 22:**   I am very close to my parents. Although I only see them three or four times a year it is rare that we go three days without talking on the phone. They are the most important people in my life.

**Jared, 22:**   This is something I have thought a lot about in the past couple years. I am very close to both of my parents, and I think that is the norm for most homeschoolers. I feel that most homeschooled kids are closer to their parents than the average kid who goes to school. However, having spent more and more time around people who went to school in the past few years, I think that many schooled kids have healthy relationships with their parents as well, but I do believe those are much more sparse in that community.

**Nathan, 22:** I love them both (obviously). My mother and I are close and usually talk a couple of times a week.

**Nicholas, 26:** My relationship with my parents is pretty good. Homeschooling helped create a special bond. Once I hit age 18, I was ready to be on my own, as most kids are.

**Micah, 16:** They are very open-minded but also strict. My mother has very high expectations of me academically which gets on my nerves at times, but it is really okay. We are all very close and I feel free to discuss anything with them which is different than many of my friends. All my friends love my parents too.

**Tori, 18:** I was close to both my parents. My mom taught me because my dad worked, but on the weekends he would spend a lot of time with us. My relationship with my mom has been changing as I have grown up and started making my own decisions. But overall, I think it's good and I know we love one another. I know she has helped me in staying focused and wants me to do well.

**Wendelyn, 34:** I was very close to my parents. My mom and I enjoyed being around each other, even as an adult. My father was always the one I could have long, deep conversations with.

**Sophie, 19:** I'm really close with my mom and dad. I feel like I can always go to my mom and tell her anything, I really want her to be involved in my life and I want her input and advice. I like being able to tell her everything and being able to talk to her about things in my life. My dad has always been the organization and discipline in my life. He always helps me out with school or any kind of life problems. I love talking to him because he's so smart and

> **Alaina, 25**
>
> I have a fantastic relationship with my parents. They knew when to give me my space and as a result I feel comfortable turning to them or helping them as the need arises.

> **Kevin, 20**
>
> We have an extremely good relationship. I still talk with them a lot – even though I live half a country away! My parents and I are very close.

> **Aiden R., 17**
>
> I think our relationship might be better than people that go to school because I get to be with them more.

he knows so much and I always learn a lot from him. I've learned how to work hard from both my parents and they have always wanted me to do my best.

**Rose, 30:**    I no longer live in the same city with my mother. I see her for holidays sometimes and we have nice conversations. My father lives very nearby and we see each other weekly. He's very involved in his grandsons' lives. They are homeschooled, too. He has a shop and teaches them woodworking and bicycle mechanics. Dad and I often pass novels on to each other or recommendations for exhibits and events.

**Rosie, 24:**    Wonderful! We are seven kids in my family and my parents knew how to raise each of us in a way that would help us to grow.

**Steen, 15:**    Our relationship is somewhat rocky but we get along pretty well and have a strong family unit. We spend a lot of time together which is a blessing and sometimes a curse but overall they are good people who care about and love me. I do feel a bit smothered at times though.

**Rebecca, 39:**    My mother has passed away. But we were very close despite some pretty big differences in personality. My father is now remarried to a wonderful woman and we continue to be a close family.

**Laura, 24:**    I have a good relationship with both of my parents. I'm very close to them and I respect their opinions. They were good about explaining things and yet still allowing me to make up my own mind and figure out where I stood on certain issues. I was never grounded and I never had a curfew either.

**Ari, 21:**    My relationship with my parents has always been good. They never made me feel bad about myself, and have only helped mold me into who I am today.

> **Sunny, 17**
>
> My parents and I are very close. I love them more than anything! They're great people and have definitely done something right!

> **Michael, 22**
>
> I think our good relations come from the fact that my parents respected me. It seems to me that parents that don't respect their kids, especially their teens, don't receive respect either, which in turns causes them to respect their kids less and they just spiral downwards.

## Trust & Respect

Mutual trust and respect are mentioned by these homeschooled teens and young adults. Our experience was that the two concepts, trust and respect, are very connected. Respecting your teenager and trusting their ability to make their own choices actually leads them to trust and respect themselves and you as their parent. This doesn't mean that your homeschooled teen will never make a mistake, but when they do, they know they can turn to you because they trust you and trust the mutual respect that exists between you.

**Crystal, 15:** I have earned my parents trust and it is worth a lot to me, I'm fifteen years old and I wouldn't think about going behind their back because of the amount of respect and care that I have received from them throughout my life.

**Tony, 15:** Our relationship is one of mutual love and respect.

**Sarah D., 19:** I really trust and love and respect my parents. They were never really strict, but they kept me from doing anything stupid. My mom and I have so much in common, and I feel like I can tell her anything. My dad is one of the smartest people I've ever known, and I know if I ever needed advice, he could give me good, objective advice.

I know they'd always be there for me, no matter what happened, and there's nothing I could ever do that would make them stop loving me.

## Enjoy Being Around Each Other

Homeschooled teens, simply because they are around their parents more, have the opportunity to get to know them as people, and not just as authority figures or adults that are fairly removed from their lives. Those creative parents that were searching for a way to help their teen have the best life possible often turn out to be pretty fun people. Homeschooled teens have the chance to get to know their parents as human beings, and according to these teens and young adults, really enjoy their company!

**Emily, 16:** My parents are my best friends. I don't mean we are on the same level or that I view them as peers. I

---

> **Molly N., 19**
>
> I have a very close relationship with my parents. It's good, open, and trusting.

---

> **Kelli, 21**
>
> My parents are two of my favorite people. Often I am asked how I dealt with being around them so often but I'm blessed with some great parents. They are respectful and open to us and our ideas. Of course we clashed but we always got through it like any other family.

mean that I have so much fun with them. They know me better than anyone else does. I don't think you can say that about most parents today. They are also my greatest role models. I want to be like them. I know I can trust them with anything and they will help me through it!

*Sarah P. and her dad, John, having a blast together*

**Joseph, 19:**    My relationship with my parents is/has been phenomenal. I love my parents dearly, and love coming home over break.

**Risa, 21:**    I am very close with my parents and feel like our relationship is one defined by trust and friendship. My parents encouraged me to pursue my passions and hobbies and guided me through my academic years. Throughout high school, however, our relationship transformed from a parent-child one to a deep friendship. I love hanging out with my parents; they're super cool and we laugh so much together!

**Rose S., 20:**    I still live at home with my mom and dad. I am very, very close to them, especially compared to other people my age. I've been close to them since I was a little

> ### Rose S., 20
> While my more traditionally raised peers were complaining about their parents, sneaking around, lying to them, and trying to keep every part of their lives hidden from them, I tell almost everything to my folks, and consider them to be my friends. I'm really happy that I've gotten to live at home with only my mom and dad. We spend a lot of time hanging out together, watching TV, playing games, going for walks, all kind of stuff.

> ### Laurel, 21
> I can't really imagine it being better. My parents support every aspect of my life, even if they would occasionally make different choices themselves. I trust my mom more than any other person in the world.

kid, and remained close throughout my teenage years. My dad and I coach soccer together, and watch it together for hours and hours every weekend. I feel much closer to my parents then most people I know.

*Rose S. and Roxana with their mom, Pam*

---

### Jackson, 21

My relationship with my parents is pretty darn good! I love the conversations we have, the support I get from them, and the choices they made in raising me. They're both very strong, intelligent people, and yet they say they've learned as much from me as I from them. Most importantly, there is a sense of mutual respect between us, rather than the one-sided respect that is too often seen with authoritarian parents.

---

### Katie F., 24

I love my parents! They were my facilitators in learning, and taught me a love of learning without lessons—just by virtue of them being genuinely excited to find new things to know. It was wonderful to know they always had an ear for listening or an answer for my questions.

---

**Rowan, 18:**  My mother passed away when I was 15 years old. My father and I enjoy being around each other, but we are not close. It was the same for my mother.

**Aiden W., 23:**  I'm really close with my mom. We're like best friends—the good kind where you give each other advice. My dad is kind of hard for me to get a hold of right now because of his work schedule and my "free minutes" schedule. But we get along really well. My parents always trusted me growing up, so I had a lot more freedom of movement than other children. They were really clear with their expectations though, and talked about them often. I liked that. They were pretty firm on safety rules, but other things they left up to me after sharing their own opinions. They supported me in my decisions, even if it they weren't necessarily what they would have chosen. I can talk to them about pretty much anything.

**Alaetheia, 16:**   We have an odd relationship. I spend more time with my parents than I think most teens do, and I get along better with them.

**Kate, 15:**   My mom is amazing. She is my role model. I hope when I have kids, I'll be as good as a mother to them as she is to me. My dad is supportive but we can't read each other's minds like my mom and I.

**Julia, 15:**   Très bien.

## Supportive Parents

Homeschooling sometimes means that priorities shift in a family. Teens sometimes have interests that can be time-consuming, inconvenient, or even expensive. Being a supportive parent means helping them find a way to explore their passions and follow their path. These teens and young adults noted how supportive their parents were. They felt that many of the benefits they enjoyed and some of the results they're seeing now in their adult lives are due to having such supportive parents.

**Roya, 27:**   My parents are the most helpful, loving, supportive, brilliant people I know. Does that say enough? The older I get the more I appreciate them, but they've always been tremendous sources of wonderfulness!

**Mike S., 16:**   First of all, our relationship is amazing. I could not be luckier. My parents are 100% supportive of me and my passions, they're helpful, informative, great people to learn from, interesting, humorous, and my relationship with them is extremely healthy. The sole thing I can think of that isn't amazing, is the slight paranoia of all mothers worried about their kids, which I understand and respect.

**Grace, 19:**   It's good. They've always been supportive of me. They've encouraged me not to rush choosing a major. My siblings and I talk about how lucky we were to have them.

---

**Alyssa P., 18**

My parents and I get along very well. I know I can always talk with them. My big thing is I can't stand when parents talk AT their children instead of WITH their children. But I have never had that issue with my mom or dad, thank heavens. They've always supported what I want to do—even if they weren't crazy about it. I knew I could trust them with anything. But they are some of the most amazing people, so open-hearted and loving toward everyone—it's pretty awesome!

---

**Anastasia, 19**

My parents are the best I could hope to have and I'm grateful for them every day.

**Katie P., 20:**    I have a very good relationship with my parents. If I have a problem, generally I can go to them for assistance. My family is very a strong one. Actually, I'm so grateful that I have the parents I have! I wouldn't be able to do all the theater and acting I've done over the years if it weren't for them sitting in the back of theaters for hours, waiting for me to finish. They never missed a show—and there were plenty! Plus, without their support, I'd never be able to study acting in NYC or LA.

**Caitlin, 27:**    I have a very good relationship with my parents and did throughout my homeschooling. They allowed me to pursue whatever I was interested in and were always supportive and helpful.

**Sarah P., 17:**    I would say that I am close with my parents and lean on them heavily for emotional and academic support. They have always been there for whatever I have needed, and have tried to give me every opportunity to socialize and participate in extracurricular things. Anything I've wanted to be has been made a possibility, princesses and airplanes aside…

**Hailey, 18:**    My dad and I are really close. He is my support system and my reality checker. We think alike some of the time, but differently enough to be able to give each other new perspectives on issues. My mom and I used to be closer when I was focused on the horses, like she is. For her it is hard to see me wanting to go so far away, but I think she knows in her heart that letting me go was the best thing that she ever did for me.

**Sarah B., 20:**    I have a good relationship with my parents. I know that I can always ask them for help, and that they are there for me if I need them. They are also really encouraging to me and have helped me to become who I am.

**Michael, 22:**    I think we get along better than most families. I love my parents and I know they love me and would do anything for me. I remember my mom telling me once that even if I killed someone she'd still love me… and would probably help me dispose of the body. Haha! But that's unconditional support! My dad and I always connected over projects and campouts. I really hope that he and I can make a trip to either Machu Pichu or the Galapagos islands in the near future.

**Sarah, 24:**    I had some rough patches with my parents during my adolescence, like any family. Today, I have a great relationship with my mom, we talk almost every day. She is the first person I call with any news, good or bad. She is the strongest, best person I know. Sadly, my dad passed away from cancer two years ago. I feel like there was a lot I never got to say to him, and I wish he was still here to give me advice or tell a joke to make me feel better like he always would. My dad was one of the smartest people I knew, and he is my inspiration for going to school and trying to help others.

## Open Communication Was Key

Homeschooling families who prioritize open communication give a gift to their children. These teens grow up understanding the world and how to navigate their way better. When teens are encouraged to ask questions and share their own ideas, parents have a more accurate idea of what's going on with them. These homeschooled teens and young adults felt that the good communication was a big factor in the positive relationship they have with their parents.

**Beth, 20:**    Our relationship is good, we have great communication.

**Caroline, 24:**    My relationship with my parents is very good. My parents were always open with us about asking questions and the reasons behind their answers. We always knew what was expected of us as kids and teens, and when we didn't behave we knew our punishments were fair. I'm currently on good terms with both my parents.

## Gratitude

It's touching to read the gratitude expressed by so many of the homeschooled teens and young adults. Anyone who might be concerned about what homeschooling might do to the parent-child relationship will be reassured to read these comments.

**Teagan, 20:**    I would be nowhere without my parents. I don't know what sort of person I would be without their support and encouragement. My mom is the kind of woman I hope I can someday be: kind, caring, strong, and smart. My dad has given me not only a strong male figure in my life, but a sharp wit and moral compass. The two of them have both encouraged me to be as smart and good as I can possibly be. We get along incredibly well, and I will always be thankful for the quality of our relationship.

**Chant, 15:**    My step dad is a great man and I love my mother very much. They have both done so much to help me through homeschooling. I owe a lot to them.

**Hannah J., 22:**    Sometimes I resented their being so involved with what I was doing, but now it is easy to see how their wisdom has helped and sheltered me when I needed it.

**Zach, 24:**    My relationship with my parents is pretty good. I think I have more respect for them then most school kids do for their parents. Especially looking back and understanding the choices they made in raising me and to teach me themselves.

**Skylar, 26:**    My dad died when I was nine, so I am so grateful I had more time with him than I would have had I attended school. My mom and I are close, but not in a creepy way! She lives about 15 minutes away and we see each other often and talk several times a day.

---

### Kristin, 19

My parents have always listened to me and encouraged me. Even though I had a lot of doubts about myself and my capabilities, they always did their best to dispel those doubts and let me make my own decisions and forge my own path. They never talked down to me because I was young and inexperienced, and they trusted my judgment.

They also always explained their rules to me, which made it easy to follow the rules, since they were clearly sensible and there for a good reason. Sometimes I disagreed with their advice or rules, but once I got older, I generally realized that they were right. I never felt any pressure from them to do things the way they did things, or the way other people did things. This meant that once I was in college, I was able to make decisions and just go out and do things much more easily than most of my friends. I would decide on something and go out to do it, and they'd say, "You can't do that," or "No one does that", and my reaction was always, "Why not?"

I've ended up doing a lot of unusual and fun things because of that attitude, all because my parents encouraged me to think outside the box.

*Zoe and her mom, Paula*

*Aiden R., Rowan, Ari, Kaci pictured here with parents,*
*adult friends and relatives*

*Did you have other adults you could turn to as a homeschooled teen?*

## CHAPTER 17

## Interacting with Other Adults

It's often helpful for teens to have adults in addition to their parents in their lives. When expanding from the safety of their homes – and their family– teens can occasionally use other trusted adults to provide new perspectives or help them develop skills as they transition into adulthood. Humans are social beings by nature who learn from watching and interacting with others. While common wisdom characterizes homeschooled teens as isolated from non-familial contact, especially other adults, nearly all of our respondents show that this is not the case.

### *91% of the teens and young adults identified other adults readily available their lives*

While parents are usually the first person that these homeschooled teens and young adults turn to for advice, other handy adults have helped them along the way. Additional adults can act as mentors, role models, or simply be available for questions, bouncing around ideas or sharing concerns.

Homeschooling families get to know each other in much the same way kids in school get to know each other – shared activities. The difference is that often the entire family is involved or somewhere nearby while the children/teens participate. In our case, we often met families at park days, or sitting outside with siblings while one child took classes or participated in a group activity. This always gave me the opportunity to talk with other parents and see who we might "click with." And, as the children get older, they have more independence; they begin to grow their own circles of adults and friends.

All three of my grown homeschoolers took this survey and identified one or two other adults they trusted during their teen years. Yet the reality was that many adults crossed their paths throughout those years: friends of the family, their own friends' parents, relatives, adults from church and I would venture to guess that this is true for most homeschoolers.

## Influential Adults

- Relatives
- Neighbors
- Family friends
- Friends' Parents
- Instructors
- Coaches
- Employers
- Church leaders
- Club/Organization Leaders
- Other Homeschool Parents

Homeschooled teens are often involved with clubs or classes outside the home that give them access to 4-H and Scout leaders, dance teachers, coaches, community college professors, and co-op teachers. Each of these adults brings a new personality into their lives. Because they have chosen to participate in most of these classes/clubs, the teens tend to be open to the relationship with these other adults. The experience of having only adversarial relationships with adults, so often seen with school teens, doesn't seem to exist in the homeschooled world. The often touted "rebellious" or "anti-authority" teenager seems to primarily correlate with those teens who are given no choice about the adults or the situations in their lives. This is simply not the case with most homeschoolers.

When my daughter decided to try high school for a year and a half, she often commented how the other students saw adults as "the enemy." She had had such a different experience with adults as a homeschooler. At the typical parent-teacher meetings at her high school, teachers spoke of how she made eye contact, spoke directly to them, and seemed to enjoy the teacher-student relationship. And they were right, she did! Evidently, this was unusual. Several teachers, unaware that she was new to the public school system, talked of how refreshing her behavior was in the classroom.

The homeschooled teens and young adults that were surveyed shared that they have a wide range of adults in their lives.

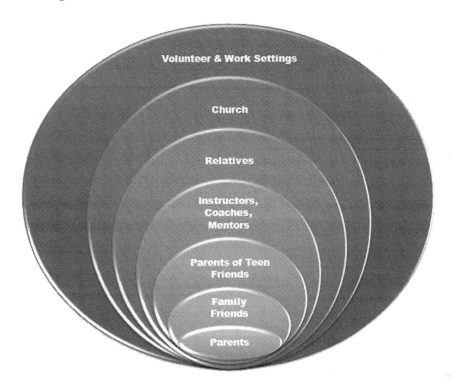

## *Family Friends*

Most of the other adults in our survey respondents' lives were considered a friend of the whole family instead of the friend only of one family member. Because homeschooling families tend to spend more time together they are more likely to spend time with each others' friends. Their mother's friend becomes the teen's friend as well through shared experiences and proximity.

Family friends can develop rapport with the teen, provide a more objective or distanced view of problems, another adult perspective, or maybe just a new ear to talk to.

**Jared, 22**

I have always felt comfortable around parents, teachers, authority figures, etc. As a homeschooler, I spent a lot of my time around my parents and other kids' parents, so it's almost second nature to feel at home around them.

**Alyssa A., 18**

I have one aunt that I turn to when I am at my lowest point. She is always there to shed comfort, and luckily she is less than 30 minutes away.

**Sarah P., 17:**    Many parents in the homeschooling community have offered me support or care whenever needed, but so far I haven't needed anything dire that my parents could not provide. I met these parents through my homeschooled friends, and I met them through social gatherings and acting classes. I know that if I need a "third parent" some are always close at hand.

**Katie P., 20:**    I probably could have turned to friends of my mom or Girl Scout leaders, but I never needed to.

**Emma, 18:**    Yes, I do have other adults in my life. One is a good friend of my mom's that we met through homeschooling. Others are friends' parents, coaches, and adult friends that I have met through horseback riding.

**Alyssa P., 18:**    My mom's best friends are like my "go to" mommies if I ever need anything. My dad's brother is always around to listen if I need someone to talk to.

**Elizabeth, 19:**    Most of the adults I would turn to if I had a question or problem are very good family friends that I've known since I was born.

**Zach, 24:**    Yes, I have three or four other pseudo-parents. Most of them are family friends or other homeschool parents.

**Grace, 19:**    I can't think of a situation that I couldn't turn to someone in my family for, but there are two adults from my childhood who I would feel comfortable going to if I needed to. Both of them were homeschool parents.

**Alsatia, 18:**    I have a few other adults I can go to. Mostly though, I don't because I tend to be an extremely private person. I met my main "other parents" (as I call them) through my siblings actually. The adults have kids my brother and sister's age (fairly close in age to mine) and we spent a LOT of time together and bonds formed through that.

**Sunny, 17:**    I do have other adults! My second set of parents whom I've kind of adopted into my life, Brye and Salem, are my best friends and I love them to death. I always call them if I need advice or have problems. I met them through traveling!

## Relatives

Some of the homeschooled teens live near their extended family, some of whom homeschool their own children while others do not. This provides another layer of variety in the homeschooled teens lives. Twenty percent of those surveyed identified that they could turn to a relative if they needed help with a problem or issue.

**Simcha, 17:**   I have an uncle and aunt I can go to for just about anything.

**Rebecca, 39:**   I always had plenty of family and close friends.

**Nathan, 22:**   I have a person who I consider my sister, although we are actually not related. She knew my sister and moved into our house to get out of a bad living situation.

**Sarah, 24:**   I usually talk to my good friends if I have a problem. I am very close to one of my aunts, but she lives in Japan, so I do not get to talk to her as often as I would like.

**Chant, 15:**   I know I can always go to my older sister if I ever need help.

**Nancy, 15:**   My grandparents will always help me if I need them.

## Friends' Parents

Homeschooled teens often spend a good deal of time in their friends' homes. The flexible weekday schedules often allow teens to "hang out" at each other's houses, giving them the opportunity to interact with their friends' parents as well. They take notice of how people in other homes react in various situations. This gives them a good indication as to whether they could turn to their friends' parents if they needed something.

**Kaci, 18:**   I definitely have other adults to turn to: my boyfriend's parents, my best friends' parents, as well as teachers I've known.

**Dakota, 20:**   I could turn to a few parents of friends. I've known some of them for a really long time.

---

**Kristin, 19**

There's a definite barrier between adults and teens at school, and I was too used to having adults as friends and equals to be able to put up with that. This was one of the reasons that I never went to school

---

**Skylar, 26**

I loved my second-moms when I was homeschooling. So many women (and men) I could turn to when I needed someone to talk to.

---

**Zoe, 22**

I have a large community of Other Mothers. In my homeschool group some of my best friends' mothers are still my friends to this day.

### Rowan, 18

I do have other adults I can turn to. They mostly came from volunteer work and our local support group.

### Roxana, 23

I have aunts and uncles, I have other homeschooling parents who I know through my mother's involvement in the online homeschooling world as well as through going to so many homeschooling park days, conferences, etc. I have former college teachers who have been extremely helpful and influential in my life.

*Friends' moms are often available to each others' teens: Aiden R. and Ari's mom (Cydney), Alyssa P., Katie P. and Michael's mom (Sue), Sarah P. and Jackson's mom (Laura).*

**Aiden R., 17:**   Yes, I have a lot of contact with my friends' parents and my bosses.

**Katie F., 24:**   I felt comfortable going to any of my friend's parents for an answer to a question or for advice.

**Skye, 22:**   Yes, primarily parents of my homeschool friends were available to me.

**Sarah B., 20:**   I have a bunch of other adults I can turn to, mostly my friends' parents.

**Tess, 27:**   I had a couple other adults in my life. The moms of my best friends (who were also homeschooled) are like extended family to me.

**Kate, 15:**   My best friend's mom is an inspiring woman—I can trust her with anything.

## Adults Involved with Their Church

Only 14% of those surveyed identified people from their church as adults they could turn to if they had a need.

**Micah, 16:**   I do have plenty of adults, but I really don't need them. I don't mind discussing anything with my parents. I would guess my church youth group leader would be next in line if my parents were not available.

**Kevin, 20:**   Yes, I had other adults in my life, mainly through the church.

**Aiden W., 23:**   Well, it depends on the question or problem. If it's a personal problem I guess I would talk to the bishop of my ward (kind of like a pastor). But I don't really tend to have those. I've always had lots of adult friends, and I go to them if they can help me with something. Generally, I figure things out on my own.

**Beth, 20:**   I could always turn to the youth ministers from church.

**Caroline, 24:**   Most adults in my life were parents of kids I babysat from my church.

> **_Laurel, 21_**
>
> I have a lot of adults in my life that I trust. A lot of them are other relatives, friends of my mom, other unschooling parents, or people I've met through work or volunteering.

> **_Risa, 21_**
>
> Yes! I turned to church leaders and other homeschool parents (many were like "other-moms").

## A Diverse Support Network

Nearly 40% of those surveyed identified more than one category of adults that they can turn to. Family friends, "other moms" and parents of their own friends were the most common. In reading the responses, it's clear that homeschooled teens have an extensive network of adults they can turn to for any assistance they might need.

**Hailey, 18:**   I have an incredible adult support system. Through mentoring websites, my own networking and resourcing, family friends, and family, I always have someone to reach out to for guidance, a place to stay, or even a foot in the door for a job. Nothing can be accomplished without a support system. Relationships bring meaning to everything that we do. The human element is the way to change the world.

**Hannah J., 22:**   My pastors, professors, and other adults I have met through college and church are available to me.

**Molly, S., 20:**   Definitely. I could turn to my Aunt Helen, who is very smart and has been the closest thing I have had to a Grandma. Or, I could consult one of the very smart, older-than-me, grown up ladies I have met in theatre. I would also feel comfortable talking to some of the faculty here at UCI. Although I have only met them this past fall, it's easy to become a family doing the things we do.

**Crystal, 15:**   Yes, I do I have people who I have known my entire life that I can go to for a question. Some are people who have been my parents' friends for a long time and some of them I've met through classes or my church.

**Laura, 24:**   I had other family members I could talk to if I needed. I also had some pretty good support from my local church and some people I could turn to there.

**Molly N., 19:**   I do have many adults I can turn to, and have had them throughout my life. I attribute this to the fact that unschooling encouraged me to build friendships with adults.

**Hannah T., 18:**   I have tons of other adults in my life! It all comes from that 'friends without age borders' thing ;). I have met friends through my mother, various academic ventures, my work, and conferences. Because of this I have a wonderfully eclectic support base from which I can draw wisdom.

*Alyssa P. and Katie P. with their dance teacher, Jeanna Phillips*

**Kristin, 19:**   I had a lot of adults whom I considered friends, since I got to meet all of my acquaintances through activities other than school. I got to know my neighbors really well, and a lot of them gave me advice on life and relationships. My physical therapist, who was a dancer, told me anything and everything about physical therapy schools and jobs, and gave me lots of resources. My lab teacher gave me science and college advice, and encouraged me to pursue science. My dance teachers were my closest adult friends, and they shared all sorts of stories and advice with me, as well as asking for advice from me.

**Caitlin, 27:**   I got to know a lot of other homeschooling parents pretty well, and I would often talk to the moms of my friends about dating problems or college plans. I also

> ### Brenna, 22
>
> I have several adults that I regularly tap for advice. One I met through a ceramics apprenticeship, some are homeschooling moms, others are former homeschoolers like me.

had adult friends form my volunteer work that I would go hiking with and talk to about almost everything.

**Cameron P., 20:** A few, I'm not super close to any of them, but I trust them enough, and know them well enough, that if I really needed to talk to/get help from one of them I could. They're also pretty high caliber people.

**Rose S., 20:** I have a large support system. First of all, at this point, most of my friends are adults, so I have them to turn to if I need something. My boyfriend, of course, is always there for me, whatever I need. I also have my parents, and my extended family. Daniel's (my boyfriend's) parents are also a resource for me depending on my problem. I also have several teachers from my community college that I feel like I could call on if I had a specific question of some kind. Additionally, I have a large group of homeschooling moms that I spend a lot of time hanging out with and talking to.

**Alaina, 25:** I was a part of the local police force as a cadet so I could turn to any of those adults. Also, there were many adults in Taekwondo that I could have turned to if I needed something. There were the parents of my friends and our neighbors. I got along with adults almost as well as I got along with kids my own age.

**Roya, 27:** Absolutely. My ceramics instructor was my number one mentor when I was younger. I had a manager at the ceramics supply store that was helpful, and the lab technicians at Cypress College were like my older brothers. I met them by being passionate about what they were trying to teach me, and it turned into more. I had my aunts and uncles, my swim coaches, directors and actors in my theater groups, and other teachers. I continued my streak of finding supportive mentors when I went into my bachelor's and master's degrees as well.

**Steen, 15:** Yes almost all my close friends are adults and a majority of them I met online through my activism and political activities. I spend a large majority if not all my time around adults and I get along great with them. My three best friends are 32, 40 and 29 years old, for example. We do

---

### Jackson, 20

I have more adults than I can count who will support me when I am in need of guidance or assistance. I met most of them through Austin Area Homeschoolers group but a few through theatre classes. I get along well with people of all ages, so I've built some really strong friendships with a lot of my friends' parents. I also occasionally befriend professors!

---

### Michael, 22

Well, yeah, if I had other questions that I felt I needed more input than just my parents, I could turn to some of my friends' parents.

But really, I don't feel like there's anything I can't ask my own parents.

all sorts of things and talk like close friends do. We can talk about anything and everything. They advise me on things and I advise them on things. I have a great relationship with my friends.

**Rosie, 24:**    Sure, I've always had many close friends of all ages. Right now I'm living in a small city in Italy and my closest friend is probably, Gaetano, a seventy-year old retired bank manager who has basically become my grandfather. We always go driving in the mountains to discuss classical philosophy and politics.

**Nicholas, 26:**    Being pretty mature for my age, I made friends with several adults. I don't recall having questions or problems specifically related to homeschooling. My mother had several adults to turn to for advice and questions during homeschooling. We plan to homeschool our children and have plenty of resources to turn to also.

**Sophie, 18:**    I have friends that I've known for a long time so I know their parents well too. I can trust them and go to them if I ever need to. I haven't had to because my parents have always been able to help me though. Also, I've met some really great adults through the horse world that I have become very close with.

**Ari, 21:**    Yes, I have several. One happens to be a homeschooling teacher/mentor.

**Sarah D., 19:**    Aside from my dad's baby sister, who I know because she's family, there are a few adults I met at church who would be there for me.

**Alyssa H., 17:**    Yes, I have ladies in my church who are always willing to answer my questions and I also had a lady who I met through the acting group, who I grew quite close to. She gave me some awesome advice during some rough years with my parents. She really made me understand and see the reason behind some of what my parents did. She was also good at pointing out what I was doing wrong, but was kind in telling me how to fix it.

> *Mike S., 16*
>
> Since I've found most everything I need in my parents, I haven't developed very many close relationships with other adults, and I find it much easier to interact with people my own age. I do have some good relationships with some adults that I've met in the SCA, but I wouldn't bring up personal problems to them, only questions about the society or something like that.

**Alaetheia, 16:**   If I want to find helpful adults, I can do that easily. I think I met them the same ways other teens meet adults: church, extended family, volunteer activities, babysitting, etc.

## *Not much need for Other Adults*

A hand full of those taking the survey did not identify other adults in their lives. Many felt perfectly comfortable with having only their own parents to advise and turn to. Many of the teens and young adults share how their relationships with their parents is one of trust and respect, making it understandable they might not need to find other adults for help, counsel, or additional input.

**Kelli, 21:**   I don't really have other adults around for advice.

**Tori, 18:**   My family and friends help me with most of my issues. I've never had something that I couldn't share with them.

**Joseph, 19:**   I love talking with my other relatives and the other adults in my life, but I find myself most often turning to my friends at school, my friends at home, or my parents.

**Trina, 16:**   No, I have just my parents for support.

**Emily, 16:**   My parents are my role models and mentors! I do not feel the need for any others.

**Anastasia, 19:**   I don't really have other adults in my life.

*Michael, Katie P., and Alyssa P. with their grandma*

*Katie graduated with an Associate Degree in Fine Arts*

*How hard was it to get into college?*
*And, can you describe your experience there?*

## CHAPTER 18

## College Experience

While parents today are becoming more aware that college isn't THE ONLY path to success, they certainly don't want to do anything during their child's teen years that might close any doors. For years, questions like "How will they get into a good college?" or "Are you ruining their chances for college?" have plagued parents of homeschooled teens. These questions and concerns tapped into fears that parents often have. The older teens and grown homeschoolers are able to put these worries to rest.

**Attended 4-year Universities**

# 82%

**18-22 year-olds**

We've already discussed how homeschooled teens are using the community college system. Here, we'll address attendance at four-year universities. Some of our survey respondents are planning to go to college, but simply haven't yet because of their age or their life's course at the moment. For this reason, we will primarily focus on the 18 and up age group from the survey respondents.

I asked if they had trouble getting into college and asked them to describe their college experience.

## *College Acceptance*

Most respondents attended community college before moving to a four-year university or other educational institution. Some took the SAT & ACT exams, while others simply transferred in as college sophomores or juniors. Many people are not aware that taking as few as 30 hours of community college, if made up of transferable courses, can easily allow transfer into the university. Some states may have slightly different rules.

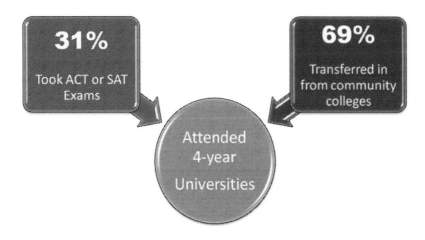

Most who tried to get into a university had no problem at all with admissions. The few who did made a few modifications and then were also successful.

**Brenna, 22:**   I applied and was accepted to several colleges when I was eighteen. I chose to attend New College of Florida. The process of getting in was fairly straightforward—I created a narrative transcript, took the SATs, solicited several letters of recommendation, and wrote an admissions essay. No college denied my application—three accepted me outright, one wanted me to take an additional math class, and one deferred my enrollment until the spring semester. My experience was that colleges have become very friendly to homeschooled students in the last decade. We've become such a large market that they stand to profit significantly from accommodating us.

**Roya, 27:**   I transferred from community college at the age of 20, as a junior, to CalState University at Long Beach (CSULB). I hadn't been intending to go to university that year, so it was a last minute decision, but I can't tell you how glad I am now that I did. My undergraduate degree was in Recreation and Leisure Studies, with one certificate in Outdoor Recreation Resource Management, and another in Non-Profit Management. I was travelling during the time I needed to apply, so I actually filled out the application over the phone from a Denny's parking lot in northern California with my mom. I was not super invested in getting in, and it was the only college I applied to.

**Michael, 22:**   I went to college and it was fairly easy to get in. I got my required 30 hours of community college so I could transfer to Texas State as a sophomore without ever taking SAT's or ACT's. That was pretty cool—people don't realize you can do that! Still, I had to take a placement test, the Accuplacer. I passed the Reading and Math components. I had to retake the Writing section and then passed on the 2nd try. I had never written a book report or a research paper. So, when they asked for a response to, "What do you think of the 'No Pass/No Play law in Texas?" luckily, I had heard of it from the news. But I just ranted about that poor kid that is only good at football, and now can't play because he failed a class? They were not looking for my real opinion. They wanted a simple persuasive paper—intro paragraph, 3 supporting arguments, conclusion paragraph. So my mom showed me how to do that, and the next time, when they asked, "What's your opinion on whether kids should be required to wear uniforms to school?" I simply spit out some ideas into the prescribed formula and VOILA! I passed. Weird that the topics are all so school related though!

**Caroline, 24:**   I completed two years at a community college and majored in engineering. The school had open enrollment, so I had no difficulty getting in. When I graduated, I was one of two students in my year to graduate with a perfect GPA. I applied to three universities to transfer to as a junior (one very prestigious) and was accepted to all three. I ended up at my third choice due to financial reasons, but never regretted that decision. I went on to graduate with a degree in Mechanical Engineering, somewhere in the middle of my class. During my senior year, I enrolled in a combined Bach-

---

**Jackson, 20**

I am currently in my senior year at the University of Texas at Austin, in their School of Communications. I was able to transfer in fairly easily from Austin Community College, even though the School of Communications is insanely competitive. The U T experience has been crazy, hectic, stressful, exciting, and fun!

---

**Skylar L., 26**

I attended UC Santa Cruz. It was easy to get in (I transferred as a junior when I would have been a Freshman). I was told by several professors of my upper-division classes that I was much more prepared than students who had attended their first two years of college at UCSC. I graduated with a 3.73 when I was 19.

elor's/Master's Engineering program and was able to go on and complete my Master's in engineering with a thesis a year and a half later.

**Molly, 20:**    I am currently just past half way through my second quarter at the University of California, Irvine as a junior transfer student in the drama department. I would not say that it was particularly hard to get in. I worked hard on my application. I had to compile information on everything I've ever done. I worked really hard on my essays. I had to write several, because I was applying to UCs and other State schools who used the Common Application. UCLA, and Oklahoma City University both required an extra essay besides the one(s) in the application, and Michigan required three. My mom helped me get my essays really tight and edited.

Coming from community college, my GPA was 3.96 and I was Phi Theta Kappa. I suppose that was hard work, as well, but I wasn't thinking about it as "I have to get good grades or I won't get into college." Instead, I thought "I want to know about this subject," "I don't want to disappoint my teachers," and sometimes just "I have to get an A or else."

What was really hard work was the audition process. I was totally unprepared when my first audition came around, which was UCLA. It was my last choice of the four schools I had applied to, so I was not that bummed when I woke up that morning and my voice was gone with no warning. Things just got worse from there, the accompanist refused to play the music I handed him and I had to change songs at the last moment, and I had to switch to a classical monologue at the last minute because I had misread the instructions. That one was all my fault, but I had read audition requirements for a lot of places. I was able to get over how terribly that went, but it would have been nice to have had a great first audition to launch me into the others.

Next, my mom came with me on my trips in Michigan and Oklahoma. These auditions were blown by the sheer force of my nerves. I have never felt such strong, paralyzing fear as I did anticipating my University of Michigan audition.

---

### Caitlin, 27

I went to a small private university and had no problems getting in. I did have a high school diploma through a correspondence course, but that was not required for admission. The admissions interview went very smoothly and my interviewer seemed impressed with the wide range of experience I had been able to have as a homeschooler.

---

### Alsatia, 18

I got into a college alright.

I simply did an updated application to finish my associate's degree at the community college where I was "Dual Enrolled."

I was shaking, unable to eat, balled up sitting on the floor. Breathing also became difficult at both University of Michigan and OCU, which is not conducing to singing. Thank goodness for the acting department of OCU for being so calm and friendly before I started, allowing me to finally relax and earn my acceptance to OCU.

UCI did not have an audition as a part of the acceptance process. It is purely grades and essay based. I pretty much assumed I would get in. Maybe that's me being cocky, but my grades are pretty awesome. Anyway, the auditions come once you're already here as a drama major and have to try to get yourself in the BFA Musical Theatre program. I am still in that process. I will be auditioning for the BFA at the end of the quarter. Although it sucks to not know if I will ever make it into the program, it is so much less stressful to audition for faculty you know in a room you are familiar with than being so displaced and foreign in Michigan.

**Hannah T., 18:**   I just finished my first college semester at UT at San Antonio. Getting into college wasn't nearly as hard as people made it out to be. While there was a ridiculous amount of paperwork, I opted to take a standardized test and it was far from being the hardest thing I've done.

**Elizabeth, 19:**   I am now at University of California at San Diego. It didn't seem too hard to get in and it helped a lot that I had been at the high school for a couple of years. The transition to college was very easy and smooth. Again, it helped that I attended high school part time and then full time during my senior year.

**Grace, 19:**   I'm currently at Sacramento City Community College, but once you're in community college you just have to transfer [if you are eligible for a Transfer Admission Guarantee (TAG)]. My sister went to a California university after community college, and a friend of mine has just submitted her transfer agreement, both homeschooled and took the California High School Exit Exam, like I did.

**Katie P., 20:**   I found getting into my community college was a little harder than my conservatory, mainly because

---

### Risa, 21

I transferred to UC San Diego as an International Studies major in the Fall of 2011 and I know that my homeschool experience and time at the community college played a crucial role in my admittance. My homeschooling years gave me an incredibly well-rounded, unique academic foundation that distinguished me from most high-school students. Additionally, my time at the community college allowed me to explore my interests and gain experience, making me a competitive applicant.

---

### Joseph, 19

I found it incredibly easy to get in—numerous people at my college, both admissions and other faculty alike, took a quick look at my transcript and noted that I would get in without issues. Even without any particularly major high school accomplishments, getting into the fairly prestigious school where I am now, was very simple and easy.

the conservatory was an acting audition, which I was familiar with. I only want to act, so the conservatory route was a much better choice for me. I decided to go to the New York Film Academy (NYFA). I had to write an essay, do some auditions, fill out paperwork, and that was it! Easy!

**Jared, 22:**   I did have to take some basic entrance exams [for the community college]. I had to take a short online math test to see where I was with that. I also had to go on campus and take an English exam. Each test places you in a specific course depending on your score.

**Katie F., 24:**   It wasn't hard to get in. The colleges I talked to actually loved having homeschooled kids attend.

Sarah B., 20:   When I first found out from a friend about the school that I go to now (Worcester Polytechnic Institute), I knew that I wanted to go there. They did have a few different requirements because I was homeschooled, but it was not too hard to complete the extra stuff on the application.

**Tori, 18:**   I am currently attending University of Alaska, Anchorage. I think it was pretty easy because I was already in the school system by the end of my high school years. I also had resources at my high school that helped me apply. College to me seems exactly like high school, I can't wait to be done.

**Kelli, 21:**   I currently attend The University of Texas at Austin and had no difficulties getting into college.

**Skye, 22:**   Easy enough, as I was accepted to all schools I applied to.

**Micah, 16:**   I was accepted at University of Tennessee and Pellissippi State. I didn't have any problems and have had some offers of scholarships to other universities. Just have to wait and see what is offered.

**Teagan, 20:**   The road to getting in to college wasn't particularly easy for me, but that also had a lot to do with my chosen field—I was intent on getting my bachelor's in the-

---

### Zoe, 22

It was not very hard to get in. The hardest part for me was getting through the SAT process. And really what I mean by that is getting through the MATH section of the SATs. I easily coasted through the English sections but studying for the math section was one of the worst experiences I've ever had. However, because I wanted to get a good enough score to get into college, I worked hard and I ended up with a very decent overall score. As it turned out, the college that I ended up going to did not even look at my SAT scores. Go figure.

atre, and eventually narrowed down my college search to a very select few. I only applied to/auditioned for four schools, three of which (University of Cincinnati College—Conservatory of Music, SUNY Purchase, and DePaul) happen to be three of the most selective theatre conservatories in the country. The fourth, Columbia College, is a melting-pot private art school with an open admissions policy. I ended up being rejected by CCM and SUNY Purchase (not on any basis of my academic record, as far as I know, but rather on my audition), and put on the waitlist at DePaul. This, in itself, gave me a strong sense of accomplishment, as they only take an incoming class of 42 into the Theatre School (out of 800+ auditionees). I didn't end up getting in, however, and I ended up at Columbia. It was, for all intents and purposes, my safety school, but it was actually one of the schools that I had always found most interesting and exciting. And upon attending, I can truthfully say that I am incredibly thankful I didn't go anywhere else.

**Molly N., 19:**   My associate's degree all but guaranteed my transfer into a state school. I transferred with all of my lower division general education courses completed. Transferring involved some logistical work within my degree program, but it was not a problem. It was and still is a successful experience.

**Nathan, 22:**   I applied to about 10 colleges and some were very understanding about the homeschooling. I don't think the experience was much different and I got into a handful of colleges who really wanted me.

**Sarah H., 24:**   Once I decided I wanted to go to college, it was actually hard to get in. Because I did not have a state seal on my diploma, many online schools would not accept me. I was finally accepted into Kaplan University Online, and I have been going for almost two years now.

**Rosie, 24:**   It was pretty difficult to get into veterinary school, but that was because of Visa problems for Italy and international complications. My documents had to pass through three different countries. None of this had anything to do with homeschooling.

---

### Hannah J., 22

Since I had my associate's degree by then, application was smooth and easy, with a lot of the normal core courses already being fulfilled. I was able to finish my B.S. in two years and am currently working on my doctorate in physical therapy. A good number of homeschooled students are enrolled at that university, and everyone I mentioned it to was supportive of it and usually knew someone who had been homeschooled.

---

### Laura, 25

I attended a four-year university and I got in by taking the ACT. It wasn't hard for me to get in and I actually really enjoyed college. I liked the social aspects and the learning opportunities. It was different from homeschooling, but I thought it was good.

> ### *Kristin, 19*
>
> The hardest thing about applying to universities was the time I spent visiting them all. I toured two of the universities I applied to, and then ended up having to go to a number of auditions and scholarship interviews as well. This was difficult to fit into my schedule. I even ended up skipping one scholarship day, because it was the same weekend that I was performing in Hamlet. I immediately decided that Hamlet was more important than that school and declined my acceptance there. Overall, applying to universities as a homeschool student was very easy. All of the universities were very helpful and accommodating with any problems or differences I might have coming from a homeschooled background.

**Sarah D., 19:** Yes, I'm currently attending East Carolina University. It wasn't very difficult to get in, except that I didn't have any geometry course listed on my transcript, so they wouldn't have accepted me. When that was brought to my attention, my mom and I made a plan for me to work through a geometry textbook in May-June the preceding spring.

**Kristin, 19:** I am currently enrolled at University of North Carolina- Asheville (UNC-A). I applied to three other schools my senior year of high school. They were all state schools, and I got into all of them. Applying to them was a pain in the neck, but after working for UNC-Chapel Hill, I was used to filling out ridiculous amounts of paperwork, so it wasn't a big deal. I was worried about writing the essays, because I disliked writing and didn't do it terribly often. However, compared to the essays that you have to write on the advanced placement exams, college essays were a piece of cake. The most fun essay was the one I wrote for UNC-A. The prompt was what historical figure would you have a conversation with and why. I chose the Chevalier D'Eon, a master swordsman and cross-dressing French spy from the late 1700s. I wanted to talk to him because no one ever did figure out why he liked to cross-dress so much (he lived the last few years of his life completely as a woman, and there was a large betting pool at his death on what his actual gender was). This was such unconventional behavior at that time that he must have felt very strongly about it to have lived his life that way despite the possible ridicule. My main problem with the essays was how short they had to be. I wanted to write page after page about Chevalier D'Eon, but I was limited to 250 words.

**Roxana, 25:** It wasn't hard at all to get in. I started out at the community college just taking the things I was interested in – opera history, web design, musical theater – and eventually sort of fell into the more 'academic' type courses, as they started to become requirements for higher level classes. For instance, I had to take English 100 before I could take the higher level history and literature classes I was interested in, so I bit the bullet and got through a boring, incredibly easy semester teaching me how to do what my mom had shown me in 5 minutes. At some point, I decided I wanted to transfer to a 4-year university. I took another year to finish up the IGETC requirements, so that I could enter a University of California school as a junior, and applied to UC Irvine as a drama major. I only applied to the one school—it didn't occur to me that there was any possibility I wouldn't be accepted, and as it turned out, there wasn't. (I had a 4.0, wasn't entering an impacted major, and was a transfer rather than freshman, all of which made my acceptance guaranteed.) Later, when talking with friends at UCI about their application process as freshmen, it occurred to me that it was arrogant not to think about 'safety' schools, but really, it wasn't necessary, and UCI was where I wanted to go.

## College Life

These college-bound homeschoolers enjoyed so many "firsts" as they ventured off on their own. Just like their schooled peers, they learned about roommates, making it to classes, adapting to a completely new environment. A few of these grown homeschoolers candidly share how they experienced a small adjustment period to the idea of school schedules and expectations—even if they attended community colleges prior to attending the university. This seems very similar to their school peers who also take a little time adjusting to the new surroundings of living on their own and going to college. Most, however, found their educational path created no additional obstacles for them. Instead, they felt better equipped to handle college life, make choices and spread their wings.

**Roya, 27:**   Once I got into the university, I discovered myself a part of a small department in a huge school. I joined the department's academic organization the first semester, and the second semester I became its President. I took amazing classes, went snowboarding for credit, learned about camp management (what I want to do when I grow up), and formed some amazing relationships. For example—my husband (I met during the first week), one of our groomsmen (I met during orientation), and one of my

> **Alsatia, 18**
>
> If anything, my homeschooling years made me more prepared than some of my counterparts. I was never the smartest person, but I was raised with a strong work ethic toward school that helped me a lot. I guess I should also mention that I'm currently enrolled in a PhD engineering program while working full-time. I certainly didn't suffer academically or socially while in college.

mentors, thesis committee members, and the person who did all the flowers at my wedding (one of my teachers). The classes I took were incredible—I went on a week-long trip to Santa Barbara Island, camped there with 15 students and no trees or natural water, swam with sea lions, jumped off of very high things into the ocean, and learned about "recreation in the ocean environment." My husband and I have since gone back as staff every year. I went backpacking in Joshua Tree for a class, I went on a month long "wilderness water expedition" where I kayaked through Lake Powell in Utah and survived off of what I could paddle. I took classes in program management and managing resources that directly applied to the jobs I had after. The culmination of my undergrad degree was a 400 hour internship—my then boyfriend/now husband and I did ours together—in the outback in Alaska. It was an amazing summer living in the spruce and alder, with moose and bears. I should do a shameless plug for CSULB's Recreation department now, because none of this would have happened without the resources and relationships I had through that department.

I am now almost finished with my Master's in Counseling. Once again I only applied to one place—I had decided on a

> ### *Alaina, 25*
>
> College was great. I was a very dedicated student and enjoyed the experience. I did not feel the need to be a party student. I made the decision to go to school anywhere but where I grew up. I feel this decision was driven by my homeschooling experience and a desire to experience as many places and cultures as possible. Also, I felt a need to go discover who I was outside of my family—I feel this was overall a good decision.

*Jared enjoying a USC game!*

specific school and program I wanted, and was not going to get my Master's just to get one. This time it was nerve-wracking. There was an interview and I found myself unexpectedly terrified and unsure of whether I'd get in. I was told that approximately 200 people had applied to this program and about 20 would get in. Even after I was accepted, there was doubt due to the huge amount of time and effort it would take, and the fact that I wouldn't be able to keep a paying job while I did it. It has consumed my life for the last two years, what with seeing clients as an MFT trainee, and working on my thesis. It has been a difficult and rewarding two years, not only because of time/finances, but because the field I am in requires a tremendous amount of self-growth and awareness.

**Jared, 22:**   I'll be honest, it was a weird experience at first. The whole idea of going to class at a certain time, waking up early, and just the way a classroom works was all fairly foreign to me. Like most everything else in life, I adapted to the new style and kept going with it. It was just something new—not something I couldn't handle.

**Michael, 22:**   When I got to Texas State University, I needed to take one remedial Algebra class. I hadn't taken any at the community college level, so I needed it for my major. I completed it easily and then went on to make an A in College Algebra. I only bring all this up, because I didn't "do curriculum," maybe a few workbook pages or a website here and there. But regular life was the prep for these classes, really.

The University campus did feel different from anything else though. In homeschooling and even community college, there are a lot of different ages mixed together. But at the university, seeing an entire campus of 18–24 year olds—that was a new experience. The dining hall was an easy place to meet new people. I didn't move into a dorm, because they were overbooked, but I lived with three roommates in an off-campus student apartment.  In my first semester, I found clubs and organizations to join. It was the first Obama campaign, so I worked on that there. That was exciting and fun. I worked as a newspaper reporter for the University Star, so I was able to

> **Katie F., 24**
>
> It wasn't too much of an adjustment. The basics of my unschooling background (making my own schedule, self-disciplined study times, research from books and not textbooks) actually helped me fare better than many of my classmates.

> **Zoe, 22**
>
> Actually being IN school was an interesting experience. It was very mixed for me, both in terms of my classes and interacting with my peers, but I feel like that has more to do with acting and actors and acting teachers then it does with me being homeschooled.

*Roxana pledged a sorority*

### Alsatia, 18

My experience with the college/university was overall very positive. While I was on the quiet side, I did always have a group of friends. At both schools, I was also in honors scholarship programs and heavily involved in some engineering clubs that competed internationally.

interview a lot of interesting people and stay on top of what was happening on campus. I got a job as a Radio DJ the next semester, and then that moved into having my own radio show for a couple semesters in my last year. I joined a group that snorkeled and cleaned the San Marcos River that flows through campus—lots of people at Bikini Hill. I had to do a lot of problem solving on my own since it was the first time to live away from home. Overall it was a fantastic experience.

**Sarah D., 19:** The college experience so far has been very good for me. It's very different than being homeschooled, and I've had a hard time getting used to the structured schedule and the deadlines. This university offers free counseling for all students, and taking advantage of that has helped me deal with some challenges I faced.

**Molly S., 20:** School has been great so far. Everyone in the arts is very welcoming and friendly. It is hard to actually be cast in productions, but I made sure it happened by auditioning for literally everything. I have been very busy and working a lot.

**Hannah T., 18:**  The college experience didn't thrill me, it was very much an institution where I was a number instead of a person, but my passion about medicine and drive to accomplish my goals make it a necessary means to an end.

**Roxana, 25:**  The college experience was, basically, pretty great. I spent three years at UCI, and loved most of it. The actual campus and surrounding area are lovely and comfortable, I was able to live on and very near campus for all three years and was thus very involved in campus activities—I never got into 'commuter' mode. I joined a sorority in my first quarter, and got extremely involved—I made some of my best friends there, as well as having countless leadership opportunities and chances to do things like plan and put on a speaker event for about 1200 people. I ended up adding a history major, and shifting the focus of my drama major to history/theory (instead of performance), but I often joke that I really majored in sorority life. That's only partly a joke. As it turns out, though, the work I did through my sorority activities have had a greater and more obvious influence in what I've done since graduation.

*Michael graduated Magna Cum Laude*

*Sophie competing with her horse*

*What became of the hobbies you discovered as a teen?*

## CHAPTER 19

## Pursuing Passions

Chapter 13, *Enjoying Hobbies*, included examples of the many passions homeschooled teens pursue. For the homeschoolers who are now adults though, they were looking back at their adolescence and sharing what hobbies they had enjoyed as a teenager. It's interesting to see if exploring their interests as teenagers would lead to pursuing these passions after the high school years.

*Did their hobbies continue post-adolescence?*

*Did a hobby from their youth lead them to something new?*

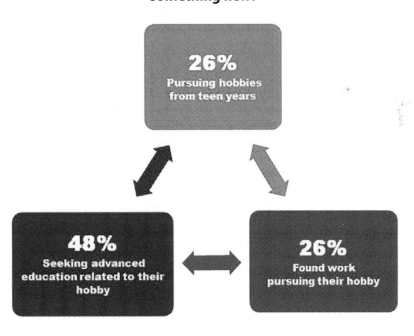

26%
Pursuing hobbies
from teen years

48%
Seeking advanced
education related to their
hobby

26%
Found work
pursuing their hobby

Sometimes they spend time on their hobbies in their spare time; others went on to practice their hobby in more depth, even enrolling at colleges and conservatories; others support themselves with their hobby. When a teen has the opportunity to find their passion early in life, they have an earlier start toward a life that brings them joy.

## Diving in Deeper

These grown homeschoolers have taken their passions into a more formal study arena. Following their hobby led them to conservatories and colleges where they had exposure to experts in their interest fields and peers who shared their passion.

**Teagan, 20:**  My passion for theatre has held fast. It is what I intend to spend my life doing. I now hold a BFA in acting, and plan to return to school in 2013 to get my MFA as well. I eventually hope to teach theatre at the college level.

**Carver, 18:**  I enjoyed theatre, music, audio engineering as a teen and I'm currently going to college to study recording engineering.

**Joseph, 19:**  My current information technology major definitely stemmed from the time I spent building/tweaking/playing with my computer.

**Kelli, 21:**  After years of performing as a teen, I am studying at the University of Texas at Austin to become a theater teacher.

**Molly N., 19:**  I was interested in theatre arts, specifically technical theatre. When I was 16 years old I was paid by the performing arts center at my community college to be a lighting technician and stagehand when the venue was rented by outside companies. I am now a freelance stage manager, with a professional resume, and I am pursuing a degree in the field.

**Sarah B., 20:**  My love for building things and taking them apart, plus the robotics I did as a teen, helped me decide to go into engineering in school.

---

### Laura, 24

As a result of my high school work (joining writing clubs, attending writing conferences, etc.) I attended college and got a degree in creative writing. I'm currently working on an MA in Professional Writing. I want to write children's/ young adult books and I'm working on making that dream a reality.

*Jackson on the drums*

**Beth, 20:** My involvement with writing and literature helped me decide to pursue a job in education. I'm finishing up an English degree, with plans to go on to a Masters or PhD.

**Molly S., 20:** Musical theatre is what I am planning on doing with my life and I started that as a homeschooled teen. Playing the piano, also something I did as a teen, is important because I compose on the piano, and also if I ever want to get into musical direction or teaching voice, I am going to need to be better at playing the piano. I am experimenting with giving voice lessons to my friend and I have seen growth, which is very exciting. I am currently working on writing the music for a new musical that I am developing with a group at school. I will also be directing a student-run musical production of "She Loves Me" in the spring quarter. I am also working on video editing clean up for a web series started by a friend of a friend. I am mostly working on fixing sound and adding music and sound effects.

**Katie P., 20:** My little backyard theatre blossomed into community theatre. And then that turned into part-time work and studying full time at a conservatory in New York

### Nathan, 22

I still read for pleasure and enjoy photography, when I find the time. As for continuing my interest in animals, I am in school and want to go into veterinarian medicine. Absolutely, my hobbies blossomed into something more.

### Skylar, 26

When I was a teen, I volunteered at a grief support center. This volunteer work dove-tailed into a full-time, six-month field study as part of my undergraduate degree requirement.

I am continuing in an MSW program in the fall.

and now Los Angeles. So yes, my hobbies turned into my career. I've done an independent film, commercials and will graduate with an associate degree in fine arts from the New York Film Academy. I still pursue writing as a hobby. I'm currently working on two books and have a third one floating around in my head.

**Rosie, 24:**   I am now studying to be a vet, so I guess growing up with animals had an influence on me. Also travel as a kid made me unafraid of even extreme styles of travel later on. I performed as a kid, and still do today.

**Roxana, 25:**   I ended up with a drama degree! I still enjoy acting, and enjoy the theatre literature and history even more, but I'm not trying to make a living out of it anymore. But who knows?

**Jared, 22:**   Homeschooling allowed me to experiment with filmmaking for years. I'm pretty certain that without it, I wouldn't be where I am today – pursuing my degree in filmmaking at USC.

**Sarah D., 19:**   My novel writing hasn't blossomed into anything more than a hobby, but it's a nice dream. I've been considering, lately, changing my major to something that would build on my love of insects & spiders.

**Hannah T., 18:**   I'm not into forensics anymore, but traveling has continued to be a passion of mine. Combining my interests in medicine and travel evolved into a desire to someday work with WHO (World Health Organization) and MSF (Medecins Sans Frontieres). I'm currently in college, working as an EMT, pursuing my goal to be a physician.

**Cameron PT., 20:**   I spent a lot of time designing derpy little games when I was a kid, and now I'm working on a computer science degree. So yeah, my hobbies grew into something more.

**Kristin, 19:**   Dance was always my favorite hobby, but I wasn't good enough at it or flexible enough to be a professional. I had known this for a long time and had decided that dance would never be my career. However, when I in-

> ### *Alyssa P., 18*
>
> When I went to high school I made the dance team, because of my years in cheer and dance. My make-up internship at age 14 led me to a career in cosmetology. I graduated from a 16-month Vidal Sassoon cosmetology course and currently work as a hair stylist. One thing always leads to another.

jured myself while dancing, and had to go through physical therapy, my physical therapist was also a dancer. She helped me recover after my injury but also taught me how to dance in the future so that I wouldn't re-injure myself. It was amazingly helpful to have a dancer as my physical therapist, and although I had other great physical therapists, none of them could help me as much as she did. Since this was so good for me, I figured that other dancers would also benefit from having physical therapists who were dancers. However, most physical therapists come from a sports background, since that's where the majority of injuries come from. Finding a dancer physical therapist must be hard. I realized that there was a demand for a particular specialty of physical therapist, and that I could combine my love of anatomy and dance to make a successful career, where I could be physically active and help others at the same time.

## Continuing Hobbies as Adults

Sometimes hobbies provide enjoyment just as they are—no extra development needed, no taking it into a money making arena. These grown homeschoolers still love the hobbies they found as teens and are continuing to have fun.

**Elizabeth, 19:**  Because of homeschooling, I was able to pursue a lot of hobbies that I don't think I would have been able to have otherwise. I learned to cook at a very young age and would cook whenever I had free time at home. I was also able to play more sports than most kids. I was able to play competitive soccer while doing level 7 gymnastics. Some weeks I would have between 15 and 20 hours of sports practice. All of these are still just hobbies for me.

**Aiden W., 23:**  I enjoyed reading like it's going out of style, writing, cooking. I was able to volunteer at a therapeutic riding stable. That gave me the opportunity to learn how to ride. I took fencing through the SCA. I was able to have a lot more babysitting opportunities than other girls my age, which gave me more spending money for the things I wanted to do. My writing is still a hobby, but it has potential and has made me a little money.

> **Tori, 18**
>
> Mushing is still pretty big in my life, although I had to slow down to get through college. I always hope to have dogs, but I don't know how competitive I will be.

> **Alaina, 25**
>
> I still play the flute and I earned my second Degree Black Belt in Taekwondo.

**Rebecca, 39:**   My library work from my teenage years fostered an interest for research that is still a passion of mine.

**Katie F., 24:**   I still pursue my teen hobbies of quilting, graphic design, photography, nature walks, and writing. I was the editor of a monthly e-mail newsletter and volunteered extensively at a riding stable for the handicapped.

*Aiden R., Ari, Kaci on a family hiking trip*

---

> ## Kaci, 18
>
> I've continued with photography and have taken several classes to educate myself further in that field. I ended up dropping most of the sports because I lost interest, besides dance and gymnastics. I am currently a gymnastics coach for a wide range of younger children – so I guess that could be blossoming into something more!

> ## Zach, 24
>
> Some of my hobbies included video editing, surfing, guitar, carpentry, home rehabbing, fitness and nutrition.
>
> Strong hobbies helped shape my life.

---

**Jackson, 20:**   Music! I play drums/percussion, and I write and perform rap/hip-hop music. I have had a lot more time than most to practice and learn. Additionally, I was able to participate in theatrical productions through Zach Scott Theatre's Performing Arts School, as a part of their homeschooler classes (held during normal school hours). We shall see if it turns into more! I'm working on a rap EP with a producer friend of mine at the moment, and we're hoping to start playing gigs soon. I've been able to continue doing theatre as a hobby in college, participating in the fantastic Shakespeare at Winedale UT Summer program, and I now have some connections in the local theatre community in case I decide to pursue any further acting/writing/directing endeavors.

**Anastasia, 19:**  Art is the most obvious to me, but I consider most of my studies to be "hobbies." I've been able to pursue them in some rewarding directions.

**Wendelyn, 34:**  I love to cook for my family and have challenged myself to cook meals for others who are in need. I don't cross stitch anymore but I taught myself how to knit 7 months ago and have knitted both of my sons a scarf and two scarves for myself. I continue to read for relaxation and for educational purposes. I still love to sing. I sing on our church's worship team and recently lead the worship for the church service. I sang the National Anthem at a Minor Leagues baseball game two months ago and tried out for a local vocal competition. I sing with my children and my students in my classroom at work.

**Rose S., 20:**  I continue to be a big soccer watcher—more and more as soccer because more accessible to U.S. fans. When I reached age 19, I was no longer able to play AYSO. I had little interest in playing for a women's league or at the college. Instead I took up coaching. Actually, my last year of playing, I coached an Under-8 girls' team at the same time. After I stopped playing, my dad coached an Under-10 team and I helped out. We ended up taking the All-Star team and playing in the spring. This year we are coaching an Under-14 girls' team, and we are, yet again coaching the All-Stars.

The martial arts interest blossomed. I started teaching unofficially at my studio when I was fifteen, a few months before I got my black belt. At this point, opening a martial arts studio of my own someday is pretty much my dream job!

My hobby of watching television has increased as I've gotten older, and become more focused. When I was little, I would spend a significant amount of time watching shows I didn't LOVE because they were pretty good. These days,

> ### Rose S., 20
>
> As soon as I received my black belt, I became an official instructor. I have been working there ever since. It hasn't always been easy, but I've learned a lot about the style, how to be a good instructor, how people learn, how to get along with bosses and co-workers and how to communicate clearly.

> ### Tess, 27
>
> As a teen I enjoyed horses and volunteer work. I now work at the veterinarian clinic where I volunteered as a homeschooled teen.

I only watch my favorite shows—but I watch those very intensely. My boyfriend and I have just about finished all seven seasons of Buffy the Vampire Slayer—in less than three months. I take great joy and even pride in watching entire series of TV shows. I love discussing the shows I love with my friends and family (and even random strangers sometimes). I spend a lot of time online reading about my favorite shows, writers, actors, directors, what have you. I still do NaNoWriMo—the National Novel Writing Month—every year, as well as Script Frenzy (another challenge presented by The Office of Letters and Light). In fact, as of this writing, I am smack dab in the middle of November and working on yet another novel. My writing continues to be a deeply personal thing—I very rarely allow other people to read my work, although this is less and less the case as I get older.

I have recently gotten more into video games, as my boyfriend is a huge gamer.

**Cameron L., 24:**  With my drumming, I formed my own band, and got paid to play with two different bands during my late teenage years. I've written a long selection of poems (in fact, one is published in an amateur poet anthology), a novella about an adventure I had in Peru, and I'm currently writing a full length novel about my travels and hitch hiking through America. I've created a blog about how I travel and my poems/ writings about my travels: www.onewanderingpoet.wordpress.com Both cooking and farming has helped fund most of my travels and living expenses as a young adult, as well as working for Unschool Adventures (www.unschooladventures. com) as a mentor and trip leader for unschooled teens.

## Earning a Living

These teens and young adults have continued with their hobbies, finding a way to make money and sometimes even careers out of following their passion.

**Laurel, 21:**  Yes, some have continued beyond my teen years. Art makes the top of this list—I've sold a lot of art.

---

### Brenna, 22

I discovered ceramics when I was 18, and I'm currently running a small business selling my functional and crystalline glazed pottery. Through my passion for ceramics, I've learned how to do all sorts of things:

- start a business
- pay business taxes
- build a website
- mix glazes
- fire a kiln
- apply for craft shows
- market my work & myself

I've also worked as a baker with two different businesses. Dancing has also become a significant part of my life. This summer I traveled across the country alone, and connected with some really great dance communities.

**Kirby, 26:**   I still do a lot of board/card gaming as a social event with friends around town. I still enjoy video games, normally played online with friends. I even did a little bit of acting for a couple of indie films that friends made. They never released. It was fun though! But my videogame knowledge and experience landed me a job with Blizzard, the company that makes World of Warcraft. I've been working for them for five years.

**Zoe, 22:**   It's hard for me to think of acting as a hobby, because now I work in theater now in New York City. I was able to devote lots more time and energy pursuing what I went to school for and what my chosen career is. I think that can be said for anything.

**Rowan, 18:**   I currently create a line of hats and accessories that I sell at art shows.

## More than Just a Hobby

Lastly, our grown homeschoolers have the benefit of hindsight. They are able to look back and share a little more about what they think about pursuing passions and hobbies during adolescence as a homeschooler was really like. I saved these for last, because I think you'll really enjoy what they have to say!

**Roya, 27:**   Every one of my hobbies turned into something more!

> *Swimming*   I was on a swim team for many years. I do not swim competitively anymore, but I do swim a few times a week for exercise. It's more than exercise, though, it's self-care, relaxation, and a reminder of how awesome my body is and how capable and strong it can be. I credit swimming with having influence over my body image.

---

### Michael, 22

The exchange student experience at age 16 changed my life forever. I fell in love with world travel and decided that I would find some kind of profession that would allow me to have my passion and get paid for it. After getting my degree in Journalism, I'm working for the Peace Corps in Nicaragua. Being a self-motivated, self-taught kid, I learned to always see the possibilities and not put yourself down. Believe that wild crazy adventures are not just possible but you can really go out and have them if you just put one foot in front of the other and do it.

> **Rose, 30**
>
> I was able to take a job as a seventeen-year-old that included travel to Europe. I spent so many hours as a teenager reading on my favorite subjects, pursuing knowledge deeper and deeper. Everything that I have done since then has been an outgrowth of that period. My life now is very much a product of my life then. My friends who went to school see that as a different them and a different life, but my interest in history informs my political activism, my love of hiking in the woods led to my sustainable living practices, the hours I spent hanging out with my grandmother grew into competence with a sewing machine, the church-hopping I did then to find the right one for me has meant a very stable faith as an adult.

*Girl Scouts*    I had been a girl scout since age 5, and once we began homeschooling we actually had a troop of all ages, of homeschoolers. I tell people that my undergraduate degree (Recreation and Leisure Studies) is actually a degree in Girl Scouts. It was the basis for my dream (running a camp with an art/wilderness therapy emphasis), and the start of so many of my other hobbies and interests.

*Theater*    We joined a Shakespeare theater group which was an amazing experience and one that we were able to spend a lot of time focusing on because we weren't in school. I also, with a group of homeschooling friends, put on the Wizard of Oz (I was Dorothy), and wrote and put on a Civil War melodrama.

*Fiber arts & Heritage arts*    Historical theme days, living history museums, Adobe Days at Rancho Los Alamitos—we jumped into these activities as part of our homeschooling, helping me create my passion for fiber/heritage arts. I love it all—crocheting, knitting, quilting, candle making, bread baking, ceramics, cross stitching—anything that Laura Ingalls had to do to survive, I think is an art form and I try to do as much as possible in my daily life. I have started to sell the items I make, but even more than that—it has turned into a philosophy about creating beauty and self-sustainability that I try to live by.

*Poetry*    I met my best friend in a poetry workshop at a homeschooling conference when we were 13. We kept journals, did poetry marathons, and hosted poetry workshops at every party, conference, and campout we went to. I remember writing poems on my pants. Today I am a co-leader in a creative expressions therapy group, where we do all sorts of art and writing as a means of self-awareness. I have seen poetry save lives.

*Traveling*    Being able to take off and travel for months at a time was life-changing. I stayed with friends everywhere I went and saw how different people lived, got inside of families and was able to witness firsthand the different systems around me. I really think this has shaped and benefited my ability to work with people in a therapeutic setting—it's easier to understand the individuals coming through the door when I have so many different lifestyles I've been exposed to. Not to mention, I saw some awesome things and did some awesome stuff. I'll never forget shearing a sheep on an island in the Puget Sound, going to knitting guild meetings in Madison, Wisconsin, salmon fishing in the Matsu Valley in Alaska, or the "gold rush" camping trip my family took through northern California.

*Dressing up*    well, I love it. I love costumes. Not going to say for sure that it has hugely impacted my life or career, except that I am pretty sure that's another reason I want to run a camp—I want to have whole historical theme days where everyone dresses up!

*Ceramics*    I lived at the ceramics studio between the ages of 13 and 20. I grew up there, learned about responsibility, clay, and ideal communities. My first job was working at a ceramic supply store, and later as the lab tech in that same college class. My philosophies about leisure, unschooling, and experiential therapy all stem from what I learned by doing ceramics.

*Camping*    my love of camping, especially with other homeschooling families, and at Not Back to School Camp, turned into my desire to run my own camp, which turned into my undergraduate degree in Recreation which turned into my Master's degree in Counseling.

*Hair dying*    I had to throw this one in there, because I LOVE to dye my hair and it hasn't been pink in way too long, and I don't think I ever would have had the rainbow of colors I have had if I went to school. Between pink hair, my poetry pants, and painting silver glitter on my Converse, I was a walking embodiment of self-expression and it was accepted, nurtured, and congratulated. Did that blossom into something more? Self-expression and my identity—they are my life, and nothing short of that. It might sound strange—being able to dye my hair pink equals who I am as a person—but yes.

*Thank you, Homeschooling.*

### Risa, 21

My involvement in competitive speech and debate gave me numerous invaluable skills. I became an effective public speaker, learned how to conduct extensive research and write persuasively, and practiced defending my beliefs. Using these skills, I was hired by the CA State Department of Parks and Recreation as a Student Aide when I was 17; the youngest aide they'd ever hired. Homeschooling allowed me the freedom to pursue my interests and hobbies, equipped me with valuable "real-life" skills I couldn't have learned elsewhere, and opened doors to amazing opportunities most high schoolers never get to take.

*Roya face-painting kids at a local festival*

*Katie P.: Playing dress up for Ikkicon in Texas can sometimes be a step on a path to an acting career in L.A.!*

*Alyssa P., cutting Michael's hair at cosmetology school*

*Did you find a career path that doesn't include college?*

## CHAPTER 20

## A Non-College Career Path

Many of our respondents are just embarking on their career path, while some are a little further down the road. Homeschooling families are in a better position to support their teen as they search for a career that really resonates with them because they apply less pressure to move on to college immediately after high school. Part of this is because the families are more comfortable spending time together and part is because there isn't the peer pressure to make a decision just because everyone else is shifting from high school to "something else.". These homeschooled teens look at what interests them, and then make the decision about whether that would include college or not.

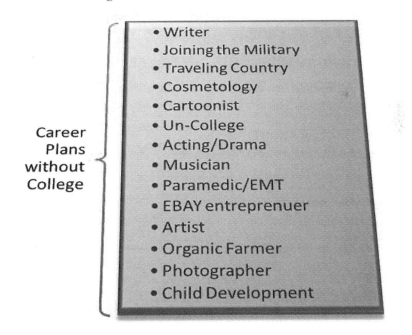

Career
Plans
without
College

- Writer
- Joining the Military
- Traveling Country
- Cosmetology
- Cartoonist
- Un-College
- Acting/Drama
- Musician
- Paramedic/EMT
- EBAY entreprenuer
- Artist
- Organic Farmer
- Photographer
- Child Development

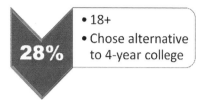

**28%**
- 18+
- Chose alternative to 4-year college

---

**Nicholas, 26**

I became a Paramedic after 1½ years part-time training through a hospital. I discovered this career by way of the dream many kids have; I wanted to be a firefighter. After talking to some current firefighters they highly recommended getting my EMT-Basic certification first. I loved it so much I continued on to EMT-Paramedic school and haven't looked back.

---

With my own three grown homeschoolers, each chose a different path post-homeschooling. And isn't that what we as parents want? Instead of pouring money into the college system, when they are unsure of their path, it seems more reasonable to give them some time, and let them explore different options. They seem comfortable with exploring their own individual path. And it has taken them to some very interesting places!

## Plans That Don't Include College

These homeschooled teens and grown homeschoolers have decided they're not going to go to college.

**Cameron L., 24:**   A career? Does anyone have only one career anymore?  I surely do not desire to do one thing for the rest of my life. Not now, anyway. Currently, I'm tasting as many things as I possibly can while I'm young and able to travel and live so freely, such as organic farming, self-leadership, communication skills, dance, writing (poetry and prose), music, Spanish, domestic and international travel, relationships, self-knowledge, meditation, culinary arts, entrepreneurship, blogging. I think, and actually know from experience, that each career I choose will involve a small piece of everything I've accumulated in my toolbox.

**Aiden W., 23:**   I'm expecting my first child in February. I know it's not really a popular thing to say, but my career is motherhood and I'm really happy with that. For my own pleasure I write poetry, and I'm working on a novel. I've made a little money with some writing and editing work.

**Anastasia, 19:**   When I was twelve I became quite set on being a cartoonist. I never changed my mind.

**Alyssa P., 18:**   Yes, I recently finished a cosmetology school called Avenue Five Institute. I'm ready for my new career to take off! I have always LOVED doing make-up and hair and making people feel wonderful about themselves. Now I will do it as my career!

**Hailey H., 18:**   I'm still on that journey now. :) But I am indeed going the un-college route.

**Katie P., 20:**   I found my career when I was 10 years old. It was when I first auditioned for the musical Peter Pan that I first acquired my love for the arts. I have loved it and been involved in it ever since. I'm currently taking classes at the New York Film Academy, which is an acting conservatory. You don't need college to become an actor. I love to write and could see myself completing a few books in the near future as well. I did take some community college classes to help me decide if I wanted to pursue a college degree or not. Obviously, I decided against it.

**Mike S., 16:**   I'm currently pursuing my passion: music. I plan on taking some music-related courses at the community college in the near future. I hope to learn from the teachers and other musicians about college options.

**Simcha, 17:**   I'm being drafted into the army and will serve the minimum two and a half years before I begin looking for a full time career.

**Rose, 30:**   I have had four jobs (excluding motherhood). I took a job at age eighteen as a tutor in a little organization that hired me because they wanted to start working with homeschoolers and figured I would know something about that demographic. I developed a reputation for being very good with the ADHD and ODD kids. They offered to send me to college to get credentials, but I met and fell in love with a professional harpist and decided to get married and have babies instead. I began to work for him as a manager, booking gigs. I taught myself to do that, using the Internet. I got pretty good at it! We supported our little family that way for a long while. Eventually, I divorced him and began to use eBay and auctions as a way to stay at home with my children and still support myself. A friend had shown me that things that go for good money at local country auctions are very cheap on eBay, whereas things that go for a lot of money on eBay are often cheap at auctions and yard sales. Moving stuff back and forth between those two outlets supported us for a long time, but my heart wasn't in it.

---

**Cameron L., 24**

College is expensive and most of my friends who went had to take out loans. It's hard to know that once they graduate, they're going to have to find a job immediately to pay off those loans. So many of them are envious that I'm constantly traveling and viewing the world face-to-face. They say they'll do it afterwards or later on in life.

But the point of life is to see it now. Do it now. Because once you have loans to pay or a family to build, adventure stands further away.

---

**Zoe, 22**

My path included college, however it was not a normal four-year program. I've known almost my whole life that I wanted to be an actor. Going to a four-year program didn't seem like the right choice for me. I ended up going to a two-year acting conservatory—the American Academy of Dramatic Arts

Now I write flash fiction and sell it to websites. I had been a fan of modern fantasy and started reading the blogs of authors. That led to reading the blogs of authors' friends -- including agents and editors. One of those posted one day about making money quick as a writer. I immediately took advantage of her system.

I'm certainly not the typical career woman that would make homeschooling look golden. It's been important to me to do what I love, to stay home with my kids, to have flexible hours. But I have a life that I love and the means to support it. That's how success ought to be measured.

**Zach, 24:** I've always been interested in computers and technology and I had a family friend and my father in the online marketing industry.

**Rowan, 18:** My main interests are tattoo art, horse work (riding, training, shoeing), and art. I grew up with all three, my sister has gorgeous tattoos, horses have been in my family years before I was born, and my mother and father were fantastic artists.

**Emily, 16:** Although I am still a student at this time, I think I am going to be a photographer. I have always loved taking pictures and through my parents' guidance I have been able to find what I really love. I have been studying photography this year and my parents have helped me get all the equipment I need. They have encouraged me to do what I love my whole life and now they are helping me do it! I have already had a few people ask me to do their pictures and I have just applied for a photographer position in an online Christian magazine for girls.

**Katie F., 24:** I began working in a nursing home coordinating activities for the residents. Though I had a degree, it wasn't a factor (or applicable); I was just looking for jobs in the paper that fit in with my years of volunteering experience.

**Alyssa A., 18:** I'm planning on getting certified in a child development program just before I graduate. I discovered the idea while volunteering at age 15. I told my mom that I

---

### Rosie, 24

While I am currently studying to be a veterinarian, I have pursued other career options before this. I was a soldier for two years and was thinking of staying and becoming an officer. They didn't mind that I was homeschooled. I have also worked in agriculture, tourism, and entertainment, and it was never a problem that I hadn't been to college. There are many jobs for which you need to have a specific skill, rather than a particular type of education. For instance, I am fluent in Hebrew, English, and Italian and now work as an English teacher and translator.

### Kevin, 20

I joined the Marines.

I've been waiting all my life to do this.

loved it and would love to learn more about how to actually work in a place similar to the one where I volunteered. We both researched it and she discovered that all I needed was a certificate to begin. Next year I am planning on getting this certification.

**Laurel, 21:** I'm not currently pursuing one specific career path. Two areas of interest (out of many!) are baking and art/illustration. I'm pretty confident I could pursue both of these career paths further without a degree, although I'm not completely opposed to going to school for either one.

## Additional Comments about Non-College Options

These grown homeschoolers have college degrees or are currently pursuing one, but college hasn't been their only career or focus. Some of their comments reflect how they came to their decisions about their career paths.

Here are their ideas about what they're doing and suggestions for anyone with similar interests.

**Roya, 27:** I've been pretty invested in the college system since I was 13. And despite the fact that I am currently working on my Master's and have a career path very entrenched with academia, I am also pursuing selling my fiber arts. I have no formal education in this at all—neither the business side of it, nor the fiber arts side of it. I learned how to crochet when I was about 8 years old, and just kept going. At some point a few years ago someone asked if I could make them an item and they paid me—and now I am a regular vendor at some local art shows, and trying to get my fledgling Etsy shop off the ground (royaboya.etsy.com).

**Cameron PT., 20:** You certainly can become a computer programmer without a degree, but I've chosen the college route towards this career because I enjoy taking college classes.

**Emma, 18:** No, my career path will definitely involve college and vet school—unless I decided to become a

> **Rose S., 20**
>
> My dream job is opening a martial arts studio that is open to people that have difficulty fitting in at more traditional dojos—homeschoolers, deaf people, people who have physical disabilities, people with developmental disabilities, etc. This career also in no way requires a college degree.
>
> So, although I am planning on continuing my college education through the B.A. and possibly beyond, the reason is really just because I want the education. Not because I need it for my career.

model down the road, although probably unlikely, which wouldn't require college.

**Rose S., 20:** My current career plan does include college, though it does not require it. I am planning on becoming an English/American Sign Language interpreter. This does not in any way require college, but I am currently going through a community college program and am planning on getting a BA in Deaf Studies to continue learning about interpreting.

**Sarah H., 24:** I worked minimum wage jobs for five years after high school, because I was not sure what I wanted to do. At the beginning of 2010, I decided I wanted to go to school for a degree in Human Services. At times I wish I had not waited so long, but I did not know what I wanted back then. So, really, it's good that I waited.

*Katie P. in her dorm at the NYC Conservatory*

*Rebecca homeschools her own children: Zach, 11. Libby, 14. Allie, 16.*

CHAPTER 21

## Will you homeschool your own children?

I wondered whether those who took the survey felt their experience was positive enough to want to homeschool their own children, if and when the time comes. For most, this was pure speculation on their part, but their responses showed that they took this question very seriously. They have reservations about the school system in much the same way the mainstream society does today.

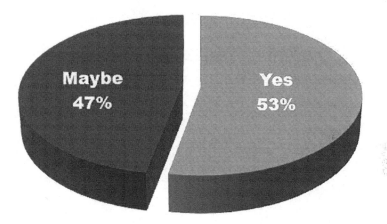

As you see, they're split fairly evenly between confidence that they will surely homeschool their own kids and hesitance about whether the situation will be right for their own family. Instead of giving a resounding "Be True To Your School" response, these homeschooled teens and grown homeschoolers examined what they liked and didn't like about homeschooling. In this chapter, they discuss the factors they consider important in their decision making.

### *Planning to Homeschool Their Own Children*

Slightly more than half feel certain they will homeschool their own children for reasons that mirror many that we hear for current families. Some anticipate that they will take this alternative path to educate their children some day because the public school systems are doing a poor job. But many more believed they would choose homeschooling because of better opportunities, happier lifestyle, fewer negative influences. As you read, you'll see that they often identify multiple reasons they want to homeschool their own children.

## Will They Homeschool Their Own Children?

### Inadequate Public Schools

Many of the grown homeschoolers believe that the public school system is not the best place for children to learn. Considering that the majority found their own non-traditional educational path to be a much more positive experience, it's not surprising that many would like to continue the same path with their own children.

**Brenna, 22:** I think that the public school system is irreparably flawed, and I wouldn't want to force my children to be part of that system. (Unless they really wanted to go, in which case I would discuss my reservations with them but ultimately allow them to make their own decision.)

**Cameron PT., 20:** Yes… I couldn't imagine it any other way, I suppose. Public schools are pretty rubbish, and quite pointless. Plus, by the time I have kids I'm going to be an excessively well-educated guitar playing half-hippie half-yuppie badass who'll probably do a much better job of teaching his kids than some crappy proxy-parent.

**Hailey H., 18:** Yes. I have read so much in the past few months about the decline of the public school system. I have personally experienced my creativity being pulled away from me and when my self-worth was centered around my test scores and my GPA. I want any future children I have to grow up and learn in an environment that nurtures their natural talents and interests, no matter what they may be. I want my children to grow up doing whatever it is that they were created to do. I don't care if it is the lowliest of trades as long as it is what makes them happy. I think that traditional schooling sucks the intrinsic goodness from children and teaches them that "the real world" consists of nerds, jocks, cheerleaders, and hippies. It does not. It should not.

**Mike S., 16:** Unless the educational system changes drastically by the time I have kids, I know that I'd rather give them the opportunities that I have had. I will give them the choice to go to school if that's what they want, but I plan on letting them lead their own life, even at a younger age when some parents feel like they should control their kids' lives.

**Sophie, 19:** Yes, I will homeschool because I see the things public schoolers get involved in and I really don't want my kids to be like that.

---

**Hannah T., 18**

I do not believe in institutionalized education. I think the statistics only show how badly the system fails kids time after time. If/when I have children, I want them to be able to experience the world around them. I want to be with them as they walk through the amazing and sometimes difficult journey of growing up, and offer my support as they explore their interests and what drives them.

---

**Aiden W., 23**

I had a really good experience homeschooling. I'm also very uncomfortable with the way schools are run. My husband is studying to be a teacher, and the system is just so broken. We both agree that this is the way to go.

*Aiden W. and her husband await
the birth of their son, Levi*

**Rowan, 18:**   If I were to have children, I would prefer that they were around things that they can learn from on their own instead of putting them with other children their age. I also want them to learn at their own pace rather than putting them through unnecessary stress to get them to pass a grade. I did not learn to read until I was 9-years-old. I was tested at Sylvan Learning center when I was 14 and the results said that I already knew 12th grade level English. That was mostly self-taught.

**Trina, 16:**   I've seen what public school does to kids, and I don't want my children to be like that.

**Simcha, 17:**   I will homeschool my children. I have very strong feelings about school.

**Alsatia, 18:**   Yes, I will homeschool my children. Because honestly? Here in Florida the public education sucks and this place is very homeschool friendly.

## Prefer the Homeschooled/Unschooled Lifestyle

This group truly celebrates the fact that they were home-schooled. They found that their entire lifestyle was influenced by the way their family chose to homeschool them, and they want to provide something similar for their own future children.

**Roya, 27:** I benefited so much from homeschooling that it does not make sense to me to not want my children to get those benefits also. My whole philosophy of living is relating to the philosophy of unschooling—to the point where even if my children were using school resources, I can't imagine not living with this lifestyle.

**Julia, 15:** I would feel terrible having experienced the joy of unschooling and then depriving them of the experience.

**Alyssa H., 17:** I chose it, because even though my child-hood had rocky places it had many more good things that probably wouldn't have ever come about if I hadn't been homeschooled. Plus, if my children are anything like me, they'd never make it!

**Laurel, 21:** My answer is yes if you change "homeschool" to "unschool." My kids will grow up with an unschooling approach to life, and they can still choose to go to school if they want to. But shush, I'm not having kids for another 10 years anyway.

**Katie F., 24:** Because I know it fits my children's personalities. They are curious, bright, and wild. I know they need, and will flourish with, a flexible learning path and lots of time to wiggle.

**Skylar, 26:** I loved the experience I had. I look around at my friends who attended school, and I know I got the better end of the deal. I even convinced my best friends to homeschool my godson!

**Rebecca, 39:** I had a very positive homeschooling experience. It is my wish for my own children to experience the

---

> ### Sarah P., 17
>
> Homeschooling has worked out very well for me and many of my friends academically. I feel that it has produced a lot of mature, abstract-thinking adults. I am so beyond disappointed with the public school system and every school peer situation I've encountered. I would feel like I was knowingly putting my child in a bad situation by enrolling them without trying homeschooling first.

> ### Sarah H., 24
>
> I actually do not plan on having children, but if it happens, I would like to homeschool them. I think it is just more freedom to learn at your own pace, or pick a day and go on a field trip if you want, or get up at 9 a.m. instead of 6 a.m., or study what you feel passionate about.

freedom and flexibility that I had to spend time with my family and to passionately pursue my interests and goals.

## More Opportunities with Homeschooling

Some of the respondents found so many more opportunities through homeschooling than they would have found if they were in school. This has had a big influence on them in determining that they would definitely want to homeschool their future children.

**Alyssa P., 18:**   I believe in letting the children of the future choose THEIR own future. I want them to learn that they do not need ANY kind of approval from anyone to be who they want. I want my babies to not be scared of the world and not be scared of taking chances. I want them to go above and beyond and get every chance life has for them, I want them to go to school for something they LOVE not something they feel they have to do simply because every other kid does it. I think they will have opportunities that kids in public school have no idea about or have no chance in trying. Kids there are so scared of things that are different. I want my kids to learn to love everyone and everything, and that everything happens for a reason. That is why I want to homeschool my kids. I want them to choose what they want to do and who they want to be.

**Michael, 22:**   I believe that I won't be having children for a long time. It's hard to see that far into the future. I think I would homeschool my children in order to make sure that nothing cramps them, nothing belittles them and no one ever tells them they can't do something they dream of doing.

**Rose S., 20:**   I really loved the way that my parents raised me, and I think that I am a better person for it. I will not be parenting my children EXACTLY the same way of course (my spouse will have an effect on it, for one thing). But I will definitely be homeschooling, or rather, unschooling, or really rather, radically unschooling my children. For sure.

> ### Rose, 30
>
> I want my children to have the opportunity to get to know themselves and their world before they are financially responsible for themselves. I want them to live a balanced lifestyle with time for work, play and learning and even some integration of that triad.

> ### Zoe, 22
>
> I simply cannot imagine sending my kids to school. Being homeschooled was so important to me and shaped me into the person I am today. I am unable to imagine that I would want to deny my kids that same experience.

**Jackson, 20:** Yes. I mean, homeschooling worked amazingly well for me! My only wishes for my future children are that they have the same fulfilling experience of childhood that I did (or better), and that they end up with similar chances and opportunities. Based not only on my own experiences but the recounted experiences of a few close "schooler" friends, I believe that homeschooling is the right way to go about having those wishes fulfilled.

**Katie P., 20:** I think homeschooling truly gives children opportunities to learn about the real world, rather than trying to learn from a desk in a prison cell. Oops, I mean classroom. Hahaha!

**Anastasia, 19:** I don't see any children in my future, but I think homeschooling is simply the best way for children to develop to their full potential. I may not have realized what a privilege I had as a young child, but I realize it now and I would not deny it to my children for the world.

### Better Influences

Some of the teens and young adults believe that homeschooling is the best path for offering better influences for their future children. Instilling good morality and satisfying spirituality, while avoiding peer pressure and negative political interference are the major determining factors for them.

**Emily, 16:** I strongly believe homeschooling is the best way to raise God-fearing children. It has been such a wonderful blessing for me! I can't imagine not doing the same for my children!

**Hannah J., 22:** It's the best option I've encountered or experienced so far regarding the goals I would have for future children—inculcating a strong moral and spiritual foundation first, then academic.

**Kate, 15:** Though there are pros and cons to homeschooling, I believe the pros far outweigh the cons. You are able to progress faster academically with homeschooling. You can avoid peer pressure and negative influences.

> *Wendelyn, 34*
>
> I say yes, because I know too much. I refuse to take away a wonderful childhood from them so they can go sit for hours in a classroom. They would be taught what someone else has decided is important and in someone else's time frame. I want a high quality and meaningful education for my children. This cannot be done away from the real world.

> *Crystal, 15*
>
> Yes, because I can't think of a better way to help your children be the best that they want to be and homeschooling has to be the best way I can think of to make sure that you know and understand your kids as much as possible.

**Nicholas, 26:**    Yes. There are several reasons:

Both my wife and I were homeschooled. We both are glad we were, and want to give the same opportunity to our children. Although homeschooling is not for every family, it should be strongly considered by all parents. It is our vocation to raise children, and we want to raise them with the best education possible. God has blessed me with a job sufficient to support our family so that my wife can be a stay-at-home mother. By homeschooling we have more control over what our kids are being taught. We don't have to worry about politics or government interfering with the schools. The local public school system is notoriously bad and private schools are pretty expensive.

---

### *Laurel, 24*

I really believe that homeschooling was the best option for me. I don't have the strict mentality that all public schools are corrupt and should be avoided at all costs—I know some great people who went through the public education system and turned out great. I just don't see an advantage to public school versus homeschooling. I think homeschooling has many great opportunities for kids and gives them the ability to learn at their own level.

---

## The Maybe Crowd

This group is carefully examining what it would mean if they chose to homeschool their own children. They're writing about some of the potential problems that could arise: finances, spousal agreement, their own abilities, as well as whether better options might be available. Some believe they will simply offer the choice to their child. None of these respondents have children yet, so listening to them speculate objectively, from their distant vantage point is interesting.

### Offering Choices

Many of those who have had wonderful homeschooling experiences, want to be able to offer their child choices for their educational paths.

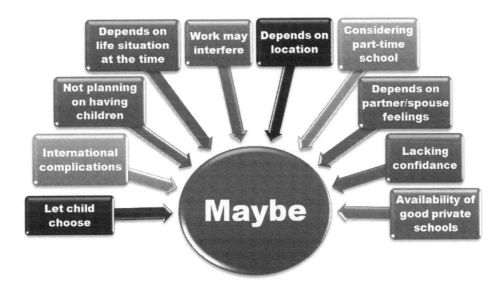

**Sunny, 17:**  I loved homeschooling, my kids might love it too! I'm not planning on forcing it on them. If they decided they want to try public school, so be it. I'd definitely love to work with them and let them choose what makes them happiest.

**Kaci, 18:**  I will share with them my experiences with homeschooling, but ultimately I will let them decide on what they want to do.

**Kristin, 19:**  Homeschooling was definitely the right choice for me and many of my friends, but for other friends of mine it would not have been the right choice. Everyone needs something different from and for their education, and if possible, they should be given that choice. Just because I liked homeschooling doesn't mean my children will. I might start out homeschooling them and give them the choice of going to school at any time. Or I might start them in something a bit less structured, like a Montessori school, and see what aspects of it they like, and whether school or homeschooling might be a better choice for them. When I have kids, their education will definitely be their choice, and something that they have the biggest say in.

**Aiden R., 17:**  I want my children to do what they want to do.

> **Carver, 18**
>
> After having been homeschooled, I think whether it is successful depends largely on the personality and work habits of the kid. It should be up to them whether they want to be homeschooled or not.

> ### *Skye, 22*
>
> I want my future children to have the opportunity to construct themselves with the best means possible. Homeschooling was the best choice for me, but it may not be for my eventual children.

> ### *Alaina, 25*
>
> Homeschooling requires synergy. If the synergy is wrong or I can't afford to homeschool my children then I won't force it.

> ### *Kelli, 21*
>
> It depends on where I'm living and if there are other options such as a one-day academy and or flexible private schools that I agree with.

## Parenting Styles

Some of these grown homeschoolers are examining whether they would have the right temperament to homeschool their own children. They've seen situations that are less than ideal, and wouldn't want to have that experience.

**Teagan, 20:** Since I had such a good experience with homeschooling, I know that it can be an incredible thing. I also know that it is delicate. If I have children, I want to make sure that I have the right level of knowledge, patience, and emotional maturity to serve them right by homeschooling. My parents did, and their choice to homeschool was the best thing that ever happened to me. However, I know some other homeschoolers that were served poorly by that choice because their parents were negligent, or overbearing, or the parent/child relationship was unstable. Also, I would want to take my children's desires into account—do they want to go to school? I would want them to do what makes them happy.

## Depends Upon the School District

While none of these grown homeschoolers have children yet, they haven't ruled out the possibility of finding a good school for their own children in the future. Private schools, One-Day Academies, innovative charter schools are all options to them at this point.

**Caroline S., 24:** I'm open to homeschooling if I could do it better than the schools in the local area. That being said, I think well-trained teachers can do better job than parents. My preference, at this moment, would be to send my kids to a private religious school. That being said, I'm, frankly, several years away (at a minimum) from having kids, and several more years after that from having school age kids. My opinion on this topic has changed drastically from one opinion to another since I was in high school. I see no reason it won't change in the future.

**Zach, 24:** Maybe. Because I would like to but I also understand the challenges and want to make sure I can give my kids the best education they can get for their personal learning style. Just in the past 5 years I've seen large innovations in learning and different types of alternative charter schools some of my friends are using for their children.

## Career Conflicts

Teenagers who are focusing on what they want to do as a career might have a difficult time imagining homeschooling their own child.

**Chant, 15:**   Maybe. Well, I may or may not be getting married and while I want my children to have the same experience I did growing up, if all works well I will have two jobs and I will be so busy it only seems logical I would not be able to homeschool them.

**Grace, 19:**   I really don't know. It depends on my job, my husband's job, how close I am to family, the homeschooling community in my area and what other schooling options are in my area. I want to give my kids the experience I had, but I don't know if it'll be feasible.

## Family Concerns

Family dynamics and situations play a large role in these homeschoolers' decisions about whether or not to choose this same path. Every family is unique, and they would have to think carefully about whether homeschooling would be a good choice for them.

**Risa, 21:**   I plan to live and work overseas. Because I am unsure which particular country (or countries), I'll be living in, I can't stay whether my children will attend school with the village children or not. I believe homeschooling is a fantastic option and it worked incredibly well for me, but at this point in my life, I'm not sure how an international context will influence the choices I make for my children.

**Sarah D., 19:**   I have anxiety issues, which led to several issues with shyness and social fears. I get that anxiety from my mom, who gets it from her dad, and we're all on medication for it. That anxiety has made it very difficult for me to adapt to the school environment. Sometimes I think that, if I hadn't been homeschooled, I wouldn't have been as shy or

> ### *Ari, 21*
> I said "Maybe" because it depends on what situation I'm in when I start having kids. Work, availability, and my spouse will be big factors in the decision.

anxious about many things in my life. So, if I have children with anxiety issues, I may consider sending them to school.

### Spouse's Input Matters A Lot

Not all grown homeschoolers end up marrying other homeschoolers. These homeschooled teens and young adults are aware that having both parents in agreement is a critical component in the choice to homeschool.

**Kevin, 20:**    Maybe. I'm not sure yet, I don't have kids, but plan to. That should be something discussed between husband and wife.

**Rosie, 24:**    Maybe. I'm not yet married, or with a partner, and eventually it would very much matter what he wanted.

**Micah, 16:**    I would like to have a wife that was interested and capable of homeschooling. My mother homeschooled my older brothers and sisters by herself as she was divorced at the time, but it would be best to have both parents cooperation to be most effective.

**Steen, 15:**    I plan to make that decision jointly with my spouse when the time comes and it depends on our life situation and how our children are. I honestly can't say one way or another what I would do right now as I am just a teen and understand that everyone is different.

### Probably Part-time or While They're Younger

Even though these survey respondents were homeschooled through the teenage years, they express some doubts that they will be able to. Nevertheless, they see the benefits of homeschooling their future children during their younger years to create a good foundation for later.

**Joseph, 19:**    Maybe. If you would have asked me a few years ago, I would have said yes for sure. However, since then (and getting to know some of my schooled friends much better), I definitely acknowledge that homeschooling is not for everybody. I do plan on attempting to homeschool my children, at least for a few years—I want them to experience the joy I had of exploratory wonder. Instead of send-

---

> **Caitlin, 27**
>
> If my husband and I could afford to give up one income and have one of us home with the children, we would homeschool. I also have a stepdaughter who goes to public school, so I do not know how I would feel about having one child that does attend school and others who do not. We have a few years to make these decisions.

---

> **Tori, 18**
>
> I really like homeschooling, especially when my kids are younger, but I know public schooling helped me prepare for college and helped me socially. I think I might do part-time because it gives you the best of both systems.

ing them off to a school right away, I want to take them to museums, teach them math, let them play with Legos, etc. However, I know that everyone is different, so depending on their learning styles, the resources available to my family in the future, and any number of other factors, I could still see myself putting my children in school. I won't do so without saying I tried homeschooling first, though.

**Beth, 20:**   I don't know if I want kids. If I do have them, I might homeschool them until 8th grade just to instill values in them and so they can be brought up right. I want them to be respectful.

## On the Fence

This last group is undecided as to whether or not they will homeschool their children in the future. As you read, you can feel them working out some of their own ideas, knowing that so many variables play into this decision. And even our last survey respondent, who initially did not think she would homeschool her own children, doesn't close the door completely.

**Jared, 22:**   Maybe. It's hard to say. I can see the pros and cons of both. Right now, I'm leaning more towards the homeschooling side of things, but who knows. Only time will tell I guess.

**Sarah B., 20:**   I feel that it depends on what is best for my future children if I have some. Though what is best for one person may not be best for another person.

**Nathan, 22:**   I agree with my parents' decision for all of us but I think it has to be on a case-by-case basis. It takes a certain person to be able to motivate themselves into actually doing the work without anyone there to punish them.

I don't think I will homeschool my kids because although I think there are many benefits to homeschooling, there are also many downsides to it. I also didn't feel that I benefited enough from homeschooling to make it worth it.

> *Alyssa A., 18*
>
> It really depends on where I am at that point in my life and what I am doing.

> *Tess, 27*
>
> It depends on the district, my financial circumstances, and what is best at the time for my children.

### Molly N., 19

It depends on my situation and career and it is also dependent on my children's particular needs, my resources. Will I have time to spend with them? Will I have money to send them to an alternative/private school? And, ultimately, what are their wishes? High school years, in particular, will be something I want my children to be empowered to make decisions about—in fact they will need to be. Education is a responsibility, something that one needs to direct for themselves.

I feel that a lot of homeschoolers don't get a good foundation in writing and English which has not affected me too much but I do wish I had more practice with it and was more skilled in that area. My writing program in college ended up being on the easier side and since I am a science major I haven't had to do too much writing. This is probably just been my circumstances and experience. I'm sure there are other homeschoolers who have an outstanding foundation in those areas.

Also, I like the social aspect of going to public school. Not for a bunch of friends or that sort of thing but just to have interactions and talk with different types of people and to get skills dealing with others. I didn't go to elementary school at all and only went to junior high part time. I made a lot of friends through sports and other activities so it's not that I didn't have friends but I am pretty quiet and can't express my thoughts that well. I have always thought maybe this was because of homeschooling because I didn't have to talk and explain myself a lot. I interacted with people but not on the same level as kids who went to public school.

Personally, I work in a pretty standard way and can adjust to different situations fairly well so I don't think the fact that I homeschooled really put me at too much of an advantage or disadvantage. I think I would have been OK with either option, homeschooling or going to public school, and probably would have turned out almost the same. My siblings however, don't really work the same way as me and have a little bit a harder time getting homework done and focusing on certain tasks so maybe homeschooling benefited them more than it did me. I also think that since I was homeschooled and went to public school part time since junior high I know the advantages of each and I will be able to give my kids some of the advantages I had during homeschooling at the same time they go to public school.

The things that I appreciate about homeschooling were some of the things I got to do such as travel, learn to cook and bake, explore different areas that weren't covered in public school (I think I might have talked about being interesting in circuits when I was younger), and explore areas that I was interested in. I think that since I had that experience I can make sure my kids also have it by taking them on trips, doing those after school activities that most kids don't do and encouraging them to explore different and alternative topics they are interested in. I hope I will be able to combine the good aspects of both a homeschool education and a public education.

Of course, there are still downsides to putting kids full-time in school. But I think putting them in public school is the best option because not too much of what I benefited from during homeschooling really had much to do with academics. I benefited from having experiences outside of academics. These experiences are just as important but I think I can give them to my kids even if they are in public school.

---

### *Elizabeth, 19*

I don't think there is really a simple answer to this question because so many factors go into this decision. How much homeschooling benefits a student depends on how they learn, what resources are available, the school system, how old they are, family dynamics, what areas the student is interested in, and a lot of other aspects. For now I would say I wouldn't homeschool my kids unless I thought they would be much better off and benefit more from home schooling than going to a public school. All that being said, I would only homeschool my kids if I thought they needed to be homeschooled for one reason or another and wouldn't do well in a regular school. It also depends on the type of public or private education that is available, how much I work, etc.

---

*Skye and her new baby Iccarus*

## Quotes from the Young People

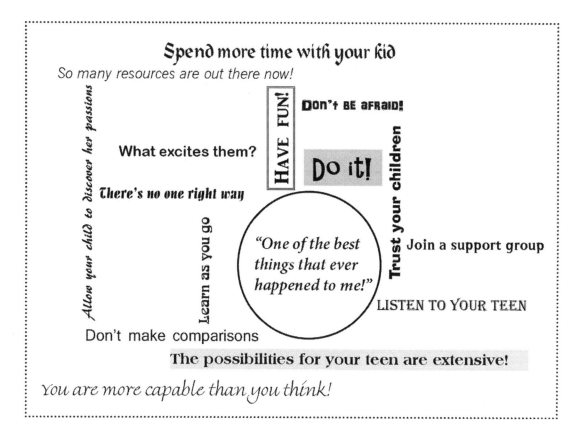

Spend more time with your kid

So many resources are out there now!

HAVE FUN!

Don't be afraid!

What excites them?

Do it!

There's no one right way

Allow your child to discover her passions

Trust your children

Learn as you go

"One of the best things that ever happened to me!"

Join a support group

LISTEN TO YOUR TEEN

Don't make comparisons

The possibilities for your teen are extensive!

You are more capable than you think!

*Do you have any words of advice for worried parents?*

## CHAPTER 22

## Words of Advice for Worried Parents

Homeschooling your teenager is a big responsibility. Most parents make the choice to let someone else be in charge of their adolescent's education during these years. It's understandable when a parent faces this task with a little bit of trepidation. Our survey respondents shared their insights on whether or not someone else should homeschool their teen. Even though most do not have children yet, they do have insights into what worked and what didn't for them.

These words of encouragement resemble so many of the panels of grown homeschoolers found at conferences nationwide. Parents ask questions about what the teen life was like and they receive the most thoughtful and reassuring responses.

### *Get More Information!*

I spent our first year reading any books I could find and picking the brains of any homeschooler who crossed my path! The Internet hadn't really taken off yet—it was the mid-90s—and finding others, especially with teenagers was much more difficult. Now, with email lists, Facebook groups, as well as the immediacy of e-books and blog articles, a parent can easily tap into a wealth of knowledge and resources to help them as they homeschool their teen.

**Kelli, 21:** Listen to your children, address their needs and don't worry. Read, read, read and then read some more. Reach out to your local home-schooling community. Knowing that you are not alone is a great weight that will be lifted. They will have an abundance of resources for you.

**Rose S., 20:** Read a lot. There is a ton of information on the internet, and some really great books out there now too. Get on the email lists, and get out to your local park day group. The support you get from other parents that are taking the same journey as you is priceless.

## Look at All the Flexibility!

No need for a one-size-fits-all approach to educating your teenagers. Homeschooling allows parents to be flexible as they decide what's best for their child. Having the ability to create, and deviate when need be, from your family's schedule is so helpful.

**Sarah D., 19:**   Every kid needs a different education. Not every kid needs to go to college to be a successful person. I never had a choice about my education until college, and I never really minded that, but your child will probably want to have a say, since it is their life. I wasn't homeschooled alone; all my younger siblings were in the house all the time.

I don't know you or your situation, but I know that homeschooling helped build a strong relationship between me and my parents and siblings. It gave us the freedom to be able to travel in case something happened, like when one of my grandparents died, we had the flexibility to pause school for a week and drive up to be there.

**Alyssa H., 17:**   There's no right or wrong way to homeschool. All kids are different and learn differently, some need everything to be structured and others, like me, need education to be a bit less organized. Some kids like text books, others need hands-on activities. Study your teen and learn if he/she would fit into a homeschool lifestyle. See if your city has a homeschool group, chances are you have one and there is probably a homeschool mother who is a veteran at this that can answer your questions and get you started.

**Rose, 30:**   The best parenting advice I ever received was, "As long as you stay conscious of where your children are emotionally and intellectually, and maintain your ability to be responsive, everything will be fine." Homeschooling gives parents more opportunity to know their children and

---

### Rebecca, 39

Ninety percent of what parents push, worry and stress about, or force teens to do in their high school years is entirely unnecessary.

Know that.

Feel confident in that.

And embrace the freedom and flexibility that that knowledge gives you and your teen.

---

### Sarah H., 24

Don't try and compare yourselves to any other type of schooling. The point of homeschooling is the freedom to be different and do what you want. Don't worry, have fun and use your imagination! And don't push college too hard if your children are not ready yet.

much much more ability to respond because of the flexibility. If you suspect it's the right thing to do, it probably is.

Because I was homeschooled, I knew how to comport myself in the world, a full decade before my friends who were very scheduled and went to college straight out of high school. I knew what my goals were and I knew how to discipline myself. It didn't look like I was learning that, at the time. I spent a good three years in adolescence failing, but every one of those days I was learning what not to do. A chance to make those initial big, adult-sized mistakes about time and career management while living at home with parental supervision, before the age of majority, is an invaluable gift. The learning curve to adulthood can be steep, and homeschooling gives teens the opportunity to do it before failure can result in poverty.

> **Julia P., 15**
>
> Remember that the point of homeschooling and especially unschooling, is that you want your children to be happy, healthy and interested. If these needs are not being met in school and you can move in a direction towards them, how can your resist?

*Jackson, Kirby, Sarah P., Kaci, Alyssa P. speaking together at an unschooling conference about their lives as homeschooled teens*

## Schools Aren't Good Enough

When we first started homeschooling, I knew I could do as well or better than the school system. After two years of my son going to school, my happy-go-lucky kid was no longer cheerful about learning. He was disappointed that information was being parceled out in small bits at a time – and was even told to stop asking questions because the more in-depth information was scheduled to be presented two grades later! The one thing I always told myself was that if homeschooling didn't work, I could always send them back. That never happened.

**Tess, 27:**   If things are not working in the public system, and you have the ability to homeschool, I would do it. My life would have been different and my relationships different if not for the opportunity homeschooling gave me to be myself. You have plenty of support out there, and so will your child.

**Sarah P., 17:**   Every child is different, and will need different things. Some may need regular schooling times, and some may need much more relaxed, at their own pace schedules. But to enroll them in school without trying other alternatives first is to put them into a categorized lifestyle blindly, and to accept the constant deterioration of the public school system. However, some children may flourish in public schools.

**Nicholas, 26:**   I'm glad my mother chose to homeschool me. I know that I did better academically because of homeschooling. I have a normal life, normal job, and normal friends. I have even met friends at work that were also homeschooled. If there are things I missed by not going to school, they were more than made up for by the advantages of homeschooling. Education is the important aspect of going to school. Everything else in school is trivial compared to the rest of your life! And, no, I didn't go to school in my pajamas… usually.

**Michael, 22:**   Homeschooling is a different life style. Taking your kids out of school is a hard first step because you've

---

### Wendelyn, 34

Schools are overrated. If you actually looked at the amount of time teenagers are "learning" in school, you would wonder why they have to go for 7–8 hours a day. With the right environment and encouragement, your teenager can become self-motivated, learn what they need to know and become successful adults who live fulfilling lives. If she's worried about not being able to do it by herself, she doesn't have to. There are so many people and resources out there that can help with this journey.

been trained to think if you want to be ok in life, you stay in school. Don't believe that. It's just the image that schools have given you so that you think they are synonymous with education and the good life. The fact is, they aren't. The majority of the people in the USA go to public schools, get out and live mediocre lives, in my opinion. I honestly don't think that I've missed out on anything, educational, social or otherwise that I would have had in school. At the same time I can point to any number of things I've done in my life that school would have made completely impossible or, even worse, made me think that I can't/shouldn't do it because it's not what everyone else was doing.

## Don't Fear Academics— Or Feeling Inadequately Prepared

This is interesting to me because I know the majority of parents who think they might not be up to the task are themselves products of the school system. If schools didn't prepare you, then either you learned it and forgot it because it had no practical use in your real adult life, or they didn't do a good job teaching you. Or, more likely but also more discouraging, your schooling wreaked havoc on your feelings of competency so that now you doubt your abilities to teach your own children. The truth is, whether or not you did well in school is completely irrelevant. Resources are all around you. You can learn right alongside your teen, or find someone (or possibly even community colleges) to handle anything you don't want to tackle.

**Katie F., 24:**   If you don't think you can teach something, go to your library. They will probably have more information about it than your kid can stuff into their brain. If you don't find it there, look into a community college for dual credit. You can't go wrong with dual credit.

And most importantly: It's okay. No, you can't teach them everything. Yes, there will be gaps. Yes, I said "gaps" just like every other high school graduate out there will have. But it's okay. You will give them the tools they need to learn

> **Hailey H., 18**
>
> If your kid is serious about this and wants it, truly wants it, then do it. Don't hold your child back by keeping them in an institution that will eventually drain her of her creativity and reduce her to a test score.
>
> Grant her wings so she can fly!

for a lifetime. They will be well-rounded adults. You will give them an education in life, and that is what they need.

**Emma, 18:**   If she's worried about classes and getting into college I would tell her that both high school and homeschool are appropriate ways to go about getting an education. There are ways to make sure he/she is getting a full education when homeschooling. Homeschooling takes away a lot of the peer pressure found at high school, but it can take a great deal of self-motivation, depending on how you do it.

**Risa, 21:**   I think one of the main reasons moms are daunted by the idea of homeschooling their teen is because they feel they are inadequate or "not smart enough." I would encourage you not to be afraid of what you think are your limitations as an educator. There are so many resources available to homeschool moms—more than ever before! – support groups are plentiful, and the possibilities for your teen are extensive. Even if chemistry or English aren't your forte, there are so many ways to ensure your student learns them and receives the strong education they need. Colleges are recognizing the strength of homeschoolers and often cater specifically to them, tailoring the application process or requirements to accommodate homeschool graduates. Your teen will still be able to take the SAT, can still have a vibrant social life, will have opportunities her public school counterparts will not, and the resulting relationships you'll be able to forge with your teenager(s) are priceless.

**Kristin, 19:**   Let the teen make as many of the decisions regarding his or her education as possible. Being able to follow their own passions and interests can lead them in interesting directions and open up new education and career possibilities that they never would have thought of. Also, if they can follow their dreams and interests, they will have a much better sense of self and idea of what they want to do with their life. Some people never actually figure those things out. By living their lives and not spending all their time on schoolwork, they know themselves better.

Don't worry too much about fitting all the academic subjects in exactly like the public schools do. I was lax in study-

---

### Sarah P., 17

If your fear is that you'll be lost or do a poor job, just listen to your child. And listen to yourself. Like countless other homeschool parents, you will find that you already know what to do.

---

### Nicholas, 26

There is no reason to worry about not being smart enough to homeschool a child. There are many books and curricula out there, geared towards a parent teaching their child. Don't forget about *Google!* It is a huge resource to anyone for anything.

ing my math and foreign languages, and so far, that hasn't been a problem at all in college.

**Micah, 16:**   Just Do It!!! By the time kids are teens they should be self-disciplined enough to homeschool themselves. There is so much available online now, they could just do college courses for all their high school courses, not to mention there are tons of high school courses available online.

## Finding Support Groups

Many shared that they loved participating in local support groups. Having a few friends nearby—for the teen and the parent—can really help with any feelings of isolation. Support groups can be as simple as a weekly get-together. Younger homeschooled kids often gather at park days, while you might find the teens meeting at nearby coffee shops. Tapping into groups that share a particular interest or even creating one yourself is a fairly simple endeavor. Local and regional groups have email lists where a simple, "Anyone with a teen interested in photography?" (or whatever interests your son or daughter) can be the first step to some life-long connections. It's not uncommon for homeschooled teens to meet at regional homeschool conferences and then continue the friendship online.

Support groups are also very helpful for parents. Meeting and talking with other adults going through the same experiences is so beneficial. When families participate in support groups, they can find out about local resources available that their teen might enjoy.

**Elizabeth, 19:**   I would tell her that it was a great experience for me and that it has many advantages. I think one important thing to consider is if the homeschool community is already established in the area. I think Davis, California has a fantastic homeschool community, full of wonderful people and that is the reason I enjoyed it so much. Make sure the child will still be able to interact and get together with many different kinds of people through taking classes with other children and parents, playing sports or doing

> ### *Jackson, 20*
>
> You are more capable than you think. Make some friends in the closest homeschooling community and make use of the resources they offer. You'll probably make mistakes, but kids are resilient, and as long as you acknowledge your errors and work to fix them, you'll be in good shape.

other extra-curricular activities. I would tell her to talk to people who were homeschooled themselves, or to parents who have homeschooled their children. Find out what has worked. It will be a different experience for everyone and you just have to find what works best for your situation.

**Alsatia, 18:**   I would say that it is the smartest way to do it but to give the kid a choice and to make sure that they get involved in a home school group or network with kids the teenagers own age.

## Socialization

Many of the other chapters focused on questions that relate to having a social life. Homeschoolers often hear, "What about socialization?" so these answers pertain to any social concerns a parent might have.

**Sophie, 19:**   Go for it. They may not like it at first, but in the end, they will realize how lucky they were that their parents decided to homeschool them. Also, get involved in recreational sports and find a homeschool group to get involved in. If you're religious, get involved in church and go to youth group. You can meet all kinds of kids so you are a "socialized" homeschooler. Parents always worry about that. It's just with homeschooling you have to actually go out and try a little bit to make friends rather than show up at school with hundreds of them already there.

**Trina, 16:**   You can see the result of homeschooled kids compared to public schoolers if you look. We are far from 'socially deprived' as some people say. Also, my advice is not to put your kids in co-ops because that's just public school for homeschoolers.

**Nicholas, 26:**   The biggest worries I have heard are about socialization and not being smart enough to teach your children. When it comes to socialization, there are many opportunities including your neighborhood, church, and homeschool groups. Homeschooling is increasing in popularity so the groups are becoming easier to find.

---

### Grace, 19

I would tell a worried mom that homeschooling has really shaped who I am. I would tell her that I'm a really social person with a lot of friends. I know that sounds funny, but parents seem to worry a lot about their kids getting "socialized" if they're homeschooled. I would tell her that people can't "tell" that I was homeschooled. I know that sounds weird as well, but people often seem to think that homeschoolers are either uber-religious or hippies. They expect them to act differently. I'm not going to say her teen will love it, because depending on why they're homeschooling, they might not. But I will say that it does impact a lot and that I wouldn't change a thing about how I was educated.

## *Get Logical*

These respondents approach the issue from a practical standpoint—aware that homeschooling through the teen years isn't for everybody, yet offering encouragement to fully consider the option.

**Laura, 24:**   I'd say she should do her research and really weigh the pros and cons of homeschooling. I'm a strong advocate for homeschooling, but I also understand that it may not be for everyone. She should take into consideration all of the aspects of homeschooling and really decide if it is the best option for her child. You can find many resources online. Don't believe everything you hear about homeschooling. You'd be surprised at how many different ways there are to homeschool too.

**Simcha, 17:**   It's up to what works for them and their kids. Try it out for a month. If it doesn't work then it doesn't work.

**Tori, 18:**   I would ask your child what they want, and consider every aspect. Is your kid doing well socially? What about academically? Will homeschooling affect what colleges they can attend? Will you have time to help your child with their education?

**Zach, 24:**   I don't think I would tell her anything. I would try to understand what was causing her to worry and see if I thought both the kid and mom would benefit from the homeschooling.

My main question would be, "Is your kid's learning or personality being stifled at school and do you think they are disciplined enough to pursue their passions without too much encouragement?"

**Nathan, 22:**   Look at me! I'm mostly normal!

But in all seriousness I would sit them down and tell them the good and the bad. The good is that it gives you the ability to learn whichever way works best for you. You aren't learning in a way just to "pass the test" but you get to actually learn the material in your own pace. The bad is I have seen kids who have no internal motivation and didn't

---

**Jared, 22**

Well first of all, I think it depends on the kid. Homeschooling isn't for everyone. It's a system that worked for me, but I understand that it wouldn't work for everyone. I would just tell a worried mom about my experiences as a homeschooler and tell her how much I appreciated being homeschooled. It was an experience that shaped and changed my life. I wouldn't be the person I am today without homeschooling.

---

**Mike S., 16**

I would tell her to trust her kid as she would trust an adult. I was raised in a very different way from most people, so I can't say that your teen will be like me, but I do know that when given choices about what to do with their life, your teen will pursue their passions with vigor, and will work hard to achieve their goals.

get much motivation from their parents. Now they have some dead end job. This is not an easy choice and it's not a one-sided thing, you have to make sure that both the child and the parent know exactly what they are getting into before the final decision can be made.

**Kevin, 20:**   Talk it over with your teenager and spouse. See what they think is best, and go from there. Something new is always hard, but try it out and see what happens.

**Sarah B., 20:**   Trust that you know what is best for your child—but they also know what is best for themselves. If they do not want to be homeschooled, talk to them and find out why. What are they worried about? What are you worried about? It is hard work to homeschool through high school, but it is also a very rewarding experience.

**Tony, 15:**   Think carefully about it. If you think about it long enough the answer will become clear.

**Katie P., 20:**   I would tell her to ask her teenager if it's something that THEY want to do. If homeschooling is something that they want to try out, you should let them try it. If they like it great, if they don't they can always go back to school.

**Beth, 20:**   It takes patience. As long as you have the patience you will be fine. And when the child reaches 12–14 let them make the decision to continue homeschooling or go to public school.

**Ari, 21:**   I'd tell her that she needs to do whatever is best for her teenager. It may be hard at times, but in the end will be worth it.

## Communicate with your Teen— It's All About the Relationships

Some felt that having good communication with your teen is what can create success as a homeschooling family. They have such remarkably good relationships with their parents, they're sure this will help reassure a worried parent.

---

### Brenna, 22

Allowing your child to discover her passions and learn how to find the advice, information, and resources she needs to explore those passions is infinitely more important and valuable than shoving Geometry down her throat.

---

### Hannah J., 22

The time you get to spend with your teen while homeschooling is invaluable, even if he or she doesn't see it at the time. Take every opportunity to build up and nurture your teen, then see the fruits of that later.

**Steen, 15:** I would tell her that homeschooling can be a positive rewarding experience for her teen as long as she takes the time to listen to her teen and understand his or her needs. If you allow your teen to have some freedom and do certain things he wants to do, you will have a much more positive relationship which will then transition into happy teen years for all involved. Education is an important part of your teen's future and homeschooling can be a great way to complete that. It is a wonderful opportunity if balanced correctly. Allow your teen to think for himself and seek out new ideas and ways of doing things. Don't always push your opinions or values on your teen but rather let them seek things out. Homeschooling should be a journey and a fun positive one for all involved. Don't get too stressed and don't get too down.

**Aiden R., 17:** I'd tell her that I think it's better because you get to spend more time with your kid. And they won't be as stressed about school because it's not like you must go to this class at this time or you will get in trouble.

**Crystal, 15:** I think that homeschooling was one of the best things that ever happened to me, and I'm so glad my parents chose it.

**Emily, 16:** Homeschooling is a calling from God! It is not easy, but has there ever been something easy that was worth doing? It's the hard things that are worth it. God calls parents to teach their own children, not school teachers! "Direct your children onto the right path and when they are older they will not depart from it!" (Proverbs 22:6) "Repeat them (scriptures and commandments) again and again to your children. Talk about them when you are on the road, when you are going to bed, and when you get up." (Deuteronomy 6:7) How are you to teach the scriptures to your children when you are only with them in the evenings? When you home school you have opportunities to discuss God's Word all throughout the day! You are your children's primary example! Not their peers.

**Cameron PT., 20:** Maybe the reason that I am so close to my mom is because I was unschooled, so we got to spend a lot of time together. That kind of turned us into close friends,

> ### Teagan, 20
> It works differently for everyone. LISTEN to your kid(s). Find out what excites them, what makes them want to learn. Let them follow what makes them happy, even if it's not "practical." Don't hover, but don't leave them completely to their own devices. Trust them, and help them grow.

> ### Molly N., 19
> Talk to your kid. Encourage them to have goals, passions, and motivations. Help them find an option that isn't school, but is something that helps them move forward.
>
> Remember, there is no one right way to do this. It's not necessary to know what you want to do with your life as a teenager – just spend time trying on things and building skills.

on top of being parent and child. The answer to this question really depends on WHAT exactly the parent is worried about.

**Molly S., 20:**    Give your child choices. If they do not want to homeschool, that should be considered, as well as if they do not want to go to school. You learn more and actually retain it if you care about what you're learning, which is much more likely if you are not forced to learn it.

If your child is planning on going to college, you should really think about it well in advance, at least a year. Not that you need to stress it for all of this time, but the information should be out there. Go to a counselor, talk to friends who have gone to school in a similar field, don't miss the deadlines.

**Skye, 22:**    Don't force your child to change their life if it will strain your relationships. Suggest a "trial run" over a summer break and see what they think. Make sure there is a good, active homeschool community in your area—and get involved!

**Laurel, 21:**    Make sure this is a mutual decision. If you're pulling them out of traditional school, learn about deschooling, and don't skip that process. Make sure they have a support network of other homeschooling teens. If that means searching for one, or helping them start their own— do it. HAVE FUN!

## Relax

Some parents are natural worriers. They want the best for their children and they have been conditioned to think that they need experts to help them. They begin to think that they are not capable of an endeavor as big as homeschooling. But it's not true. Parents are capable. They simply have to relax and remember that they were their child's first teacher. They can handle the next steps along the path.

**Caitlin, 27:**    Don't worry. Give your teen a lot of time, maybe a whole year, to adjust to the freedom of being out of school. Even if you think they aren't learning anything, it's

---

### Kirby, 26

Don't panic. Take some time to think about what your child is going to miss out on without attending high school. Also you can make a list—compare the benefits to what you think they might miss out on. This part should be easy, if you're already homeschool or are unschooling.

But also:

▲ Encourage their interests.

▲ Introduce new things into their lives often.

▲ Go to museums, parks, stores, whatever.

▲ Let them go on their own if they want! Some might do better without you looming, no offense!

▲ Be interested and involved, but not commanding and/or a burden.

okay. They're learning how to figure life out for themselves, which is way more important than algebra.

**Skylar, 26:**   I had a wonderful experience homeschooling. It worked for the way I learned and for my family. It doesn't work for everyone. Connect with other homeschooling families. Be OK if your kid just stops for a month or two. Detoxing from traditional high school is rough and a lot of healing is happening if it seems like your teenager is not engaging much.

**Chant, 15:**   I would tell her to go for it, at first it may be a little difficult but her teenager will end up liking it.

**Roya, 27:**   TRUST YOUR CHILDREN.

**Rowan, 18:**   School shuts down the genius within. Unschooling lets the genius develop.

**Caroline, 24:**   I'd tell them not to worry. As a homeschooled teenager, I knew many many other homeschooled teenagers by the time I graduated high school. Many are now married with a few kids and stay-at-home moms. A few are like me and have careers. Almost all went to college and, of those that did, almost all graduated (the ones that didn't, did not drop-out for academic reasons). I'd also tell her to give her teen the option of activities where they can hang out with others their age (sports, youth groups, etc.), but not to worry if they don't want to go. Always be aware that at some point the teen is going to want more independence than the parents are ready for and will probably say a lot of very mean and idiotic things to you because of it. Discipline them as necessary, but try not to take it to heart. You are doing fine as a Mom, you're teen won't feel that way forever, and one day they'll actually realize how awesome it is that you actually cook and do the laundry for them.

**Joseph, 19:**   I would tell her my story, and explain all the details that helped me turn out how I am now (which may be described as "normal" and/or "successful"). I would reassure her that her teen's social life will likely stay intact—I can say from experience that teens always manage

> ***Anastasia, 19***
>
> I would tell her not to worry. I was a terrible student for years before I found my educational "groove" and even if you don't think your children can make it without structured instruction, they can, they probably will. Anyone can thrive when they find what they love; it's just a matter of looking at as much as humanly possible. To the teens themselves, read everything. Watch everything. Study everything. It's all beautiful!

to find a way to stay social if they want to. Academically, the sky's the limit. If her teen is motivated and passionate, that teen is going to thrive. As far as college is concerned, some of the stuff that can be accomplished while homeschooling (personal projects, in-the-field work early on, early college classes) is *ridiculously* impressive to college admissions people.

## Some have lists!

**Alyssa A., 18:**

1. Talk with your teenager first! Is this something they really want to do or are you pressuring them? A lot of times kids will say something just to please their parent if it will get them something else.

2. Think about what type of homeschooling you will be doing; talk with your teen about it. My mom made sure I was part of the whole homeschooling process, from curriculum selection, to making the portfolios and transcripts and filling out the application for my graduating class. I felt more connected with my school work and it helped me to think about what I did since I was the one who picked it out to begin with.

3. Join a support group. Wherever you are there is a group out there. If not, then make one! I'm sure there are other homeschool moms with teenagers in your area desperate for someone to lean on and vent about their teen. And I'm sure there are homeschooled teens who need to vent to people their own age about being with their parents.

I speak from experience, I have been homeschooled my entire life, so I know the ups and downs all the way. There are positives and negatives in everything. Just think about everything before you make the decision.

**Alaina, 25:**

1. Not every parent should homeschool and not every child should be homeschooled. If you don't enjoy

---

### Kaci, 18

I'd tell a worried parent that no one goes into homeschooling knowing exactly what they're doing. But it's a process that you learn as you go.

It's benefited a lot of people—including me! As long as you are committed and you want your child to learn better than they would in public schools, I say go for it!

---

### Kate, 15

Does your teen want to be homeschooled? Why? Is it because of education, social problems, etc.? For homeschooling to work, you will have to make an extra effort. It takes work and responsibility from both the child and the teacher. But if you both have goals and expectations, it can work out for the best.

your child, if you don't like to teach, if your child doesn't get along with you at all, if something just isn't working, then this might not be a good match. Don't take that personally, it doesn't mean you aren't a good parent. I would like to say it works for everyone, but it doesn't. I watched parents who did not take the time to educate their children or raise their children and it did not work. Make sure the synergy is right.

2. If you decide to homeschool your child, let them sleep in! Their body is going through a lot of changes and they need to sleep. There are no actual demands that they be up by 7 and start school by X time. Let their bodies establish their own rhythm

3. Finally, enjoy yourself. You're attempting something that many parents now wish they would or could do. Have fun thinking outside the box for ways to learn something. You aren't tied to school books. This isn't about power or who is in charge, it is about meeting your child and stimulating their thought process and creativity. Admit that you don't know everything and there are things for both of you to learn together.

**Aiden W., 23:**

1. Socialization. School is not how you learn to socialize. People who learn school socialization have to unlearn it and relearn real life interaction when they graduate. If they don't, they're miserable. Yes, if you don't get out of the house and do things so that your children get to interact with people, they could turn out weird. So don't do that.

2. Testing. Your children don't need to be tested constantly. If you're involved in their life and talking to them and aware of them as a human being, you will know how they are doing, and a test is moot. A test cannot accurately measure where someone is at. Mostly it measures one's ability to take a test. Trust me. I read my husband's textbooks. If you're really

> ### *Hannah T., 18*
> Think about your child as a person—a whole person who has interests and needs just like you. Think about how extra time might afford your teen the opportunity to explore their interests and grow as a person outside of standardized tests and meaningless busy work. Giving a child freedom may be the best gift a parent can give, and just from my own experience I can tell you how grateful I am to have been given that gift. Finally, trust yourself and your child, and make the leap. I don't think you'll regret it.

> ### *Alyssa P., 18*
> Do it, you will be surprised what your teen will learn. And also who they will turn out to be. I think it's the best thing for teens because these teen years are so difficult. Your teens grow at the speed they want to grow and not be rushed.

freaked out about it, pretty much every state offers tests you can have your children take.

3. Math. Math anxiety is common in America. It's BECAUSE of SCHOOL!!! Get out there and read what the education experts are saying—not the ones who sell curricula to schools. Read Lockhart's Lament [A Mathematician's Lament: How School Cheats Us Out of Our Most Fascinating and Imaginative Art Form by Paul Lockhart]. It's great.

4. Reading. If you read to your kid, your kid will want to learn how to read. If you don't read to your kid, even though school will hammer the basics into their head, they probably won't care. Simple as that. (Yes, there are studies, I'm not just talking air). Also, in hammering the basics into a child who is inclined to read, school may just hammer that inclination out. So you might as well save yourself the trouble and just read to your kid. Also, if your kid isn't reading by first grade age, (whatever that is...) that doesn't mean you're doomed—unless you force the issue. Many children's brains haven't developed the areas necessary for reading yet. It's normal. So don't make your kid feel stupid. Just let him enjoy reading time with Mom or Dad and when he's ready, then he'll learn.

5. My kid won't keep up with the others! Chill. Just because the school kids are reading or whatever so early doesn't mean it's good for them or that they're smarter. School keeps pushing things earlier and earlier for kids, but it's not good for them. Some of them may be ready developmentally. I was an early reader, but most are not. The messages they're getting are that learning is hard, they don't like reading, and they're dumb. It's heartbreaking. Every kid develops at a different pace in different areas. It's pretty much impossible for a teacher to keep track of all their kids' progress. So we have a standardized process for non-standard product, and the result is the kids that most closely resemble the standard do okay, and the rest get beat up and then rejected for being who they are. Some manage to make it anyways, such as Einstein, but the rest are miserable. Do your kid a favor and spare them that.

*Alyssa P. and Kaci speak to parents at an unschooling conference*

*Jared editing a film*

*What are you doing now? What makes you happy?*

## CHAPTER 23

## What Are They Doing Now?

The people I surveyed who homeschooled during their high school years are absolutely inspiring! Consider this final chapter an informal "Meet & Greet" where you have the opportunity to find out what all of these individuals are up to in their lives today. Some overlap exists, as those building a family now, are also working or going to school simultaneously. But here is how they self-identified:

**What Are They Doing Now?**

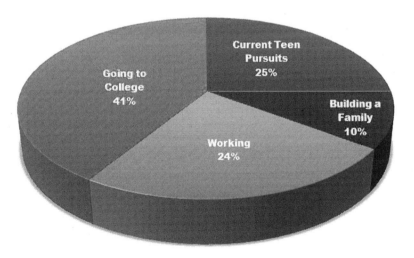

In the end, as parents, we want our children to be happy. We want the decisions that we've made, those that have hugely affected their lives, to all work out for the best. When we think of them being happy, we might visualize them as successful, confident, living their days full of joy. And, for many parents, that's one of the reasons they've chosen to homeschool. The familiar school-focused approach simply isn't measuring up anymore.

When we asked the surveyed respondents what made them happy, you might find some of their answers to be philosophical, some rambling, and some downright silly. But how wonderful is that? They're able to look at their lives and share honestly with all of us. Whether they're still in their "high school" years, or whether those years are behind them, you'll find their interests considerably varied. Many share an introspective quality of knowing themselves a bit better than most people their ages because they've been afforded the time to do just that—figure out who they are and what interests them.

This chapter will give you another glimpse into the people that these homeschooled teens and young adults have become. I find it fascinating because in some ways, their answers resemble those of any American teenager or young adult. In spite of parental worry, criticism from society or maybe even initial self-doubts, they've moved—or are moving now—through adolescence with a sense of self that we sometimes don't see until later in life. They were asked to explain what they're doing now and share what makes them happy—and every one of them had an answer!

## Our Younger Crowd

25% of those surveyed are working on high school credits, looking to the future, making plans and setting personal goals.

**Alaetheia, 16:**  I am planning and plotting and wondering. There's a bunch of different things I'd like to do: study cosmetology, more music, volunteer work, classes I'd like to take. I'm trying to figure out where I want to devote my time. Music, family, art, warm cookies, sci-fi, friends, my animals, glow sticks, and the Occupy movement all make me happy.

**Aiden R., 17:**  Well I might go bike after this, but I have work at 3:30 everyday (but not on weekends—so that's

---

> **Emily, 16**
>
> I am working towards graduating early and starting my photography business.

---

> **Tony, 15**
>
> I am currently planning to go into the music business and am working towards that goal. Music and friends make me happy.

good!) These things make me happy: my family, biking with my friends, and sunny days.

**Alyssa A., 18:**  I am completing my final year of high school and trying to figure out the next step in my path. The people I love, friends and family, make me happy. Also, playing and listening to music, dreams of the future, the idea of traveling around the world, make me happy too.

**Alyssa H., 17:**  I'm saving money to attend our community college to get my diploma in cosmetology and then hopefully work my way through college and major in history and minor in theater. Those are my plans and that is what I'm working toward.

Sitting, writing in one of my novels or researching a historical period make me happy. Planning a costume to be worn in a show, playing basketball with friends, being able to do what I want and to study what I want—These are what makes me happy!

**Emma, 18:**  I'm finishing high school and thinking about college. I'm trying to figure out what path I'm going to take to college. I'm also moving up in the levels of [Three-Day Horse] Eventing.

It makes me happy to make my parents proud as well as make myself proud. I'm also happy when I'm hanging out with friends or my horses.

**Crystal, 15:**  Right now, I'm doing high school!! And I'm trying to balance school and work with kung-fu and my other hobbies. Life makes me happy! So does the smell that you get in the morning after a cold front, watching my little brothers playing in the yard, Thanksgiving, hanging out with friends at youth group, making bread, reading a really good novel, climbing as high as I can in a tree, musicals, rain, great weather, Shakespeare, finally finishing a math problem that I was having trouble with, overcoming an obstacle in Kung-Fu, hot chocolate.

**Hailey, 18:**  I am going to finish this semester of community college and also the spring semester. I will take two

---

### Kate, 15

I have completed seventeen college credit hours through CLEP testing for a B.A. in History. I plan to graduate from college before I turn nineteen. I'm also 'Alice' in *Alice in Wonderland* at our community theater.

---

### Mike S., 16

I'm currently working on my short novel, planning an album release for early next year with a friend of mine, constantly producing music content for my many music websites, among many other things.

Music, mostly, makes me happiest. I get a huge amount of joy out of creating music and seeing other people enjoy it. I also enjoy reading and writing a great deal, but what makes me happier than anything is being with my closest friends or family.

more online classes to fulfill the standardized Florida graduation requirements, and then, by May, I will be finished with my official high school education. I will leave the nest then. There is a possible paying internship awaiting me in Bavaria, Germany, and a lot of interesting and beautiful places to go see even if that falls through.

I am happy living! Cooking with friends, cuddling with my sisters, reading books out loud in the barn to the horses when it's raining and listening to the symphony of the raindrops hitting the tin roof make me happy. I also like being in nature, any sort, and feeling humble beside a tree. Backpacking for the sake of the journey, not the destination, getting lost in European cities, and telling stories that make people laugh makes me happy. I love making people feel better about themselves, and getting a smile from a frowner. I really like libraries and the smell of old paper, and finding out something incredible and needing to tell others about it. Dreaming makes me happy, but making those dreams into reality is what I am living for.

**Emily, 16:**   I love seeing God work! I love spending time with my family! I love riding and working with horses, anything outdoors, raising animals, reading, drawing and painting, and photography! I could go on and on with things that make me happy...

**Julia, 15:**   I'm taking dance classes, and about to start a job this year.

**Chant, 15:**   I am trying to work hard in school and study hard at college and see where I go from there. I love to dance but I also love to study plants and their medicinal properties. Reading, acting, writing, watching 'The Princess Bride' over and over, and hanging out with friends, make me the happiest.

**Nancy, 14:**   I'm figuring out what I want to do with my life trying to find God's calling in my life. Books, I love books! I love reading them and sometimes just looking at how older books were so beautifully made.

### Steen, 15

I am currently an activist and in addition doing my political activities of all kinds I am very active in social media (Facebook, Twitter etc.), and investing. I write a weekly political opinion column. In addition I am in the 10th grade and continuing with my normal education.

### Trina, 16

What make me happy? Doing anything that ends with 'board'.

*Rose S., and Roxana at Roya's wedding*

**Trina, 16:**   I'm working on getting my homework done so that I can be free during the summer, and pursuing wakeboarding.

**Micah, 16:**   I am waiting to make a decision about more college as the TSSAA (sports ruling board in our state) has to decide how many college credits I can have and still play on a high school team. Most everything—family, friends, church, video games, sports, etc.—makes me happy.

**Steen, 15:**   I like to do things that are fun and be around my friends. I like to see the efforts that I make on things lead to success.

**Sunny, 17:**   I graduated early, so at the moment, I'm working at my family's coffee shop and helping with the sale of it! After that, I plan on getting solid on what I want to do as an individual, career-wise, living-wise, etc. A lot of things make me happy! I'm a very happy person in general.

## *Going to College*

**42%** are currently attending college, but as you'll see, that's not all they're doing! Many are maintaining jobs and active in hobbies and community work at the same time. They have incredibly busy and full lives.

**Elizabeth, 19:**   I am a Physiology and Neuroscience major and pre-med at UC San Diego and hopefully going to medical school after I graduate.

> **Caroline, 24**
>
> I'm currently a PhD student in Mechanical Engineering. I work full-time in the defense industry. I rock-climb several days a week after work and play "Go" when I have time. I read occasionally and in spurts. I enjoy doing well in my work and making others happy. Having my room uncluttered and being on time for events also makes me happy.

> **Hannah T., 18**
>
> Right now I just finished my first semester of college, I'm working as an EMT and a nurses' aide, I'm volunteering with an AIDS and substance abuse organization. I'm living on my own for the first time, and learning what it means to be out in the world without a visible net. It isn't always easy, and some days it seems downright impossible, but no matter what I'm grateful to be here living and learning everywhere I go.

It sounds cliché but I really love helping other people. I am pre-med at UC San Diego and I really want to become a physician in the future.

**Alsatia, 18:** I am finishing my associate of arts degree and then transferring to a bigger college to get my bachelor's degree in public relations.

What makes me happy? Reading a good book, making critters out of Sculpey Primo clay, eating yummy food, staying up late and sleeping later, warm blankets, *Glee* (the TV show), and the StarKid Produtions musicals (*A Very Potter Musical*, *A Very Potter Sequel*, and *StarShip*), make me happy.

**Beth 20:** I am a certified medical assistant, a store manager, finishing up my English degree, soon to be moving on to get my masters or PhD. I am doing missions trips to Mexico and will be going to India soon. Books, writing, family, friends, waking up every day, make me happy.

**Carver, 18:** I'm currently attending college.

**Cameron P., 20:** I'm learning how to be myself. Being alive makes me happy.

**Grace, 19:** I'm going to community college, currently undecided. I'll probably take one more year before I transfer. I don't want to make a bad call on this big of a decision. I work over the summer as a manager at a pool, I bought myself a car in February, sort of looking for a winter job, but not too intensely. I'm happy. Music, reading, spending time with friends, spending time with my family—normal stuff makes me happy.

**Hannah J., 22:** Learning and applying information, spending time with one or a few friends at a time, and nurturing my spiritual life makes me happy.

**Hannah T., 18:** What makes me happy is my community, the people I spend time with, the ones both far away and next door. I like getting thoroughly engrossed in a subject or discussion for hours on end, making good food and sharing it with others, helping others whenever I can, smiling children and their parents, playing games with my nephews, reading medical journals and talking to experts in the field I someday hope to be a part of.

**Jared, 22:** I'm studying at USC in filmmaking. But I'll probably have to go a 5th semester so I can get all my classes in and keep my sanity! As of now, I hope to be working in the film industry in some capacity. We've developed a great network here at USC, and we hope to all pitch in and make a feature film once we graduate. I have several ideas for features that I'm currently working on, and I hope to pursue them once I've graduated. In addition, I hope to find some sort of job working in the industry so I can pursue my personal projects on the side.

**Joseph, 19:** Right now, I am in my 2nd year at RIT [Rochester Institute of Technology] as an Information Technology major. I am exploring other interests through my minor and other college courses and maintaining a high GPA. I am also looking for co-op work, to get credit, money, and experience in my field of interest. I'm also considering a number of entrepreneurial ventures, but I'll keep those details private for now. All of the above, plus enjoying my social life, messing around on the Internet, and playing plenty of video games is probably the best way of summing up my life right now. Wonder, amazement, excitement about learning/experiencing something new, in both adults and children alike make me happy. I love that feeling myself, and I love seeing it in others. It's that feeling that reminds me exactly why I want to be a father someday.

**Tori, 18:** Right now I'm going to college, and trying to figure out what I want to do with my life. I've never really found my passion and that's what I'm trying to do right now.

I love being around my friends or family. I love my dogs and mushing. Dancing is another thing I really enjoy doing. Also just doing stuff around the house keeps me pretty content.

**Kelli, 21:** I am starting my junior year at UT-Austin, living on my own and loving life.

---

### *Katie P., 20*

I am currently taking classes at the New York Film Academy. I've just finished up in New York and now preparing for the second year in Los Angeles at Universal Studios! I plan to stay in LA and work in the film industry. It's incredibly fun, and it's a dream come true. I'm learning more about how to use my craft to convey a story. Also, I am currently working on two books and I have plenty more ideas floating around in my head.

I enjoy storytelling. Whether it's writing ideas down on a piece of paper, acting in a film or on stage, or singing a song—all of it fills me up with the greatest feeling in the world. It's pure joy!

God, my family and friends, being creative, acting, collaboration, laughing, my pets, our country's National Anthem, reading, debating and swimming on a warm day, make me happy.

**Kristin, 19:** I'm pursuing a Cell and Molecular Biology degree at UNCA, with a Dance minor. I'm still planning on going to physical therapy school and becoming a dance physical therapist. At UNCA, I'm involved in numerous clubs, such as Swing Dance Club, Biology Club, and the Baptist Student Union. I'm the founder and leader of the Dance Club, and I frequently make up and teach dances, sometimes to people who have never danced before. I have a close group of friends, and we live, eat, and hang out together all the time. They are invaluable as my family away from home, and there are a lot of things I couldn't have gotten through without them. Next semester I will start working on research with the Biology department, and I'll be staying in Asheville next summer to do summer school and work on research.

Dance and spending time with my family and friends makes me happy. Dancing with my family and friends is my absolute favorite thing to do. My mother and older brother were in a musical with me last summer, as were a lot of my friends. We all got to dance in a big, ridiculous disco number together, and being able to share that with the people I love was one of the best things I've ever gotten to do.

**Laura, 24:** I'm actively pursuing a career in the publishing industry. I'm in graduate school right now and I'm working towards becoming a better writer.

These things make me happy: photography, writing, reading, laughing, stupid youtube videos, blogging, dictionaries, vocabulary words, poetry, picture books, fried chicken... not sure where you wanted this question to go—but I kind of took the nonsensical route. My family, my friends, my girlfriend, my dogs, making and listening to music, writing (poems and plays, mostly), video games, and good eats, all make me happy.

---

### Jackson, 20

I'm finishing up college! I'm starting my last semester at UT, and I'm on track to graduate with a 4.0. As well as preparing for the start of the semester, I'm writing and rehearsing lyrics for the aforementioned rap EP and spending some quality time with my girlfriend.

---

### Rosie, 24

I'm a vet student in Italy.

I work as a English teacher, part time farm hand, and sometimes work as a juggler/entertainer. I am pretty active politically (Israeli and Italian politics) I think that happiness is about deciding to be happy.

**Molly N., 19:** Completing my bachelor of fine arts in theatre with an emphasis in stage management, and on my breaks working professionally in theatre to build my resume. Next year I will graduate. Doing what I love makes me happy.

**Hannah J., 22:** I am halfway through my doctorate in physical therapy, and after licensure hope to get married, attain a strong financial base, and start a family of my own!

**Molly S., 20:** I am finishing my second quarter as a transfer student at UC Irvine. This quarter I am taking 30 units. Last quarter I got all in the A range, some minuses and one plus, but in the range.

I am in rehearsal for my fourth (sort of) production at school so far.

I am composing for a new musical that a group of us are writing at school. The woman leading the group is a graduate directing student who is talking about taking the show with her to LA to be produced when she graduates at the end of the year.

I am trying to get into giving voice lessons. I have started my first student, and have seen improvement, and am planning on adding a second student next quarter.

I will be musical directing a student-run musical next quarter.

I have been, and will continue to audition for paid or union summer theatre in and around California.

I will be auditioning for the BFA in musical theatre at the end of this quarter.

Happiness: Music. Writing it, playing it, singing it, discovering it, sharing it—this all makes me happy. Acting and performing—bringing something to life—getting in the mindset of a character and understanding everything about them, makes me happy too. So does swing dancing, listening to swing music, putting on make-up and a stylish outfit that I can feel proud to wear, Stephen Sondheim, talking about Sondheim and/or music, recognition, music theory, and sleep.

**Sarah P., 17:** Attending Austin Community College in the Early College Start program, looking to learn other

---

**Skye, 22**

I am currently working toward a Bachelor of Science degree in Anthropology (focus in forensics), with minors in Geography and Psychology. People, learning, growing, make me happy.

---

**Sarah D., 19**

I'm currently in my second year at East Carolina University, majoring in Sacred Music, pipe-organ concentration. I've been thinking about changing my major to something with science or maybe creative writing or teaching.

What makes me happy? That's a loaded question. Family makes me happy. Being creative makes me happy, and learning new things makes me happy. Meeting new friends and singing at the top of my lungs and curling up in my bed with a good book!

dance styles, improving my mental and physical health, and supporting (or at least trying not to be a further burden on) my family and their numerous health issues.

These things make me happy: dancing (well,) music, cold winter evenings, Andy Samberg, 40s music, milkshakes, milkshakes, father-daughter lunches, getting good grades, exercise, Doctor Who, and milkshakes.

**Risa, 21:**   I'm a Junior at UC San Diego studying International Studies and minoring in Global Health pursuing a career in international public health. Currently, I intern with the International Rescue Committee in San Diego teaching English to newly arrived refugees, helping them transition into their new lives. Through a program at UC San Diego, I'm going to Honduras over spring break to build a sustainable water infrastructure in disadvantaged communities in order to prevent waterborne diseases. Additionally, this summer I'll be studying public health in Amman, Jordan, and working in the Wihdat Refugee Camp conducting statistical research on the health care available there. Life is incredibly exciting right now and I'm eager to see what the next few years hold!

What makes me happy? That's a tough question! I really love life. I love the feel of sunshine and the sound of my camera's shutter clicking. I look for the beauty in small details. I love the sigh of relief from an anxious mother or a child's smiling eyes when I work in health clinics. I love trying to make a difference, even if it's one antibiotic at a time.

**Rose S., 20:**   I currently live at home with my mom and dad. I go to Golden West Community College, and I'm one semester away from completing my AA, my certificate in Interpreting in American Sign Language, and being certified to transfer as a Junior to a Cal State. My plan is to go to Cal State Northridge and major in Deaf Studies, with the career goal of becoming a full time interpreter, although my dream job would be opening my own martial arts studio that is accessible to all—deaf, hearing, physically or mentally delayed in any capacity, homeschool, etc.

---

### Sophie, 19

I put all my time and energy into horseback riding and showing horses. I don't take that many classes so I can keep up with the school work and be very involved in horses. My job is riding horses and also I work as a working student for local trainers and in exchange I get lessons on my own horse.

Horses make me happy, although, I would consider myself a happy, positive person naturally.

I coach soccer with my dad. I've been a coach on my own, and for the last two years I've been his assistant coach. I teach martial arts, as I have been for the last five years. I still game about once a week with a group of friends. We mostly stick to *GURPS* and *Magic: The Gathering* these days. I have a boyfriend. We just celebrated our three year anniversary. I still write a lot, read a lot, play a lot and watch a lot of television.

These activities make me happy: playing/coaching/watching soccer, teaching/doing martial arts, signing, singing, dancing, watching television/movies, and playing games. These people make me happy: My family, my boyfriend, my gaming friends, my interpreting friends, my martial arts students, the kids I babysit. And also, these things make me happy: My books, my Xbox, my computers, my Nook, my iPods, my DVDs.

**Sarah H., 24:**  I am attending Kaplan University Online for my Bachelor's Degree in Human Services with an emphasis in child and family welfare. (It's a mouthful, I know!) I work as a server to pay the bills until I finish school. When I graduate, I want to become a counselor or work for a non-profit organization. Lots of things make me happy. Reading, watching good movies with my husband, playing with my dog, going for walks, hiking, biking, rollerblading, hanging out with my family and friends, taking photos, drinking coffee, going to concerts, listening to music, having a stimulating conversation… I am a pretty happy person. :)

**Sarah B., 20:**  I am a sophomore in college where I am studying to become an electrical and computer engineer.

**Roxana, 24:**  I'm sort of in a limbo-y crossroads space right now. Right after graduation, I went straight into a grad program, intending to get an MA in history and then apply for Ph.D.s in the same field. During my first semester, between one thing and another, I decided that was no longer the path for me, and I left the program. I've applied for some graduate programs in museum studies, wanting to move into that line of work, but I'm still waiting to hear back (as of this writing). In the meanwhile, in my first non-collegiate semester in some years, I'm re-discov-

---

### Nathan, 22

I am a Junior at the American Jewish University where I am studying Bioethics. I live with two of my friends from school and work at the school bookstore. I also volunteer with animals when I can find the time. I am getting ready to take the GRE in preparation for applying to vet schools. I just got out of a year and a half relationship. I'm a B student but that is fine with me. I have a nice group of friends at school and around the LA area. Life is good and I am where I am today because of my past which includes homeschooling. Books, friends, animals, TV, make me happy—the normal things.

ering how to unschool myself, basically. I've been doing a lot of social media and digital marketing work with a few different volunteer-based organizations, including the Homeschool Association of California. I recently applied for a summer internship at my sorority's national museum. I'm trying on a bunch of different hats and trying to figure out how to wear them all at once.

## In the Working World

**24%** One quarter of all those who completed the survey are finished with homeschooling and out in the working world now. Some went to college first, while others went straight into careers after homeschooling. I think it's interesting how different they all are!

**Alaina, 25:**   My family and friends make me happy. I also am happy being busy, learning, educating others, working, living by my rules and respecting others for living by theirs.

**Ari, 21:**   I'm focusing on work, my health, moving out on my own. My relationship with my girlfriend, being active, friends and family, working, make me happy.

**Brenna, 22:**   As I write this I'm staffing at a writing retreat for 19 teenage homeschoolers in Durango, Colorado. In the past year I've started a sole proprietorship to sell my pottery, traveled to India, organized and participated in a pottery apprenticeship, worked a part time job in a restaurant, and written a non-fiction manuscript about self education in the visual arts. Throwing pots makes me happy!

**Dakota, 20:**   What really makes me happy is: biking, music, trying something new and getting it perfect on the first try.

**Kaci, 18:**   Right now I'm working at a gym teaching gymnastics. I'm trying to save money to move out so I can embark on being an adult. Swimming, photography, being downtown, going to concerts, friends, family, animals, reading, learning things I'm interested in, all make me happy. A lot of things make me happy though.

---

### Zach, 24

I'm working as a freelance internet marketer. Finishing up the post production on a movie some of my friends and I made. Rehabbing an old Victorian house. And trying to start a production company.

The things that make me happy: earning, creating, laughing, problem solving, surfing… in no particular order.

---

### Alaina, 25

I have been working in nonprofit program review and recently completed my MBA in nonprofit management.

*Michael in the Peace Corps stationed in Nicaragua*

**Anastasia, 19:**   I am developing my painting and cartooning career on several fronts, planning for the future always, and lurking in pretentious cafés with my sketchbook.

The things that make me happy: painting and drawing and tea and good beer, long conversations and handmade paper and stop-motion films and films in general and well-written non-fiction and museums and God and politics and cities and history and music and power lines and lots of other things. I am a very happy person.

**Cameron L., 24:**   Freedom is what makes me happy. I'm traveling, meeting people all over the country.

**Laurel, 21:**   I'm looking for work in Portland, Oregon so that I can move there to live with some friends by the end of the month. I'm also involved with an LGBT non-profit, I regularly do 4 different kinds of dance, and I am constantly learning and growing as an artist, and getting involved with different projects.

Feeling loved, expressing love, seeing and helping other people and animals be happy, and expressing myself and connecting with people through art, dance, or anything that takes me by surprise—these things make me happy.

---

***Alyssa P., 18***

I am following my dream in making people feel beautiful! I graduated from cosmetology school in May, and currently work as a stylist in a salon. I just got engaged over Christmas, so I'm planning a wedding for 2013! Basically, I'm getting ready for what comes my way in life!

My fiancé makes me happy. My family, when they're acting crazy, and my baby puppy, Gracie-loo, make me happy too. Doing the work I love also makes me really happy.

> **Skylar, 26**
>
> I am the Program Coordinator at Reading to Kids, a grassroots non-profit in Los Angeles that serves seven schools west of Downtown Los Angeles. I organize all aspects of the monthly reading clubs, with assistance from an AmeriCorps fellow and interns. Spending time with friends and family, my dog, mastering a new skill, cooking, reading a good book, make me happy.

> **Michael, 22**
>
> I finished college and am currently living in Nicaragua, teaching English as a Peace Corps Volunteer. And that's where I'll be for the next 2 years.
>
> Good adventure, good food and good company make me happy. I don't feel like I need anything else in life. I know that's a simple answer but it's really true.

**Kirby, 26:**    Career/life-wise, I'm working the late late shift at Blizzard, which is a phenomenal company to work at. I'm on the graveyard shift due to a recent promotion, which resulted in my being the "new guy" again and not taking priority. (But not this next shift bid!). I work within Customer Service, but cannot go into detail of what exactly I do. I spend my "evenings" at home on the computer most days. I like watching TV series (far too many to name, currently on the 5th season of *The West Wing*), playing games, reading up on friends' Facebooks, and hanging out with my two roommates, along with the animals in the house. I live in a house that my roommate of five years has just purchased with his fiancé. There are two dogs and two cats here as well. On the weekends I go out to friends' houses to play games, eat, drink, be merry in general and all in-between. I go to a Karaoke Bar every week. Once I'm working "Day Walker hours," I'll add more to the list, hopefully martial arts once again, if I can find a school I like.

**Rowan, 18:**    Creating art and teaching others who want to learn. I really like living in the moment.

**Simcha, 17:**    Getting ready for the army and then I want to get married. I am happy with long walks, quiet time for reading, music.

**Zoe, 22:**    I currently live in New York City. I have a wonderful apartment which I share with three roommates. I work at an off-Broadway theater called New World Stages. I help run events/I'm a receptionist/I cocktail serve/I work as security (true story). I try to audition and work as an actor as often as I can. I spend lots of time with my friends. Most of my best friends work at New World with me. I spend an obscene amount of time in Midtown Manhattan. I read as much as I can—mostly on the train and before I go to bed. When I work my desk job I look at so much Facebook I think my eyes turn into a Newsfeed. Mostly I am happy, but sometimes I am sad. And that is what I am doing with my life.

Lots of things make me happy, but the two most important are my friends and my family.

**Teagan, 20:**   I'm living and working in Chicago. I'm an office temp by day, and I rehearse and perform theatre at night. I recently produced and starred in a play called *This is Our Youth*. Over the course of six months, one of my closest friends and I came up with a plan for the show, assembled a production team, raised $1,500 via the fundraising website Kickstarter, rehearsed, and put up the show. It was incredibly tough (and unfamiliar) territory, as it was my first time working in a producer's capacity. But I was incredibly proud of what we accomplished, and I look forward to moving ahead to my next self-produced show (which will likely be at the beginning of the new year) with more insight and a better sense of what I'm doing. I'm thrilled that I am able to be doing the kind of work I want with the people I want. I plan to go to graduate school to get my MFA in acting. I am still compiling a list of schools I intend to audition for, but I do know that the Yale School of Drama is at the top of my list. These things make me happy: art, learning, creating things, performing, reading (as much as possible), really good conversation, theatre that makes my heart beat faster, my family, my friends, being busy, being in constant forward motion, and accomplishing something I didn't think I could do.

**Kevin, 20:**   I'm currently in the Marines. Just doing what I love. It has its ups and downs, of course, but I love what I do. Being with family and friends makes me happy.

**Tess, 27:**   I am living every day to the best of my ability. I work hard, I apply myself independently. I own my own home, am going for a second degree, and have done it all on my own. Homeschooling taught me independence, focus, and that I make my own success. Family, friends, and my pets make me happy.

### Building a Family

**10%** taking the survey have or are becoming parents themselves. These seven homeschooled adults are raising their families from perspectives that might be quite different from other new parents their age. It's fascinating

> ### *Caitlin, 27*
>
> I work as an oncology nurse at a university hospital. I recently got married and am pregnant with our first child.
>
> I have a wonderful husband and stepdaughter, we just bought our first house, and I have a job that I love. Overall, most things in my life are making me happy right now.

to hear what they're doing in their lives. Their unique experiences will undoubtedly impact the way they interact with their own new families.

**Aiden W., 23:**  I'm getting ready to have my baby, learning as much as I can about breastfeeding, cloth diapers, childbirth, parenting. I am doing everything I can to save money and help my husband get through college. (baking our bread from scratch, making him lunches, doing the laundry, making diapers, etc). I am also writing poetry. I'm thinking eventually we'll run a bed and breakfast, so I'm learning about that and figuring out what skills I need to acquire.

Well, happiness is a decision. So when I decide to be happy, I am. Some things that make it easier to decide in no particular order: Spending time with my husband, cooking, eating tasty food, watching other people enjoy tasty food I made, long walks in the woods, writing, reading a good book, accomplishing a goal, knowing I did something well, spending time with children, flying kites, making things, helping people, scoring a good deal on groceries, horseback riding, butterflies, prayer, scripture study, feeling my baby kick, talking to a friend, kneading bread, waking up in the morning, snow…I should probably stop listing things…

**Roya, 27:**  I am about to finish up my thesis, and then graduate with a Master's in Counseling. At that point, I'll be an MFT intern, hopefully work in an agency and private practice, and also teach adults with disabilities. After 3000 client hours, I'll take my licensing exam, and then be a Marriage and Family Therapist. The goal is to run an art and wilderness therapy camp one day with my husband, gather everyone I know and love on my property, and live as self-sustainably as we can, with my Yarn Barn, herb spirals, and many unschooled children! The process of figuring out what makes me happy makes me happy. Hah. Also—being outside, camping, my German shepherds, Joshua Tree, research, swimming, alpaca yarn, anything related to Alaska, traveling with my husband, watching my sister's shows, taking photographs, weddings, exercising, swimming with sea lions, cooking on camp stoves, collaging, organizing my

---

### Katie F., 24

I am a stay-at-home mom with small children. Though we don't "do school" yet I am always teaching that life is for learning.

I am currently enjoying myself by working through the literary classics. Reading, especially reading to my children, makes me really happy.

---

### Wendelyn, 34

I am in the middle of my work season and missing the pace of being a stay-at-home mom. I started a blog to journal and in the hopes of inspiring others.

We're in the process of buying a house and I am making plans to start some businesses so that I can be a stay-at-home mom year-round.

Happiness:

- Being with my family.
- Sharing ideas with other people.
- Singing and gardening,
- Making my house into a home.

embroidery floss, big giant sparkly rings, musicals, pink hair, clay, country music, singing, picking fruit from our trees, being in art supply stores, watching seeds sprout, playing in mud, crossing finish lines, driving on Pacific Coast Highway in the summer, being in sunshine, making connections, doing group therapy, going to therapy, sunscreen, pears, being around unschoolers, looking at my honeymoon pictures, crossing things off my to do list, making decisions, being in charge, hanging out with my family, watching my dad coach soccer, going to the gym with my mom, the little kids who run into your legs in hotel hallways at homeschooling conferences, teaching other people how to crochet, watching an entire TV show series from beginning to end, anything relating to Harry Potter, and oh so many more things.

**Nicholas, 26:**   I am a father and husband with 3 children ages 5, 3, and 3 months. We have already started working on reading and writing with the 5 year old and the 3 year old. When I think about happiness, ice cream is the first thing that comes to mind. But the happiness it creates is so temporary! Separate from that, I want to see my children be faithful Christians and to be successful in life!

**Rose, 30:**   I just moved to a downtown apartment with my sons, so we're getting used to urban life. My youngest isn't a baby anymore, and it's just settling in to my soul that the baby-raising part of my life is over and I get to have big kid adventures now. I'm looking for someone to barter with me for fiddle lessons; I've decided I really want to learn. I'm looking for some kind of permanent-ish volunteer opportunity. Writing is great, but doesn't take up all my time, and I want some way to engage with the community that can develop into a specialty so I can become more valuable wherever I'm volunteering as the years go by. I'm homeschooling three sons, too! Life is busy and full and ever-changing. What makes me happy is knowing my values and goals and seeing myself accomplish them, and sharing that work with like-minded loved ones. I also really like chai tea and playing board games with my sons.

> ### *Rebecca, 39*
>
> I homeschool my children using an interest-led, unschooling approach. I spend my time actively and joyfully facilitating their interests and helping them achieve their goals as well as passionately sharing my own interests with them. I also work part time at a group home for troubled teenage boys, help my mother-in-law out with her tax business during tax season and do whatever odd jobs come my way to help make ends meet… i.e. pay for all my kids' sports-related activities!
>
> Things that make me happy: my family; my children; spending time with them; living life together; talking and laughing with them; seeing them happy; watching them passionately pursue their interests and goals, seeing how focused and intense they can be. And cheesecake. Cheesecake makes me really happy.

*Cameron L., traveling the country, seeing the world*

# EPILOGUE

Well. There you have it. Years of conversations and introspection.

These teens and young adults have pored out their thoughts and ideas for you in hopes that you will be able to see the advantages and benefits of homeschooling through the teenage years. They hope that you'll be able to overcome your own fears and embrace these ideas, creating a wonderful joyful educational path for and with your own teen. Maybe we'll even talk to them again in another five years and see how life has changed and hear what their perspectives are!

It's my hope that you've found the reassurance you were looking for. I imagine your faces at both the start and the end of this book, being similar to that of the conference-goer who would enter the teen panel presentations at homeschooling conferences across the country. Parents entered the room nervous, worried, concerned that they maybe couldn't—or shouldn't—try to pull off this homeschooling thing. But after the session, their faces told a different story. Their concerns were addressed. Their questions were answered. Their confidence was restored. Their faces more relaxed and smiling. They were enthusiastic about facing this new adventure awaiting them with their teenagers.

As a homeschooling parent, it's not that we never had fear or worry. But we continued to explore our own thoughts about how children learn best, and undid some of the preconceived ideas we had that simply weren't valid or even true. This allowed us to continue to trust our children, learning and growing right alongside them.

I hope you've found what you were looking for! Maybe we'll meet in the future and you can let me know how it's going for you and for your teenager. I wish you well.

# ABOUT THE AUTHOR

*Sue Patterson*, wife and mom to three grown homeschoolers, is as busy as an "empty nester" as she was while the kids were all still home! Her kids are off on adventures of their own now, weaving in and out of her life. Sue and her family began homeschooling in 1996 when they found the local public schools simply weren't good enough. They participated in support groups at the local, state and national level, as her husband's military career moved them from state to state. Now, nearly two decades later, she feels she's seen enough and knows enough to help people understand more about how to homeschool successfully.

Sue, a perpetual volunteer, is also a life coach and homeschooling mentor, hosts the Unschooling Mom2Mom website/Facebook group, and is the managing editor of *The Homeschooler Post*. Sue is a well-loved speaker at conferences around the country and enjoys talking to people as much as she loves writing—she combines the two whenever possible! She is excited to share the results of her new book, *Homeschooled Teens*, three years in the making! She is sure that your fears will be allayed and after reading this, you'll be inspired and ready to dive into homeschooling your own teens!

For more about Sue's projects, go to www.SuePatterson.com.

26614288R00191